PHOTOSHOP® CS

DOWN & DIRTY *Dirty* TRICKS

SCOTT KELBY

The Adobe® Photoshop® CS
Down & Dirty Tricks
Team

CREATIVE DIRECTOR
Felix Nelson

TECHNICAL EDITOR
Chris Main

EDITOR
Richard Theriault

PRODUCTION MANAGER
Kim Gabriel

PRODUCTION LAYOUT
Dave Damstra

COVER DESIGN
Felix Nelson

The New Riders Team

PUBLISHER
Stephanie Wall

EXECUTIVE EDITOR
Steve Weiss

PRODUCTION MANAGER
Gina Kanouse

SENIOR PROJECT EDITOR
Sarah Kearns

PRODUCTION LAYOUT
Gloria Schurick

PROOFREADER
Linda Seifert

STOCK IMAGES
The royalty-free stock
images used in this
book are courtesy of

www.brandx.com

PUBLISHED BY
New Riders Publishing

Copyright © 2004 by Scott Kelby

FIRST PRINTING: October 2003

Photoshop is a registered trademark of Adobe Systems, Inc.

International Standard Book Number: 0-7357-1353-7

Library of Congress Catalog Card Number: 2003111987

05   9 8 7 6

Composed in Myriad, Minion, Cronos, and Helvetica by New Riders Publishing

Trademarks

Warning and Disclaimer

www.scottkelbybooks.com

For my close friend Dave Moser,
because he wants the same
thing I want—to make everything
we do better than anything
we've done before.

ACKNOWLEDGMENTS

I consider myself very, very blessed. Each day I get to work with such a wonderful group of people, and when I'm not working, I'm surrounded by family and friends whom I dearly love, all of whom come together to help and enrich my life in so many ways. There's not a printed acknowledgment I could write that would honor them in the way they deserve, but one of the benefits in writing a book is that at least you get to try.

Kalebra: My wonderful, beautiful, amazing, hilarious, fun-filled, loving wife. You're the greatest thing that's ever happened to me, and asking you to marry me, almost 14 years ago, was clearly the single best decision I've ever made. Your spirit, warmth, beauty, patience, and unconditional love continue to prove what everybody always says—I'm the luckiest guy in the world.

Jordan: Little buddy—you're just the greatest. A father couldn't ask for a more fun, more crazy, more lovable, or more loving son than you. I'm so thrilled and proud of the little man you're becoming, and you're so blessed to have your mom's heart, compassion, and spirit. You're a very special little boy, and you've already touched so many people, that I can't imagine all the wonders, adventure, and happiness life has in store for you.

Dad: You've blessed me with an unfair advantage in life by being such a great parent, for raising me in such a loving home, for always supporting everything I've ever done, for always taking the high road, for sharing your patriotism, moral and business ethics, and for being the dad all other dads should be judged by.

Jeff: I can't tell you what a blessing it's been having you as a brother, and how thrilled I am that for the past three and half years you've been part of our team (plus, I love getting to sneak out for lunch with you every day). You've had an amazing, wonderful, and important impact on life, and just hearing your voice brings a smile to my face. I love you, man.

Dave Moser: What can I say—I dedicated this book to you. I truly value our friendship all these many years, and I'm thrilled with all the fun and the exciting things we're able to do together. There are few people with your passion, guts, integrity, vision, and unflinching dedication to quality, for always insisting on raising the bar; and I have to thank you for totally sharing my "what we do next has to be better than what we did before" credo. It sometimes annoys the hell out of everyone around us, but it is who we are, and "it is what it is."

Felix Nelson: I don't know how you do it, but you always do. If you had nothing but your amazing Photoshop talents, you'd be in the top one quarter of one percent of Photoshop designers in the world; but your creativity, talent, ideas, discipline, and humor put you in a league all by yourself. I remember Jack Davis asking me "Where in the world did you find Felix?" I can only figure God sent you our way. Thanks for everything you do—here in the book, in leading our creative team, and for your friendship and dedication to everything we do. You da man!

Chris Main: You don't have an easy job (tech editing my books) but you do it with grace and charm, and make it look easy (and believe me, it isn't). You were there from just about the very beginning and I'm honored to still have you on our team, and I'm delighted I get to work and hang out with you, doing lots of very fun stuff. Well done, Mr. Main!

Dave Damstra: If they ever have a competition for best page layout guy in the business, I'm sending you to steal the show. Having you lay out my books is definitely a strategic advantage and you set the standard, not only in your work, but in your amazing attitude in life as well.

Richard Theriault: OK, Dick, this is the eleventh of my books you've edited. I don't think you can really call yourself retired any longer (and that's fine by us). It's really been a blessing having you editing my writing all these years, first in the magazines and now in the books; and you continually make me sound better, smarter, and much more eloquent than you darn well know I am. That's the mark of a truly great editor, and you sir, are indeed that.

Jim Workman and Jean A. Kendra: I'm very fortunate to have business partners who understand what it takes to do what we do. I can't thank you enough for your constant support, understanding, freedom, and help in accomplishing my goals. You guys rock.

Kathy Siler: You make my job so much easier (partially because you do so much of it for me) and you do it with such great ease, such a great attitude, and you really look out for me; and I can't tell you how thrilled I am that you're on "my team." You've made my job so much more enjoyable, and I have more fun doing it. So much so, that I'm willing to say "Go Redskins!"

Kim Gabriel: I don't have to tell you—it ain't easy putting together one of these books, but you keep a lot of plates in the air, you keep the trains running on time, and you do a marvelous job of keeping it all moving ahead. I can't thank you enough.

Steve Weiss: You "get" me, you get what we're trying to do, and that's why we have the great relationship we do. Your unwavering commitment to "create great books" is what sets you apart and makes authors want to work for you. My heartfelt thanks to you, and to Nancy Ruenzel, Scott Cowlin, and everyone in the Peachpit Publishing Group who've made me feel so at home.

Adobe: Thanks to all my friends at the mothership, including Barbara Rice, Julieanne Kost, Rye Livingston, Russell Brown, Terry White, Kevin Connor, Tanguy Leborgne, Karen Gauthier, Gywn Weisberg, Russell Brady, and Addy Roff. Also, a special thanks to John Nack for his invaluable help with this book. You're very special people, doing very important stuff, and I'm delighted we get to work together.

My personal thanks go to Jeffery Burke at Brand X Pictures for enabling me to use some of their wonderful images in this book.

Kudos and continued thanks to my home team: Julie Stephenson, Barbara Thompson, Stacy Behan, Ronni O'Neil, Melinda Gotelli, Pete Kratzenberg, Margie Rosenstein, Ted (T-Lo) LoCascio, Dave Gales, Dave Cross, and Sarah Hughes.

Most importantly, I want to thank God, and His son Jesus Christ, for leading me to the woman of my dreams, for blessing us with such a special little boy, for allowing me to make a living doing something I truly love, for always being there when I need Him, and for blessing me with a wonderful, fulfilling, and happy life, and such a warm, loving family to share it with.

ABOUT THE AUTHOR

Scott Kelby

 Scott is Editor-in-Chief and co-founder of *Photoshop User* magazine, Editor-in-Chief of Nikon's *Capture User* magazine, and Editor-in-Chief of *Mac Design Magazine*. He is President of the National Association of Photoshop Professionals (NAPP), the trade association for Adobe® Photoshop® users, and he's President of KW Media Group, Inc., a Florida-based software education and publishing firm.

Scott is author of the best-selling books *Photoshop 7 Down & Dirty Tricks, Photoshop Photo-Retouching Secrets, The Photoshop Book for Digital Photographers*, co-author of *Photoshop 7 Killer Tips*, and creator and Series Editor for the *Killer Tips* series from New Riders Publishing. Scott has authored three best-selling Macintosh books: *Mac OS X Jaguar Killer Tips* and the award-winning *Macintosh: The Naked Truth*, both also from New Riders; and the new *Mac OS X Conversion Kit: 9 to 10 Side by Side* from Peachpit Press.

Scott introduced his first software title in 2003: "Kelby's Notes for Adobe Photoshop," which provides the answers to the 100 most-asked Photoshop questions, accessed from directly within Photoshop.

Scott is Training Director for the Adobe Photoshop Seminar Tour, Conference Technical Chair for the PhotoshopWorld Conference and Expo, and speaker at graphics trade shows and events around the world. He is also featured in a series of Adobe Photoshop training videos and DVDs and has been training Adobe Photoshop users since 1993.

For more background info on Scott, visit www.scottkelby.com.

TABLE OF CONTENTS

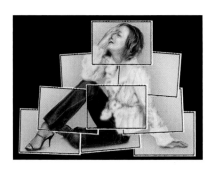

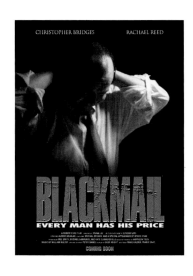

TABLE OF CONTENTS www.downanddirtytricks.com

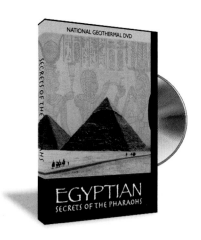

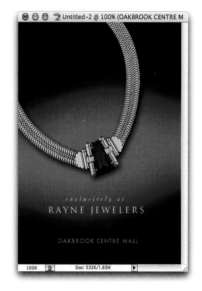

THIS IS NOT THE INTRODUCTION

Every book has an introduction, and virtually nobody reads them. That's why, instead of including a boring introduction that nobody will read anyway, this is actually "the Preamble" to the book. That's right, baby—a preamble. This is more important than it may sound at first, because as you're probably aware, not many printed documents these days have a preamble (thought this could certainly start a trend). In fact the only document that I can think of that has a preamble is the U.S. Constitution (and it's done pretty well thus far). So I'm following in the footsteps of our forefathers by trying to create a piece that will endure for more than 200 years (or until the next version of Photoshop is released. Whichever comes first).

When you break it down, the word "Preamble" is really ideal because, as you know, the prefix "pre" means "before the fix" (which, in layman's terms, means this all occurred before something was broken), and the word "amble" is the root of the Latin word "ambulance" which is what you'd need if you were to break your foot while reading this book. So, in short, this Preamble is what to read before you break your foot. Ah, it all makes perfect sense now, doesn't it?

So now that we've established that this is clearly NOT an introduction, what will reading this do for you (you being the wonderful, multi-faceted, truly unique, genius-type person who bought this book)? Reading this will help you "get inside my head" (Don't worry. I've got a huge bobble-head with over 120,000 square feet of contiguous air-conditioned warehouse space, so climb right in).

All kidding aside, taking a quick moment to read this preamble will make using this book much easier and much more enjoyable for you. Primarily because you'll then understand how and why it was written, why I did certain things the way I did, and then how to get the most from this book. Plus, it says something about you, and the kind of person you are (the kind of person who will continue reading this preamble, knowing full well that it's really the introduction, simply because you don't want to hurt my feelings. I dig you, man). Now, on to how to use this book.

...there are techniques in this book that I've never seen anybody, anywhere, showing how they're done!

100% all cool new stuff!

If you're one of the people who bought the Photoshop 7 version of this book, I have good news and bad news. First, the good news. This new version of the book kicks that book in the butt (I didn't want to say butt. I wanted to use a stronger word with one less letter, but my Editor wouldn't let me. He's so "Sassy" [note: drop the "s," drop the "y"—you get the picture]). Rather than updating the old book, I tossed every effect from that book straight into the trash and started from scratch, bringing you all new, way cool, cutting-edge Photoshop special effects.

That's because I wanted this book to reflect what people are really doing with Photoshop today. I wanted it filled with step-by-step tutorials on the same effects you see *today* on TV, in the movies, in print, and on the Web, so you can go and apply these same techniques to your own work *today*. To do that, I had to trash every technique from the Photoshop 7 version of the book, and start over creating entirely new cutting edge tutorials. Although starting from scratch was a pain in the butt (again—wanted to use another word) now that it's done, I'm so glad I did. Honestly, I'm more excited about the effects that I'm getting to share with you here than anything I've written before. I think the reason I'm so excited is that I learned so much while doing this book. I had to figure out effects that I honestly had no idea how they were done; but now that I know them (and soon you will too) it has reignited my passion for special effects (hey, anything that ignites passion can't be bad. At least, that's what they're always saying on Cinemax). So that's the good news—this book is packed with all new effects, and they reflect what the professional Photoshop designers and photographers are doing with Photoshop today.

So what's the bad news?

Well, since I wrote *Photoshop 7 Down & Dirty Tricks*, I've received literally thousands of gracious letters from people all around the world who had bought the book, telling me how much they learned from it (it was translated into ten languages, including Chinese, Russian, Japanese, and of course, the languages of love). As an author, I can't tell you how fulfilling it is to get that kind of feedback. But the bad news is, after they have this new book and try all these all-new, much cooler, never-shown-before techniques, they'll look back at that (once beloved) book and think, "What a piece of crap!" (They'll actually think of a different word. Stronger, but with the same number of letters.)

...I had to trash every technique from the Photoshop 7 version of this book and start from scratch, creating entirely new cutting-edge effects.

That's because that book reflected what was happening a year and a half ago (when I wrote it). Back then, it was cool—it reflected what was happening in 2001. But now, those effects have been done to death. They're tired. Played. So yes, I know full well that you're going to look at that old book with total disdain, and yes, on some level, it hurts (me anyway), but it's part of our growth. Part of our walk down this path, which leads to a world of enlightened and totally unbridled special effects that dare not speak its name.

So now that you know what my plan was in creating this new version, it's time to look at how this book works:

How this book works:

I wrote this book so any user, at any level of Photoshop experience, can jump right in and create these effects. For most people this is a blessing, but if you've been using Photoshop for umpteen years, there's something you should know: I spell everything out (at least, the first time, in every tutorial). And just because I do that (making the book accessible to everyone) you shouldn't let it "get to you." For example, in a tutorial, the first time I have you make a new blank layer I write "Create a new blank layer by clicking on the New Layer icon at the bottom of the Layers palette." If you've been creating layers since *Roseanne* was a top-rated TV show, you're going to be like "Oh, this is for beginners." Don't let that throw you, because for the rest of that technique, I just say "Create a new layer." I had to do it that way. Since this isn't a "Start at Chapter One and read it cover-to-cover" book (you can jump in anywhere), someone who's new to Photoshop (like a professional photographer who's now shooting digital) might not know how to create a new layer. There is no "Here's how Photoshop works" chapter at the beginning, like every other Photoshop book. Because of that, the first time a command appears, I write the whole darn thing out. Again, it's just a few extra words, and you can bounce right by it if you already know how to do it, so don't let it slow you down.

Q. So is this book full of advanced techniques?

A. Well, in a way yes, in a way, no. Here's the thing: the techniques you're going to learn in this book are the very same techniques used by today's leading Photoshop designers, digital photographers, Web wizards, and video gurus. They use these effects every day, and you can be sure if they're working for some major TV network, a Hollywood studio, or a worldwide ad agency, these people are definitely advanced. But although these techniques were created, and are used daily by advanced users, that doesn't mean they're hard or overly complicated. In fact, my goal was to make these advanced techniques as easy as is humanly possible. That's because I want every reader of this book to be able to easily pull off every single technique in the book. That's my goal. It's supposed to *look* like it was hard to create—it's not supposed to *be* hard to create. That's the beauty of it, and that's why I call the book "Down & Dirty Tricks." There is nothing I love more than finding out that the effect that I thought would be so complex is actually a 60-second quick trick. I love that, and sharing those secrets is what I love even more, and that's exactly, precisely, what this book is all about.

Think of it this way: This book is packed cover-to-cover with stuff that makes it look like you really broke a sweat. Like you spent weeks crafting the effect (because after all, you're going to charge the client like you worked on it for weeks, right?) but most of it requires you to just follow the simple steps. That's it.

Here's an example: in this book, I'm going to show you what is probably the most popular technique used in Hollywood movie posters today. You know, and I know, that the Hollywood studio hired some big muckity-muck designer to do their posters, but absolutely, without a doubt, if you follow the instructions you'll be able to create the exact same effect. Does that make it a beginner's book—because a beginner can "pull off" the same technique used by the top pros? Or does this make it an advanced book, because you're learning techniques used by some very advanced Photoshop users? So basically, you're going to learn advanced techniques that are so easy to pull off, and it's going to make you look advanced even if you're not. If you're already an advanced user, the benefit to you is you'll be able to pull these mini-miracles off even faster, by skipping the extra descriptive copy and getting right in and getting your hands dirty. It's all how you look at it.

Next, I included a quick Q&A (Quebec & Albatross) session to answer some of the questions that are probably racing around in your mind:

Q. Where should I start in the book?
A. It doesn't matter. Jump in at the technique that interests you most. Wherever you start, because everything is spelled out, you'll be able to do the technique right on the spot.

Q. Can I get the photos used in the book?
A. You're kind of pushy. I like that. Actually, thanks to the wonderful people at Brand X Pictures (www.brandx.com) you can download low-res versions of all the photos used in the book, so you can practice right along using the same photos.

Q. Why Brand X?
A. Because, in my humble opinion, they've got the best, coolest, most relevant royalty-free stock images in the market today. I came across them when their catalog came in the mail. I looked at it for about 30 seconds and I knew right then "These are the images I want in my next book." We called them out of the blue, and convinced (OK, we begged) them to let us (and you) use their amazing stock imagery for the book, and I am absolutely thrilled that they did. They offer over 20,000 images, and best of all, they're totally not the schlocky "two men shaking hands" standard stock photos that permeate the stock agencies. Their stuff rocks because it's so usable, so "non-stock," and I encourage you to visit their site at www.brandx.com to

There is nothing I love more than finding out that the effect that I thought would be so complex is actually a 60-second trick.

see for yourself. I know this sounds like a big plug for Brand X (it is, and they deserve it), but I can assure you that outside of their graciously letting me (and you) use their photos, it's not a paid plug. I don't get a kickback—not a nickel, whether you buy one or 1,000 of their images (and CDs, did I mention they sell collections?), but I am indebted to them, especially since they didn't know me from Adam (apparently, they know Adam), and I wanted to let them (and you) know how much better this book is because of their generous contribution. OK, now I'm "un-plugging."

This book is packed cover-to-cover with stuff that makes it look like you really broke a sweat. Like you spent weeks crafting the effect...

Q. Is the book for Mac or for PC?
A. Both. Since Photoshop CS is identical on the Mac and PC platforms, this book is identical for both. However, because the Mac's keyboard is slightly different from the keyboard on a PC (three keys have different names) I give both the Mac and the PC keyboard shortcuts throughout the entire book.

Q. What's the volumetric conversion of 7 cubic yards to liters?
A. Glad you asked. Seven cubic yards equals 5351.99 liters. Other Photoshop books just don't give you this kind of in-depth, seemingly useless information. See, I care.

Q. I noticed you mentioned Felix several times throughout the book. Who's Felix?
A. Felix is Felix Nelson (yes, *that* Felix Nelson) and he's about the best, most creative, most talented Photoshop artist in the known universe, and I'm about the luckiest guy in the world to get to work with him every day. He's the Creative Director for *Photoshop User* magazine, he co-authored my *Photoshop 7 Killer Tips* book, and honestly, I learn more about Photoshop from Felix than any other person on the planet. He's just brilliant at taking techniques to the next level, and coming up with inventive and creative new ideas.

For example, I'd ask him to look at a new technique I'd come up with for the book, and he'd look at it and say, "Hey, that looks slick. Ya know, if you added a...." and then he'd mention that one little thing that takes the tutorial from a pretty cool technique to a totally awesome technique. In fact, during the past few months, Felix showed me two techniques that were so cool that I said, "You've gotta do those in my book." So he wrote two amazing tutorials here in the book (the "finally real neon" and the "how to age a photo" tutorials) and I can't thank him enough for his many tweaks, ideas, and insights that have made this book much better than it would have been.

Q. What are those sidebars on every page?
A. Those are tips. Cool tips. Tips to make you faster, better, more productive. Sometimes they relate to the effect shown in the main portion of the page, sometimes they're just cool tips that I had to stick somewhere, so they wound up there. Some of these tips haven't changed since back in Photoshop 7, and they work exactly the same in Photoshop CS, but I was able to add lots of cool new tips for the amazing new stuff in Photoshop CS too, so make sure you read them (or I did all that typing for nothing).

Q. What's the capital of South Dakota?
A. Pierre.

Q. What if I'm still using Photoshop 7?

A. Dude. That's just wrong. Photoshop CS is the best Photoshop there's ever been. You'll work faster, have more fun, and you'll be able to do more cool things with it than ever before, so in short—it's upgrade time. Remember that I mentioned how out-of-date the effects in the Photoshop 7 book are now? Well, that's how old Photoshop 7 is. Although most of the effects in this book will still work in Photoshop 7, you're missing out on much more than special effects if you don't upgrade to CS, so…get on it.

Q. Where do I download the photos from the book?

A. Go to the book's companion Web site at www.scottkelbybooks.com/csphotos.html

Q. How many fingers am I holding up?

A. Three. No, four!

Q. Is the rest of the book as down-to-earth and straight-to-the-point as this non-introduction?

A. Sadly, no. The rest of the book is pretty much written like this: Step One: Go under the Filter menu, under Blur, and choose Gaussian Blur. It's all step-by-step from here, giving the exact steps necessary to complete the effect, so there's not much interference, uh, I mean, ancillary instruction, from me. Well, except I am able to share some carefully crafted insights during the intro of each chapter, so please take a moment to read them, if you want the full Zen-like experience that comes from reading chapter intros that are as meaningful and thought-provoking as those found in the opening paragraphs of this preamble.

Q. Hey, I just realized something.

A. What's that?

Q. If this is the Preamble, the rest of the book must then be the "Amble," right?

A. That's right my friend. You are indeed worthy of this book. I mean, this "Amble."

Q. So, is it safe to continue on to the "Amble" now?

A. Wow, you've really bought into that whole Amble thing—I'm proud of you. (Note: the interjection "Wow" is a registered trademark of the Jack Davis Corporation, and is used in the previous sentence with Jack's express written permission. All rights reserved. For details, see in-store display. Not valid where prohibited.)

Well, you've done your duty. You've read the Preamble, you know what the book's about, how it was written, what to look for (what you're in for), and how to make the most of it. Armed with that knowledge, go forth, and follow in the footsteps of our forefathers, who once wrote, "We, the Village People…" no that's not it. Anyway….

Turn the page, my young apprentice. It's time for you to "effect" the world.

1

Don't let the title of this chapter fool you—the photographic special effects here don't take one hour.

One Hour Photo
Photographic Effects, Part 1

Most take like three minutes. Well, four if you're Photoshopping with one hand, eating a sandwich with the other. If you charge by the hour, this is the last thing you want to hear, but there's a way around that: If the photo effect you want to use has 12 steps, do only the first 10 steps. Then drive to your client's office and present it as your "initial proof." Then, drop off your dry cleaning, go to a museum, have some dinner, catch a movie, etc. Then go back to your office, complete steps 11 and 12, and return to your client with your "second round of proofs." The effect will look like you worked on it for weeks. Give the client your invoice (include the movies and dinner receipts) and you're a hero—you delivered the effect that knocked their socks off in just one day (but it only took you three and half minutes to create it). Ahh, now you have a moral dilemma. You feel bad. Guilty even. So you go back to your client, and refund everything but a pro-rated three and a half minutes of your hourly charge. Ya know, looking back, if you charge by the hour, you should probably skip this chapter altogether.

Quick Tip:
**The rasterized
type insurance
policy**

My buddy Dave Cross
taught me this valuable
tip: If you rasterize a Type
layer and you need to re-
create that type at a later
time, you probably won't
remember the exact point
size, leading, and tracking
you used. In fact, you might
not even remember the
font name. That's why Dave
always renames a raster-
ized layer with the stats
of the rasterized type. For
example, he might name it
"Minion, 14 pt. Auto leading, -50 tracking." That way,
if he ever has to update
or re-create the type, he
knows precisely how to format it for an exact match.
Those Canadians—they
know all the cool tips.

Snapshot Focus Effect

I first saw this clever, yet amazingly simple technique used in a brochure for Orlando, Florida's SeaWorld theme park. It focuses the viewer's eye on one area of the photo by using a snapshot effect, but rather than cropping the photo to fit inside the "Polaroid" snapshot frame, they left the rest of the photo visible and applied a filter to it, creating a very appealing photographic effect. Here's how it's done:

STEP ONE: Open the photo you want to have the snapshot focus effect.

STEP TWO: Press the letter "m" to get the Rectangular Marquee tool, and draw a rectangular selection around the area you want to use as the focal point of your photo. Give the rectangle the same basic proportions as those of a Polaroid photo (as shown here).

STEP THREE: From the Select menu, choose Transform selection. This brings up what looks like the Free Transform bounding box; however, this differs in that it doesn't transform what's inside the selection (like Free Transform), but transforms the selection itself. Move your cursor outside the bounding box and click-and-drag to rotate the selection until it's angled like the one you see here. When it looks about the same, press Return (PC: Enter).

Quick Tip:

How to hide your floating palettes, but keep your Toolbox and Options Bar still visible

Try pressing Shift-Tab. When you do this, the Toolbox and Options Bar remain visible, but all the floating palettes are hidden from view. Want them back? Press Shift-Tab again.

STEP FOUR: Now, press Command-J (PC: Control-J) to copy this selected area onto its own separate layer above your Background layer (as shown here in the Layers palette).

STEP FIVE: Choose Stroke from the Add a Layer Style pop-up menu at the bottom of the Layers palette (the black circle with an "*f*"). When the Stroke Layer Style dialog appears, increase the Size to 9 pixels. This will put a red nine-pixel stroke around your layer (as shown). The stroke is red because that's the default stroke color, but notice how the corners have become rounded. We'll need to fix that.

continued

Quick Tip:
If it doesn't have a keyboard shortcut, give it one!

One of the coolest things about Photoshop CS may well be the ability to assign a keyboard shortcut to just about anything. For example, if you find yourself using a particular filter all the time (such as Gaussian Blur or Unsharp Mask), you can assign a keyboard shortcut for either one of them by going under the Edit menu and choosing Keyboard Shortcuts. This brings up a dialog box where you can choose whether you want to create a shortcut for a menu command, a tool, or a palette (from the pop-up menu at the top). Once you choose one of those categories, find the command you want to assign a shortcut, click on it, and type in the shortcut you want to use. Adding the shortcut is easy, but finding one that's not already taken is the hard part because there are already so many. Why, even the Keyboard Shortcut command has a keyboard shortcut. It's Shift-Option-Command-K (PC: Shift-Alt-Control-K).

STEP SIX: While you're still in the Stroke dialog, change the Position of the stroke from Outside (which gives you the rounded corners) to Inside (which removes the rounded corners by placing the stroke inside the layer, rather than extending out from it). In the Fill Type section, click on the red Color Swatch and when the Color Picker appears, choose white as your stroke color (as shown here). Don't click OK yet in the Layer Style dialog.

STEP SEVEN: In the list of Styles on the left side of the Layer Styles dialog box, click directly on the word Drop Shadow to make the Drop Shadow options visible in the dialog. Increase the Opacity setting to 90%, set the Angle to 118°, the Distance to 12, and the Size to 12, to create a dark drop shadow that's down and to the right from your snapshot. Now, the rest of the tutorial is about adjusting the background to focus more attention on the snapshot you just created.

STEP EIGHT: Here's one way of focusing attention on the snapshot: In the Layers palette, click on the Background layer to make it active. Press Command-L (PC: Control-L) to bring up Levels, then drag the bottom right-hand Output Levels slider to the left (as shown here) to darken the background.

On the next page, you'll find some other options for focusing attention on the snapshot.

OPTION ONE: Another option is to lighten the background using Levels. Just press Command-Z (PC: Control-Z) to undo the darkening of the background from the previous step. Bring up Levels again, but this time, drag the bottom *left* Output Levels slider to the right to lighten the background (as shown here).

OPTION TWO: Press Command-Z (PC: Control-Z) to undo the background lightening. This is the effect SeaWorld's designers used on the background—a Zoom blur. To apply a Zoom blur, go under the Filter menu, under Blur, and choose Radial Blur. When the dialog appears, choose Zoom under Blur Method, increase the Amount to 35, and click OK.

OPTION THREE: Undo the Zoom blur effect, and try this simple technique that focuses the viewer's eye to the snapshot by removing all color from the Background layer. Just go under the Image menu, under Adjustments, and choose Desaturate. This leaves just the snapshot still in color and immediately draws the eye to it.

Quick Tip:
Naming your layers as you duplicate them
Although the fastest way to duplicate your current layer is to press Command-J (PC: Control-J), it doesn't give you the option to name the layer—it just duplicates it. If you want to bring up the Duplicate Layer dialog, just Control-click (PC: Right-click) on the layer and choose Duplicate Layer from the pop-up menu. This will bring up the Duplicate Layer dialog box where you can name your layer before it's created.

Quick Tip:
**Turning a path
into a selection**

Once you have part of a
path selected using the
Direct Selection tool, you
can turn it into a selec-
tion by going to the Paths
palette and choosing
Make Selection from the
palette's pop-down menu.
The advantage of using
this method is that you can
add feathering (among
other options) in the Make
Selection dialog box. The
disadvantage is that if you
don't want feathering or
some of the other options,
you waste time in a dialog
box you don't need.

   Another method (if
you don't want feather-
ing) is to click on the Load
Path as a Selection icon at
the bottom of the Paths
palette. It's the third icon
from the left that looks
like a circle of dots.

Trendy Fashion Blowout Look

This is probably the hottest trend in fashion portrait retouching right now, and you see it everywhere,
from CD covers (like Madonna's "American Life") to print ads, to movie posters (like Jet Li's movie
Cradle 2 the Grave), and everything in between. The effect you're going for is one where the skin tone
turns completely white, leaving subtle shadow areas to reveal just the eyes, nostrils, lips, and outline of
the face. Here's the trick!

STEP ONE: Open the photo
you want to apply the effect to.
This technique works best on
images with a very light background, or a white background
(because it usually blows out
whatever background is present) and it works best with men
or women with darker hair.

© Brand X Pictures

STEP TWO: Press Option-
Command-~ (PC: Alt-Control-~)
[that's the key above your Tab
key]. This loads all the highlight
areas within your photo and
adds a slight feathering effect
at the same time, which is ideal
because it helps blend your
tonal adjustments in with the
rest of the photo.

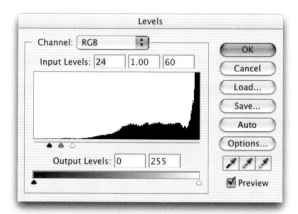

STEP THREE: Press Command-H (PC: Control-H) to hide the selection border from view, then choose Command-L (PC: Control-L) to bring up Levels. Drag the far right highlight Input Levels slider (the white one directly under the Histogram) almost all the way to the left to blow out the highlights. Then drag the shadow slider (the black one) to the right a bit to keep any shadows intact.

STEP FOUR: Click OK and you can see that her skin is considerably lighter, but you can still see her skin tone (it just looks like a very light flesh tone), so we have to keep going and pushing it further.

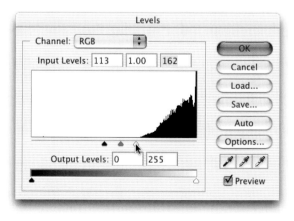

STEP FIVE: Press Command-L (PC: Control-L) to bring up Levels again. Drag the same highlight slider (the white one, under the Histogram, on the far right) to the left again (as shown here) to blow out the highlights even more. Drag until you don't see a change anymore, then drag the left black shadow slider to the right a bit to keep any stray shadow areas.

continued

Quick Tip:
Quick access to the Direct Selection tool

When you're using the Pen tool, you adjust points and path segments using the Direct Selection tool (which looks like a white, hollow arrow). You can temporarily switch to this tool any time you're working with the Pen tool by holding the Command key (PC: Control key). When you're done, release the Command key (PC: Control key), and you'll jump back to the last Pen tool you were using.

Quick Tip:
Rotating through the pens

In Photoshop, you can only toggle between two of the Pen tools found in the Toolbox with a keyboard shortcut: the regular Pen tool and the Freeform Pen tool. To toggle between these two, press Shift-P.

However, when a path is selected, you can actually access other pens that don't even have keyboard shortcuts. For example, if you have an active path and you move the Pen tool over a line segment—look at your pointer—it changes to the Add Anchor Point tool. Then, move the Pen tool over an anchor point and it changes into the Delete Anchor Point tool.

STEP SIX: Click OK and evaluate the photo. You can still see a little bit of skin tone, especially in her eyelids, around her ear, etc. The shadows under her chin are fine; so are the ones under her arm—you have to have some shadows to outline her face and arms (that's why we keep moving the shadow slider up—to keep those details somewhat visible).

STEP SEVEN: Let's push it some more. Bring up Levels again, and do the same thing—drag the highlight slider to blow out even more highlights (if you know anything about reading a Histogram, the one shown here lets you know there's simply not much there—it's almost all highlight).

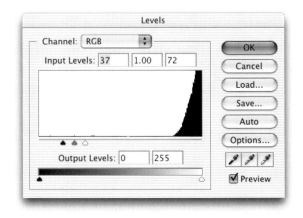

STEP EIGHT: Click OK and you're about there. If you were really anal, you might take one more pass at it to see if applying it one more time might make a difference.

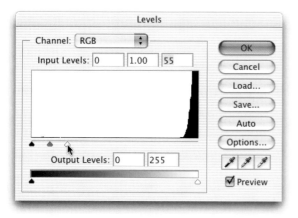

STEP NINE: Bring up Levels one last time, drag the highlight slider to the right, and see if it makes a difference. If it doesn't, press Cancel, if it does, go with it and click OK. Then press Command-H (PC: Control-H) to make your selection visible again, then press Command-D (PC: Control-D) to deselect. In the next step, you're going to bring back some of the original color in highlight areas outside the skin that were affected by your applications of levels.

STEP TEN: Get the History Brush from the Toolbox, and choose a medium sized soft-edged brush from the Brush Picker. Paint over the areas that aren't skin tone, but now look blown out. For example, paint over her top, and the clip for her headset (which both got blown out). As you paint with the History Brush, the original image you first opened (before Levels) is painted back in.

STEP ELEVEN: Next, take the History Brush and paint over the MP3 player to bring back its original detail, and then you can paint along her hair, near her shoulder, where the blue shadow looks kind of ratty and blown out. As you paint, the original image is painted back in. You might also want to paint in some of the shadows beneath her chin, and her ear buds.

continued

Quick Tip:
Where the tablet controls are hidden

Back in Photoshop 7, Adobe moved the controls for pressure-sensitive tablet users (generally just called Wacom Tablet users) into the expanded Brushes palette. On the left-hand side of the palette, you'll see a list of options. If you click on any of these options, their settings will appear in the palette. In many of the options' panels you'll find a pop-up menu for Control. That's where you'll find Pen Pressure, Pen Tilt, Stylus Wheel control, and more.

Quick Tip:
Loading
Action sets

When loading Action sets in older versions of Photoshop, you had to do more digging than an archaeologist to find them (they were buried deep within your drive, nested inside folder after folder). Not so in the latest versions of Photoshop; now they're just one click away. Here's how to load Actions: From the Window menu, choose Actions to bring up the Actions palette. From the palette's drop-down menu, choose one of the Action sets at the bottom. They'll appear as a folder in your Actions palette. Click the right-facing triangle beside the folder's name to show the contents of the folder. Scroll down to the Action you want and click on it. Then click the Play button (the right-facing triangle at the bottom of the Actions palette) to run it. Pretty sweet! Some of the Actions are pretty decent. Others are…well, let's just say they rhyme with "fame."

STEP TWELVE: That's it—the effect is complete. To show how it could look as a CD cover, I placed the photo into a CD jewel case cover (shown here) and added some type. Her fictitious name "Laura T" is in the font Mata (from House Industries) and the CD title "In the Name of Love" is in the font Skia. And of course, I added a drop shadow behind the CD box. Why? Because I could. ;-)

Before

After

The Shadow Tells the Story

This technique tells a story, and the idea of casting a shadow that reveals the real person, or their real intention, is starting to pop up everywhere. I recently saw this effect used in a magazine that showed a corporate CEO casting the shadow of a jester, making a stronger editorial statement than a thousand words.

© Brand X Pictures

STEP ONE: Open the photo you want to add a "storyteller" shadow to. In this instance, we're going to add a shadow of a full-grown bodybuilder, to illustrate the future man inside the little boy.

© Brand X Pictures

STEP TWO: Open the photo that you want to turn into a shadow. (Here's the bodybuilder photo we'll use as our shadow.)

continued

Quick Tip:
Using the new Fill control

Back in Photoshop 7, Adobe added a field in the Layers palette called Fill. This has actually been in Photoshop since version 6.0, but previously it resided in the seldom-seen Blending Options dialog (which appears within the Layer Styles dialog box. Go figure!). What this puppy does is enable you to lower the Opacity (or fill) of a layer while leaving any Layer Styles applied to the layer at full intensity. Here's how to see it in action (and then it will make more sense): Create some type, add a Drop Shadow Layer Style, then lower the Fill (in the Layers palette) to 0% and all will become clear (young grasshopper).

Quick Tip:
Clearing out all those guides

If you use Photoshop's non-printing guides, they can sometimes really clutter up the screen. If you want to get rid of them all quickly—don't drag them one-by-one back to the Rulers (from whence they came)—instead, just go under the View menu and choose Clear Guides.

STEP THREE: You have to start by putting a selection around the bodybuilder. Since this photo was taken on a white seamless background, selecting him will be fairly easy. Start by pressing the letter "w" to get the Magic Wand tool, and then click once on the white background. This will select everything except the area between his legs, so hold the Shift key and click the Magic Wand once within that area to add it to your selection (as shown).

STEP FOUR: Now that the entire background is selected, you're going to use an old selection trick—if you inverse the selection, you get everything *but* the background. So, go under the Select menu and choose Inverse, giving you a selection around the bodybuilder.

STEP FIVE: Once you have just the bodybuilder selected, press Shift-Command-J (PC: Shift-Control-J) to cut him from the Background layer, and copy him onto his own separate layer above the Background layer (as shown here).

STEP SIX: Press the letter "d" to set your Foreground color to black, then press Shift-Option-Delete (PC: Shift-Alt-Backspace) to fill the bodybuilder image with black (as shown here).

Quick Tip:
Aligning objects on different layers

You can align objects on different layers by linking them together (click once in the center column of each layer you want linked in the Layers palette), going under the Layer menu, under Align Linked, and choosing how you want your layers aligned from the menu.

STEP SEVEN: Now, switch back to the little boy photo. Press the letter "L" to get the Lasso tool (or choose any selection tool you're familiar with—in the example shown here, I'm using the Magnetic Lasso tool). Make a selection around the little boy and the weights that he's holding up.

STEP EIGHT: Press Command-J (PC: Control-J) to put a copy of the little boy onto his own separate layer. This is just a copy; the original little boy is still on the Background layer.

continued

Quick Tip:
**Another
Photoshop
prank**

Thanks to a feature added in Photoshop 7, you can now pull one of my favorite Adobe Illustrator pranks on your Photoshop coworkers or friends that will drive them just this side of insane. Adobe put a pop-up list of language dictionaries in the Character palette for hyphenation and spelling. The simple trick is to change the dictionary from English USA to English UK. The next time they create some paragraph type, or run the spell checker…well, you get the picture. I've pulled this prank and in each instance, if they see the word English when the glance at the palette, they assume it's correct, and so far they've never noticed it was changed from English USA to English UK. Eventually, they just give up and do a full reinstall of Photoshop. It's a great way to turn somebody's day upside-down.

STEP NINE: Press the letter "v" to switch to the Move tool. Then go to the bodybuilder document, click anywhere within the black shadow image, and drag-and-drop that shadow over on the photo of the little boy. When you drag the shadow over, it will appear in front of the little boy (as shown here).

STEP TEN: To get the shadow behind the little boy, just go to the Layers palette, click on the shadow layer, and drag it directly below the little boy copy layer (as shown). Your Layers palette should now have the little boy copy layer on top of the layer stack, the shadow in the middle, and the original photo on the Background layer.

STEP ELEVEN: While you're still on the shadow layer, press Command-T (PC: Control-T) to bring up Free Transform. Hold the Command key (PC: Control key), click on the top center point of the bounding box (as shown here), and drag to the right to skew the shadow over to the right. When it looks like the one shown here, press Return (PC: Enter) to lock in your transformation.

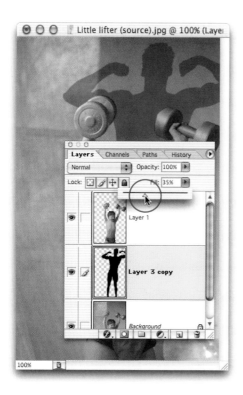

STEP TWELVE: To make the shadow less intense so that it's more natural and blends in with the background, go to the Layers palette and lower the Opacity setting of the shadow layer to around 35% (as shown here).

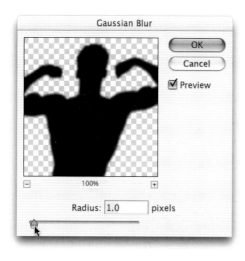

STEP THIRTEEN: To soften the shadow, go under the Filter menu, under Blur, and choose Gaussian Blur. When the Gaussian Blur dialog appears, add a slight amount of blur (1 pixel for low-res, 72-ppi photos, or 5 pixels for high-res, 300-ppi photos). Click OK to complete the effect. A before and after is shown on the following page.

continued

Quick Tip:
Speeding up Photoshop by merging layers

Photoshop is a slave to file size: the larger the size of your file, generally speaking, the slower Photoshop goes (especially if you're short on RAM). Every time you add a layer, it significantly adds to the overall file size of your image. That's why it's sometimes a good idea to merge together layers that you don't think you'll need to adjust later on.

For example, if you have ten layers of type, you can save a lot of file size by rasterizing each of the Type layers and merging them into one layer. Do this by clicking on the top text layer and pressing Command-E (PC: Control-E). This takes the layer you're on and merges it with the layer directly beneath it. Keep pressing Command-E (PC: Control-E) until all the text layers are merged. Your file size will shrink, and in many cases, Photoshop goes faster. Be careful when merging layers with Layer Styles applied, though, because they have Blend Modes assigned by default, and merging them can change or hide those effects.

Before

After

Painted Edges

This technique, where you essentially erase the photo and then paint it back in, is particularly popular for landscape and portrait photographers, but it works so well, for so many different style photos, that you'll be amazed at how many other uses you'll find for it. In fact, at the end of the technique, I show how you can turn this into a template, and then drop any photo you want right in.

© Brand X Pictures

STEP ONE: Open the photo you want to apply the effect to.

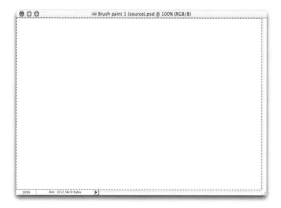

STEP TWO: Press Command-A (PC: Control-A) to put a selection around the entire photo, then press Delete (PC: Backspace) to erase the entire photo (as shown here). Create a new layer by clicking on the New Layer icon at the bottom of the Layers palette.

STEP THREE: Choose the History Brush from the Toolbox (as shown here). Go up to the Options Bar, and bring up the Brush Picker by clicking on the down-facing triangle directly to the right of the current brush tip thumbnail.

continued

Quick Tip:
What's in a name?

Adobe made a tiny change to a menu item that makes a whole lot of sense. To hide any of Photoshop's visual indicators (such as type highlighting, the Free Transform bounding box, non-printing guides, Slice borders, etc.) you would choose Show Extras from the View menu. That's right, to hide the extras, you'd choose Show Extras. It was one of those menu commands that really made you scratch your head. Adobe changed that, and now it's just called "Extras." Either you want them or you don't, and as always, a checkmark next to the menu item lets you know if it's toggled on or off.

Quick Tip:
**Brush changes
update in two
places at once**

Now that Photoshop has
brushes available to you
in two places (from the
Options Bar and from the
floating Brushes palette),
you'd think that you'd have
to go back and forth updating one or the other when
you save or edit a brush.
Luckily, Adobe designed
it so changes you make in
one palette are automati-
cally carried through to the
other palette, so that when
you're editing and creating
brushes, fear not—the
other palette will know
what you're doing and will
be updated appropriately.

STEP FOUR: You're going to
load a set of brushes, so go to
the Brush Picker's pop-down
menu (click on the right-facing
black triangle in the top-right
corner of the Picker) and choose
Thick Heavy Brushes (as shown).

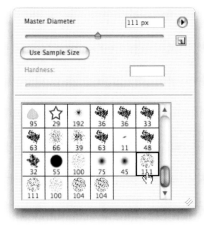

STEP FIVE: When the dialog appears, click the Append button
to add these Thick Heavy Brushes to your default set (they'll
appear at the end of your set of
brushes, as shown here). Click
on the first Thick Heavy Brush,
the 111-pixel brush.

STEP SIX: Start painting a few
strokes with this brush from left
to right across your image area.
As you do, the original photo
will paint back in (as shown).
One of the cool things about
this brush is that it has some
gaps in it (like painting with
a real dry brush), which helps
give it a real painted look. Take
a look at the bottom stroke in
particular and you can see the
gaps (the upper areas don't
have it, because I painted over
the stroke more than once).

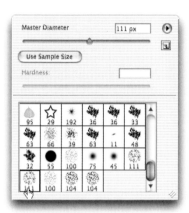

STEP SEVEN: Now, go to the Brush Picker, and choose the next 111-pixel brush in the Picker (as shown).

STEP EIGHT: Paint with about 7/8 of the bottom of the brush tip inside the already painted area and the other 1/8 of the brush (the top of the brush tip) extending over the top of the painted area. This adds a more random, spattered look. If you look at the top of this photo, you can see some spattering and specks, which were created with this brush.

nantucket seafood festival

STEP NINE: Here's the finished piece, with a line of text added, using all lowercase and the font Minion (from Adobe) with the tracking set at 400. Now, remember how we created a layer at the very beginning of this project? We did that so that we can now use this edge effect as a template for other photos (as you'll see in the next step).

Quick Tip:
Renaming brushes

Don't like the name you gave your brush (wish instead of "39-pixel soft-edge," you had named it "Frank," or "Cathy," or "Snoop Dogg")? Just Control-click (PC: Right-click) on the brush, choose Rename Brush from the pop-up menu, and when the dialog box appears, type in a new name and click OK.

continued

Quick Tip:
The secret to Batch Ranking

If you're using Photoshop's handy File Browser, you probably already know that it allows you to rank images to help you sort and organize them. However, what if you need to rank 50 or 60 images all the same? Do you have to go to 50 or 60 images individually and rank them one-by-one? It would seem so, because there's nothing in the drop-down palette about it, but here's the little secret tip that will make all your dreams come true (okay, it's something short of that, but it's a good tip). First, Command-click (PC: Control-click) on all the images you want to rank (if the images are contiguous, you can Shift-click on the first and last images to select all), and then Control-click (PC: Right-click) on one of the selected images to bring up the contextual menu. Choose Rank and then type in the rank you want to use in the Rank Files dialog, and it will automatically rank every file you chose. Thanks to Adobe's Graphics Evangelist Julieanne Kost for sharing this cool inside tip.

STEP TEN: Hold the Command key (PC: Control key), go to the Layers palette, and click on your photo layer. This puts a selection around your entire image (as shown here). Once the selection is in place, go under the Select menu and choose Save Selection. When the dialog appears, click OK. You can now drag this photo layer into the Trash icon in the Layers palette to delete it.

STEP ELEVEN: Open a different photo, press the letter "v" to get the Move tool, and click-and-drag this photo onto the document with the saved selection. Go under the Select menu and choose Load Selection. Choose Alpha 1 from the Channel pop-up menu, then click OK to load the selection onto your new photo. Then, go under the Select menu and choose Inverse to select everything but the center area (as shown here).

© Brand X Pictures

STEP TWELVE: Press Delete (PC: Backspace) and the outside areas are deleted, giving you the same edge effect applied to a different photo. The only thing left to do is to change the type to match the photo (which I did here using the Font ITC Bradley Hand).

Popping Out of a Photo

This is a surprisingly easy effect that gives the impression that the subjects in the photo are popping out (okay, in this case, walking out) of the photo. This popular effect is probably used the most in print advertising campaigns, but now I'm starting to see everyone from wedding photographers to children's studio photographers use the same technique, because it adds 3D depth to a 2D image.

STEP ONE: Open the photo you want to use in this effect. In this example, we're using people, but I've also seen this effect used in photos of products. Press Command-A (PC: Control-A) to select the entire photo, then press Shift-Command-J (PC: Shift-Control-J) to cut the photo from the Background layer, and copy it onto its own layer.

STEP TWO: Use the Selection tool of your choice (such as the Magnetic Lasso tool, Pen tool, etc.) to put a selection around the object you want to "pop out" of the photo (in this case, the bride and groom). Once they're selected, press Command-J (PC: Control-J) to put them up on their own separate layer. Click back on Layer 1 in the Layers palette to make it active (this is the layer that still contains the entire image).

STEP THREE: Press the letter "m" to get the Rectangular Marquee tool and drag out a selection around the area of the background you want to remain visible (make sure you include your subject in this selected area). Then go under the Select menu and choose Inverse, to select everything except that area you want to keep (as shown here).

continued

Quick Tip:
Paint tools have Blend Modes too

You're probably familiar with layer Blend Modes, where you change how a layer interacts with the layers beneath it. In Normal mode, it doesn't interact; it just covers whatever's beneath it. Well, Photoshop's paint tools have the same feature, and choosing any Blend Mode (other than Normal) allows your paint to interact with (be affected by) the colors in the image you paint on. These Blend Modes are accessed from the Options Bar when you have a paint tool selected.

STEP FOUR: Press Delete (PC: Backspace) to delete the area surrounding your protected area (as shown). Then choose Stroke from the Add a Layer Style pop-up menu at the bottom of the Layers palette. Increase the Size to 11, change the Position to Inside, then click on the Color Swatch and change the color to a very light gray (as shown). Then, in the list of Styles on the left side of the dialog, click on the word Drop Shadow. Increase the Size to 10 and click OK to give your background a Polaroid effect.

STEP FIVE: Go to the Layers palette, click on the word "Drop Shadow" attached to your photo layer, and drag it to the layer with just the bride and groom to apply that same drop shadow to them. Although you want the shadow of the bride and groom to appear above and below the photo, you don't want it to appear on the photo itself, so click on the bride and groom layer, go under the Layer menu, under Layer Styles, and choose Create Layer to create a separate layer with just the drop shadow.

STEP SIX: In the Layers palette, click on this shadow layer. Then, hold the Command key (PC: Control key) and in the Layers palette, click on the photo background layer to put a selection around your photo (remember, you're still on the shadow layer—don't change layers). Now, press Delete (PC: Backspace) to remove all of the shadows that fall on the photo itself, and complete the effect (as shown here).

Photo to Sketch in 60 Seconds Flat

I learned the basics of this technique from Rich Harris, the creative guru over at Wacom Technology Co. He sent me a bunch of PDFs with some special effects he had come up with, and this one just blew me away, so I asked Rich if I could include it in the book. It does the best job I've seen yet of converting a photo into a color pencil sketch. But then, not one to leave well enough alone, I added some texture effects, and a mat border to create the effect you'll learn here.

Quick Tip:
F5 is still here, baby!

Back in Photoshop 5 and 5.5, to bring up the floating Brushes palette, you'd press the F5 key on your extended keyboard. Well, when Photoshop 6.0 came out, the floating Brushes palette went away, and pressing F5 was just an exercise in futility. (When Photoshop 6.0 first came out, you could see Photoshop users pressing F5 over and over again, sobbing, "Why? Why!!!") Thankfully in Photoshop 7, the floating Brushes palette came back and along with it Adobe resurrected the classic F5 shortcut. Life was good again, and thankfully, F5 still works in Photoshop CS.

© Brand X Pictures

STEP ONE: Open the photo you want to convert into a color sketch.

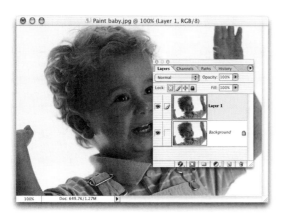

STEP TWO: Press Shift-Command-U (PC: Shift-Control-U) to remove the color from the photo (technically, this is called "Desaturating"). Then press Command-J (PC: Control-J) to duplicate the layer (as shown here).

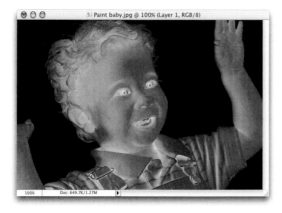

STEP THREE: Press Command-I (PC: Control-I) to invert the photo (giving you the negative look shown here).

continued

Quick Tip:
Starting from scratch with your brush

You want to edit a brush, or create a new one for that matter, and you want to start with a clean slate (i.e., you want all the option settings for the various brush controls set back to their defaults). Then, in the Brushes palette, click on the options you want to edit (e.g., Brush Dynamics, Scattering, Texture, etc.), and from the palette's drop-down menu choose "Clear Brush Controls." This will clear all the current settings and it also deselects the entire panel, so you may have to click on the option you want again; but when you do, all the default settings will be in place.

STEP FOUR: Go to the Layers palette and change the layer Blend Mode for this layer from Normal to Color Dodge. Doing this turns your photo completely white (it looks like a blank document, but in the next step, you bring back the photo).

STEP FIVE: Then go under the Filter menu, under Blur, and choose Gaussian Blur. When the dialog appears, drag the Radius slider all the way to the left, and then start slowly dragging back to the right, and as you do your sketch will begin to appear (as shown here). Click OK when the lines look dark and the photo doesn't look too blurry.

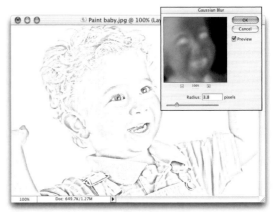

STEP SIX: Get the History Brush from the Toolbox. Go up in the Options Bar and lower the Opacity of this tool to 20%, then choose a large, soft-edged brush (from the Brush Picker up in the Options Bar) and begin painting over the photo. As you paint, a faint version of the original color in the photo will appear (as shown). Keep the mouse button held down the entire time as you paint.

STEP SEVEN: Release the mouse button, then just click once on both cheeks to bring out extra color (every time you click the mouse and paint again, it paints darker). Then shrink the size of the brush (press the left bracket key "[" on your keyboard) until the size of the brush matches the size of the child's eye, then click once on each eye to bring back more color.

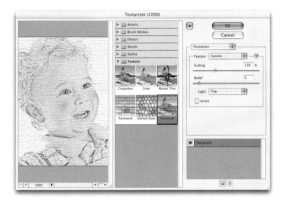

STEP EIGHT: Press Command-E (PC: Control-E) to merge the top layer with the Background. Now you'll add some texture to your sketch, to enhance the effect. Under the Filter menu, under Texture, choose Texturizer. When the dialog appears (shown here), for Texture choose Canvas, then set the Scaling at 100%, the Relief at 4, and the direction to Top. Click OK. When the canvas texture is applied, it's usually way too intense, but you can adjust that.

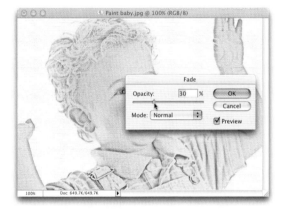

STEP NINE: Right after you apply the filter, go under the Edit menu and choose Fade Texturizer. When the Fade dialog appears, lower the Opacity to 30% to decrease the intensity of the effect. Next, press Command-A (PC: Control-A) to select the entire photo, then press Shift-Command-J (PC: Shift-Control-J) to cut the photo off the Background and put it on its own layer.

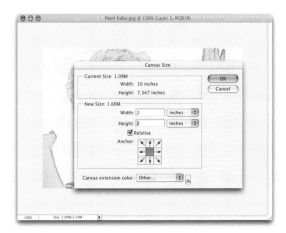

STEP TEN: Now to add a mat around the photo. Go under the Image menu and choose Canvas Size. When the Canvas Size dialog (shown here) appears check Relative and enter 2 inches for Width and Height. At the bottom of the dialog, click on the Canvas Extension Color Swatch to bring up the Color Picker. Choose a light beige as your Canvas (mat) color and then click OK to expand your canvas area to create a mat (as shown here).

Quick Tip:
Want to increase your Canvas Size? Check Relative.

Want to stop doing so much math when you go to the Canvas Size dialog box to add some extra space? Just check the Relative box (added in version 7) and type in how much space you want to add, rather than trying to determine how much to add to your current dimensions. Try it once and you'll see what I mean.

continued

Quick Tip:
Creating your own textures

If you want to create your own textures in Photoshop, here are a couple of tips that might help:

• The Clouds filter is a great place to start building your textures because it already has a texture.

• Many textures are built using the Add Noise filter as a base. Generally, you'd start by filling the Background layer with a color and then running the Add Noise filter.

• Use Gradients as your base and build upon that. You can run filters, such as Polar Coordinates, Waves, Ripple, Glass, etc. on top of gradients to create your own custom textures.

• If you started with a noise background, try adding the Motion Blur filter to enhance your background.

• Use the Texturizer filter to add texture to flat colors or to enhance a noise background.

STEP ELEVEN: In the Layers palette, click back on your photo layer, then choose Inner Shadow from the Add a Layer Style pop-up menu at the bottom of the Layers palette. Lower the Opacity to 40%, set the Distance to 2, then click OK to add a slight drop shadow on the inside edges of the photo, as if it was behind a real mat.

STEP TWELVE: Press Command-A (PC: Control-A) to put a selection around the entire image. Create a new blank layer, then choose Stroke from the Edit menu. Set the Width to 1 pixel and click OK to apply a thin black border around your beige mat. In the Layers palette, lower the Opacity of this layer to 50%, to make it appear thinner. The final effect is shown below.

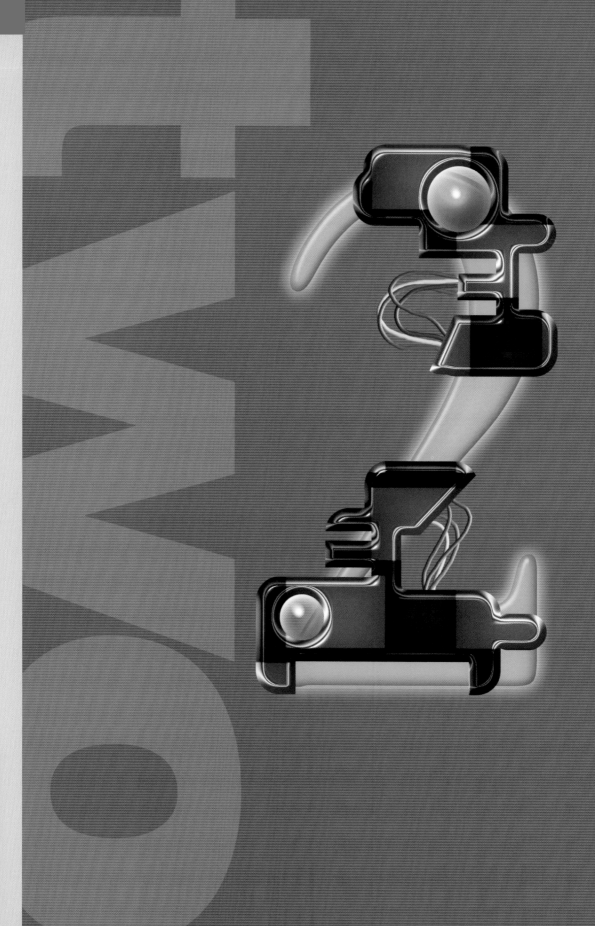

I'll bet you thought you were done with photographic effects when you finished the last chapter.

Photo Finish
Photographic Effects, Part 2

Well, my friend, there's more. Much more! One chapter just couldn't hold all the cool photographic effects, so I was forced (by the Senate subcommittee on not having too many photo effects in one chapter) to create "Part Deux." By the way, the word "Deux" is French for "doo," which my 6-year-old son tells me is half a word. As I'm sure you're aware, it's not really "doo." That's totally a joke. Deux is French for "du," which as everyone knows is short for "dude." So if you're in France (perhaps on your way to someplace that doesn't hate Americans, like Russia) and you see a long-haired surfer-looking Frenchman, say something like "Bonjour, du." Chances are he'll usually answer back with something like "Die American, die!" but at least he didn't just sneer at you and say, "My name isn't Dude." It's at that moment you realize that you're actually speaking French to a real French surf dude. Right then you'll know—this chapter was all worth it.

Quick Tip:
How to navigate your image when you're zoomed in close

When you've zoomed in on an image, trying to navigate using the scroll bars is frustrating at best, because when you're zoomed in really close, even a small move with the scroll bar can move the area you're working on totally out of the image window. Instead, when you've zoomed in, hold the Spacebar and your pointer will temporarily change to the Hand tool, and you can click-and-drag around your image. This is an ideal way to move quickly around your zoomed image, without the frustration of the scroll bars. When you release the Spacebar, you immediately switch back to the tool you were using.

Creating a Sense of Motion

This is a very popular technique for photos taken for editorial purposes (for example, if you're shooting a CEO for a magazine or newspaper article about his company). It's also popular in high-end executive portraits, because the effect leaves the subject totally focused but adds movement through the rest of the photo. The effect is so simple to apply, you're going to wonder, "Is that all there is to it?" Yup, that's all there is to it.

STEP ONE: Open a photo that you want to add movement to.

© Brand X Pictures

STEP TWO: Duplicate the Background layer by pressing Command-J (PC: Control-J).

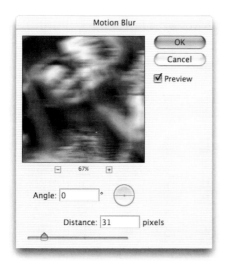

STEP THREE: Go under the Filter menu, under Blur, and choose Motion Blur. Set the Angle to the direction you want to have motion applied (I usually use a horizontal setting), and use the Distance to control the amount of effect. (I chose 31 for this low-res, 72-ppi photo. Try 100 for a high-res, 300-ppi image.)

In Photoshop CS you no longer have to choose a Background color before you enter the Canvas Size dialog (Image>Canvas Size). Now you can choose the color you'd like your increased canvas area to be from the bottom of the Canvas Size dialog. You can click on the Color Swatch and pick a custom color, choose white or black from the pop-up menu, or choose to use the current Foreground or Background color.

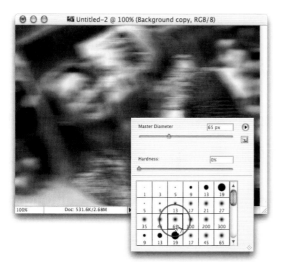

STEP FOUR: Press the letter "e" to switch to the Eraser tool. Then go up to the Options Bar, click on the down-facing arrow next to the Brush thumbnail to get the Brush Picker, and choose a soft-edged brush (as shown here).

STEP FIVE: Now for the fun part—just erase over the areas that you want to retain detail. As you erase, the original layer beneath your blurry layer will be revealed. I generally erase the person's face, clothes, and anything else they might be holding, but I stop right before the edges.

Adding Side Lighting After the Fact

If your subject needs more side lighting, or you just wish you had added a sidelight before you snapped the photo, this is a pretty cool way to add the effect back in. In the example shown here, we're applying it to a person, but the technique would work pretty much the same way for product shots as well.

STEP ONE: Open the photo you want to give additional side lighting. In the photo shown here, we're going to add some back/side lighting to the left side of his face.

© Brand X Pictures

STEP TWO: The original Background layer has to stay intact for this technique, so you'll need to work on a copy. To duplicate the Background layer, simply press Command-J (PC: Control-J), and a duplicate will appear (named Layer 1 by default) as shown here.

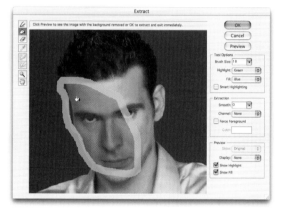

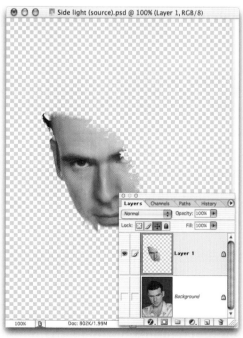

STEP THREE: Go under the Filter menu and choose Extract. You're going to use Extract to cut out a copy of the left side of his face, onto its own separate layer. In the Extract dialog, press the letter "b" to choose the Edge Highlighter tool (the top tool in the Extract Toolbar) and use it to trace along the left side of his face. Once that's traced, make a loop back to where you started, fully enclosing the left side of his face (as shown).

STEP FOUR: Press the letter "g" to switch to the Fill tool (it's the second tool in the Extract Toolbar and it looks like a paint bucket), and click it once within your marker-encircled area (as shown). Since you already defined the edges of what you want to extract, clicking the Fill tells Photoshop which areas you want to retain in the extraction.

STEP FIVE: Click OK in the Extract dialog to extract that part of his face. Since the Background is still visible, you won't be able to see your extraction, so go to the Layers palette and click on the Eye icon in the first column of the Background layer to hide it from view. Now you'll see the extracted face (as shown here). As you can see, little parts of the left edge of his face got erased during the extraction process. We've got a quick fix that will take care of most of the "dropping out."

Quick Tip:
Defining patterns

In older versions of Photoshop, you could only define one pattern at a time. When you created a new pattern, the old pattern would disappear, never to be found again. Photoshop 6.0 and 7.0 came with a number of preset patterns that you could use time and time again. You can also define your own patterns and add them to the Pattern Picker so that you can go back and use them whenever you want. Just go under the Edit menu, choose Define Pattern, name your pattern, and click OK to add it to the bottom of the Pattern Picker in the Fill dialog.

continued

Quick Tip:
Saving selections for later use

If you have a selection that you think you can use later in the same project, you can save and store that selection until you need it. Here's how: While your selection is active, go under the Select menu and choose Save Selection. When the dialog box appears, just click OK. Your selection is now saved.

If you want to get that selection back onscreen at any time, go under the Select menu, but this time choose Load Selection. When the dialog box appears, chose your saved selection (named Alpha 1) from the Channel pop-up menu, and click OK. Your saved selection will then appear within your image.

STEP SIX: To bring back details on the left edge of his face, press Command-J (PC: Control-J) two times, to make two duplicates of this layer (as shown here). This has a multiplying effect, and brings back quite of bit of the area that had dropped out. (Compare it with the previous capture and you'll see what I mean.)

STEP SEVEN: Now that the duplicate layers have done their job, you don't really need three separate layers, so to combine the three into one, press Command-E (PC: Control-E) twice. This merges the three layers into one (as shown here in the Layers palette).

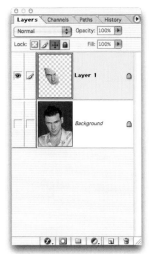

STEP EIGHT: We need to put a selection around this "left-side-of-the-face" layer, so hold the Command key (PC: Control key) and click on the layer in the Layers palette. This puts a selection around the entire object on the layer. Now you'll need to save that selection, so go under the Select menu and choose Save Selection. When the Save Selection dialog appears (shown here), just click OK. Then, press Command-D (PC: Control-D) to deselect.

STEP NINE: In the Layers palette click where the Eye icon used to be for the Background layer to make it visible again. Then, press the letter "d" then "x" to set your Foreground color to white. Press Shift-Option-Delete (PC: Shift-Alt-Backspace) to fill your face layer with white (as shown here).

STEP TEN: Press the letter "v" to get the Move tool, then press the left Arrow key twice to nudge the white layer over to the left.

STEP ELEVEN: Go under the Select menu and choose Load Selection. When the Load Selection dialog appears, from the Channel pop-up menu choose Alpha 1 (that's the original selection of the face that you saved earlier). Click OK and that original selection will appear onscreen (as shown). As you can see, because you nudged the white part over to the left, the white part extends slightly outside your selection.

continued

Quick Tip:
Getting rid of the checkerboard pattern

This should really be called "How to get rid of that annoying checkerboard pattern." I'm talking about the gray-and-white pattern that appears behind transparent layers to let you know which parts of the layer are transparent. In most cases you don't need this pattern, because you already have something that lets you see what's transparent on a layer—they're called your eyes. Because of that, I constantly have people asking me how to turn it off, so I thought I'd better include this information in the book. You go under the Photoshop menu (PC: Edit menu), under Preferences, and choose Transparency & Gamut. Under Transparency Settings, choose None for Grid Size, click OK, and the pattern will be gone.

Quick Tip:
Making Color Overlay work

If you've ever tried Photoshop's Color Overlay Layer Style, you may have been disappointed in how it works (I know *I* was at first), because rather than overlaying a transparent color over your object, it pretty much puts a solid fill over it. To get this Layer Style to work the way it probably should, all you have to do is change the Blend Mode in the Color Overlay dialog box from Normal to (get this…) Overlay. That way, the color doesn't obliterate the effects you've already applied. Try it and you'll see what I mean.

STEP TWELVE: While your selection is still in place, press Delete (PC: Backspace), then deselect by pressing Command-D (PC: Control-D). You'll see some of the "junk" left over in the middle of the his face, but don't sweat it—you'll remove those "leftovers" in the next step.

STEP THIRTEEN: Press the letter "e" to switch to the Eraser tool, and erase all those leftover white areas on his face (as shown). Also use the Eraser to remove the white area in his hair (above his ear), leaving just the left side of his ear and face with the white extending out. Lastly, lower the Opacity setting to 80% in the Layers palette. As you can see in the before and after below, the left side of his face now looks lit from behind.

Before

After

Edge Collage Technique

I saw this technique used on the contents of *Surfer* magazine, and I thought it was so well done, I wanted to show you how to get a similar effect. What's nice is—the photo never moves an inch, and you only use one photo, but when you're done, it has the look of a complex collage. My hat's off to the designers at *Surfer* who came up with this slick treatment.

STEP ONE: Open the photo you want to apply the effect to. You can set that aside for now, because first you need to create the torn-edge template that you'll use for the rest of this technique. So open a new document, 7″ wide by 5″ tall, in RGB mode, in a resolution that matches the resolution of the photo you just opened.

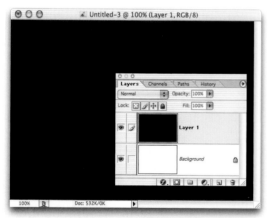

STEP TWO: Create a new blank layer by clicking on the New Layer icon at the bottom of the Layers palette. Press "d" to set your Foreground color to black, then press Option-Delete (PC: Alt-Backspace) to fill this layer with black (as shown).

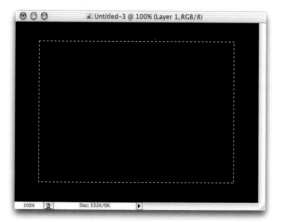

STEP THREE: Press the letter "m" to get the Rectangular Marquee tool, and drag out a rectangular selection that's about 75% as large as your original (it should look something like the selection shown here).

Quick Tip:
Esoteric-selection shortcut of the month

Okay, this one's pretty freaky: You probably already know that if you hold the Command key (PC: Control key) and click on a layer's name (in the Layers palette), it puts a selection around the objects on that layer. So for example, if you had type on a layer and Command-clicked (PC: Control-clicked) on the Type layer, it would put a selection around all your type. But here's the "esoteric-selection" short-cut of the month: If after loading that selection, you then press Shift-Option-Command (PC: Shift-Alt-Control) and click on another layer (in the Layers palette), it will load a selection only where it intersects with your original selection. Try it once, and if you're like me, you'll wonder, "When in the world would I use that?" Hey…I don't make these keyboard shortcuts, I just share them with my "peeps."

continued

Quick Tip:
Canvas Size lies!

Okay, this is really more of a half-truth. Here's the scoop: When you shrink the Canvas Size of your document (basically, you're cropping down the image without using the Crop tool), you get a warning dialog that reads "The new canvas size is smaller than the current canvas size; some clipping will occur." If you go ahead and click the "Proceed" button, your new smaller, canvas size will appear. Here's the thing: Let's say you had a Type layer with the word "Washington," on it, and when you took 3 inches off your Width in the Canvas Size dialog, all that was left on screen is "shingt" (it clipped off the left and the right side), you're really not as out of luck as Photoshop's warning dialog makes you think. That's because although you can't see it, the rest of the word was not deleted—it's just hidden from view. Grab the Move tool and drag your type left (or right) and you'll see the rest of your supposedly "clipped-off" word.

STEP FOUR: Press the letter "q" to switch to Quick Mask Mode so you can apply a filter to your selection (one of the benefits of using Quick Mask). A red border will appear around your unselected areas, so don't let that throw you—it's just a visual cue—you can pretty much ignore it.

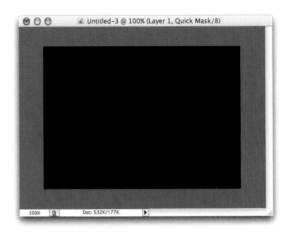

STEP FIVE: Go under the Filter menu, under Sketch, and choose Conté Crayon. When the Conté Crayon dialog appears (shown here), use the default settings (shown in the dialog), and click OK to apply a rough edge to your selection. Because we're in Quick Mask Mode, after you click OK, you'll be able to see the rough edge effect applied to the black area of your Quick Mask selection (see the capture in the next step).

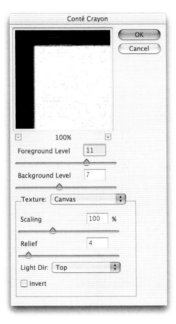

STEP SIX: Running this filter once is not enough to get the edges as rough as we need them, so repeat the filter several times by pressing Command-F (PC: Control-F) five times in a row. (The Command/Control-F keyboard shortcut simply repeats the last filter you applied, using the exact same settings.)

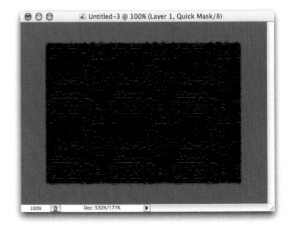

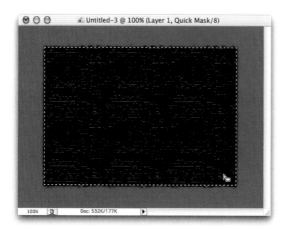

STEP SEVEN: Running this filter five times causes the effect to be applied not only to the edges but to the center of your selection (the black area) as well—but that's easy to fix. Just take the Rectangular Marquee tool and drag a selection that's just a tiny bit inside the rough edges (as shown here). Don't select all the way to the edge—just to the inside of it.

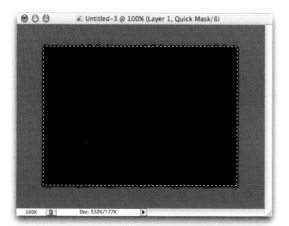

STEP EIGHT: Press Delete (PC: Backspace) to fill your selected area with black (as shown). Now you can deselect by pressing Command-D (PC: Control-D).

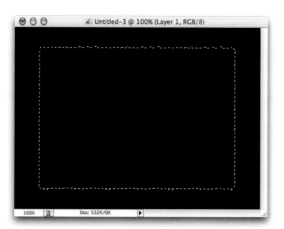

STEP NINE: To leave Quick Mask Mode and to see your final selection (with the rough edges), press the letter "q" once again. You'll see your regular black layer with your rough edge selection in place (as shown here). Next, you'll need to remove the black around your selected area.

Quick Tip:
Controlling your tracking

Tracking is the space between a group of letters or words (kerning is the space between just two letters).

To visually (rather than numerically) set the tracking tighter (removing space between a group of letters), take the Type tool and highlight your text, then press Option-Left Arrow (PC: Alt-Left Arrow) to tighten. Press Option-Right Arrow (PC: Alt-Right Arrow) to add space between a selected group of letters or words.

continued

Quick Tip:
Importing artwork from Adobe Illustrator

There are at least five different ways to import artwork created in Adobe Illustrator but frankly, there's only one *good* way to do it. In Adobe Illustrator, save the file as an EPS, switch to Photoshop, open the document you want to import your artwork into, and go under the File menu and choose Place. Choose your saved EPS Illustrator artwork and click OK. A bounding box will appear with a preview (if you saved it with a preview), and you can scale the image to any size you'd like (it's still EPS vector artwork at this point). When you get it to the exact size you like, press the Return or Enter key, and only then will it rasterize and become a pixel-based Photoshop image. When it rasterizes, it takes on the exact resolution and color mode of the document it was imported into. That's all there is to it.

STEP TEN: Go under the Select menu and choose Inverse. This inverses your selection, which means everything is selected except your middle area. Press Delete (PC: Backspace) to knock out these extra areas. Deselect by pressing Command-D (PC: Control-D). In the Layers palette, hide the Background layer from view by clicking on the Eye icon in the first column of the Background layer.

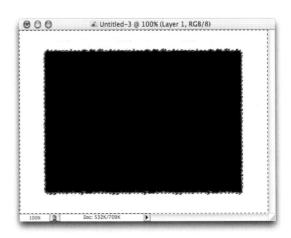

STEP ELEVEN: Hold the Command (PC: Control) key and click on the New Layer icon in the Layers palette. This creates a new layer directly beneath your black edge layer (rather than above it). Now take the Rectangular Marquee tool and draw a selection that's a bit larger than your black edge area (as shown). Press "x" to make your Foreground color white, then fill this selection with white by pressing Option-Delete (PC: Alt-Backspace). Deselect by pressing Command-D (PC: Control-D). Choose Merge Visible from the Layers palette's pop-down menu to merge these black and white layers.

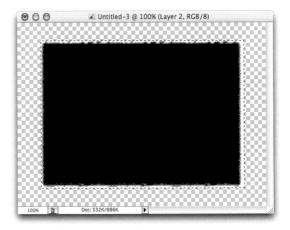

STEP TWELVE: Next, you'll knock a hole out of the middle. Take the Rectangular Marquee tool and drag out a selection that's just inside the black edge area. Press Delete (PC: Backspace) to knock out a hole (as shown). Deselect by pressing Command-D (PC: Control-D), and believe it or not, your edge is finally complete, and we can get on with the effect.

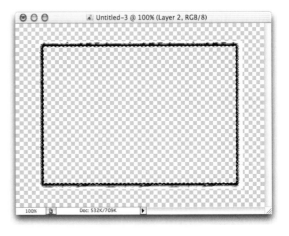

STEP THIRTEEN: Press the letter "v" to get the Move tool, click on your edge layer, and drag-and-drop it onto your original photo layer (as shown here). Chances are the edge is too large, so in the next step, you'll scale it down to size.

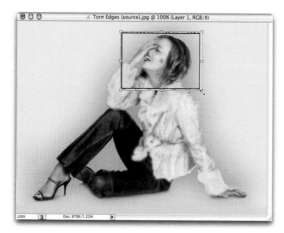

STEP FOURTEEN: Press Command-T (PC: Control-T) to bring up Free Transform. Hold the Shift key, grab a corner point, and drag inward to scale the edge down until it covers her head and part of her shoulders. (To reposition the edge, click-and-drag anywhere within the bounding box.) Press Return (PC: Enter) to lock in your transformation. This is your edge template, so go to the Layers palette, double-click directly on the name of this layer to highlight it, and then type in the name "Template."

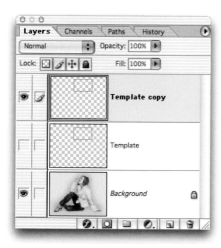

STEP FIFTEEN: This step is really important because you'll be doing it over and over again during this technique. Duplicate the Template layer by pressing Command-J (PC: Control-J) as shown here. Then hide the original Template layer by clicking on the Eye icon beside that layer. Now, press Shift-Command-[(PC: Shift-Control-[) to send this layer to the bottom of the Layers stack, but right above the Background layer.

continued

Quick Tip:
Other color models

When you're in the Color Picker and you click on the Custom button, by default the selected color swatches are the PANTONE Solid Coated set. However, Photoshop comes with a host of other color sets built right in. To choose a different color set, click-and-hold on the Book pop-up menu and you'll find a list of color sets to choose from.

Quick Tip:
Layer Set tip

If you have a bunch of layers to which you'd like to apply the same Blend Mode (or the same Opacity setting for that matter), link them all together, then choose "New Set from Linked" from the Layers palette's drop-down menu. All the linked layers will be put into a folder (Adobe calls it a Set) within your Layers palette. That's no big deal, but the big deal is that whatever Blend Mode or Opacity setting you choose for your Set is applied to all the layers automatically, as long as they remain in the Set. Makes you stop and think, doesn't it?

STEP SIXTEEN: In the Layers palette, click on the Background layer to make it active. Take the Rectangular Marquee tool and drag out a selection along the midline of the black part of the edge (as shown). Now, you're still on the Background layer, right? Press Command-J (PC: Control-J) to duplicate the selected area up onto its own separate layer. Now, click back on your Template copy layer (right above the Background layer).

STEP SEVENTEEN: Press Command-E (PC: Control-E) to merge your Template copy edge and photo copy layer into one layer. To see what you've got on this layer, hold the Option key (PC: Alt key) and in the Layers palette, click on the Eye icon beside this merged layer. All the other layers will be hidden, and you'll see your photo chunk with edge effect all by itself (as shown here). Make all your layers visible again by Option-clicking (PC: Alt-clicking) on that same Eye icon again.

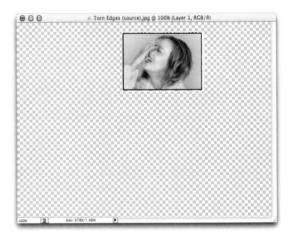

STEP EIGHTEEN: Now, hide Layer 1 from view (click its Eye icon), then repeat Step Fifteen: Duplicate the Template layer, hide the original Template layer from view, and then use that keyboard shortcut to move the Template copy layer to the bottom of the layers stack (but above the Background layer). From here on out, just to save space, I'll refer to this sequence of steps as "the move." (Cool, eh?)

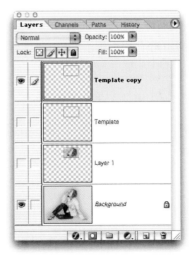

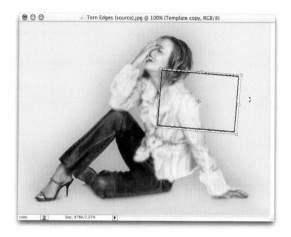

STEP NINETEEN: Each time you make a copy of the Template layer, it will appear in the exact same position (over her head and shoulders). We want to move it to a new location and rotate it a little, so press Command-T (PC: Control-T) to bring up Free Transform. Click-and-drag *inside* the bounding box to move it, and click-and-drag *outside* the bounding box to rotate. When it looks right, press Return (PC: Enter) to lock in your rotation.

STEP TWENTY: Since you rotated the edge, you can't just use the Rectangular Marquee tool to make your selection of half the black edge on the Background layer like we did previously. Instead, use the Polygonal Lasso tool (hidden in the flyout menu of the regular Lasso tool). Just click once in a corner, move to the next corner, and click again, and it draws a straight selection. When you get back to where you started, just click once and it becomes a selection.

STEP TWENTY-ONE: Now you'll repeat the second half of Step Sixteen (copying the selected area of the background onto its own separate layer) and Step Seventeen (clicking on the edge layer Template copy right above the Background layer, and merging it with the photo chunk by pressing Command-E [PC: Control-E]). You can skip the whole "viewing-the-new-layer-by-itself" thing—that was just a learning tool. Now it's time for "the move." (I couldn't wait to use that piece of cool Photoshop lingo. Sad, isn't it?)

continued

Quick Tip:
Make multiple Lasso selections

You can make multiple selections with the Lasso tool by making one selection, then holding the Shift key while you make subsequent selections. There's another way to do this that you might find easier than holding down the Shift key the entire time. After you've made your first selection, go up to the Options Bar and click on the second icon from the left (called the "Add to Selection" button), and now you can add additional areas to your selection without holding the Shift key.

Quick Tip:
Photoshop's Glass filter

If you've ever tried to use Photoshop's Glass filter (found under the Filter menu, under Distort), then you've already found that it doesn't work worth a darn (and that wording is overly kind). It just shouldn't be named "Glass." It should be named something like "Mess up your image" or "Junkicizor"—something more indicative of the real effect it has on your image. There's one instance where you might consider using the Glass filter, and that's when creating a Glass effect on type. You start by creating an Alpha channel of your type, blurring it a pixel or two, and saving it as a Displacement Map. Then when you use the Glass filter, choose "Load Texture," and load the map you saved; it applies a glassy look to your type. It almost looks decent. It doesn't look like glass, mind you, but it looks decent.

STEP TWENTY-TWO: You're going to keep repeating this process of duplicating the edge template, moving it down in the layers stack, dragging it to a different area, rotating it a bit, using the Polygonal Lasso tool to select a corresponding chunk of the background, copying that up onto its own layer, then merging the edge copy with the chunk, and then starting all over with "the move."

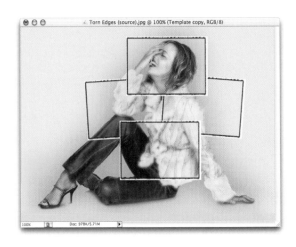

STEP TWENTY-THREE: Here's the photo after I've done this several more times (the number of edges you create depends on the photo).

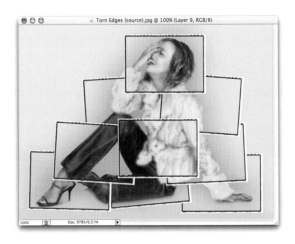

STEP TWENTY-FOUR: Now we need to combine all the edge layers into just one layer. To do this, hide the Template layer and the Background layer (click on the Eye icon beside each), then choose Merge Visible from the Layers palette's pop-down menu (as shown).

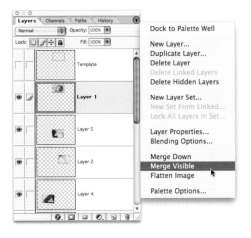

STEP TWENTY-FIVE: Now that all your edges are combined into one layer, click on the Background layer to make it visible and active. Press Option-Delete (PC: Alt-Backspace) to fill the Background layer with white, giving you the final effect shown here.

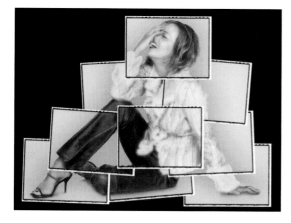

OPTION ONE: Press the letter "d" to set your Foreground color to black, and then press Option-Delete (PC: Alt-Backspace) to fill the Background layer with black, for the effect shown here.

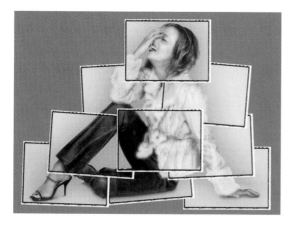

OPTION TWO: Another option (and the one used in *Surfer* magazine) is to pick a different color for your Foreground color and fill your background with it (an example is shown here).

Quick Tip:
Filters

• To change values in certain filter dialog boxes, use the Up/Down Arrow keys on your keyboard.

• To change the values in whole numbers, or in increments of ten, hold the Shift key along with the Up/Down Arrow keys.

• Once you've made changes in the filter dialog, if you want to reset them to where you started, hold the Option key (PC: Alt key), and the Cancel button changes to a Reset button. Press it and you're back where you started.

• To return to a 100% preview, click on the zoom percentage below the preview window in the filter dialog box. (This works in most filter dialogs, but not all of them. Go figure.)

From Photo to Oil Painting

I had heard that Ted LoCascio (our Senior Associate Designer at *Photoshop User* magazine) had come up with a pretty amazing technique for turning any photo into an oil painting, and as soon as he showed it to me, I asked him (okay, I begged him) to let me share it here in the book. It's without a doubt one of the best-looking, easiest oil techniques I've ever seen.

STEP ONE: Open the photo you want to apply the effect to.

© Brand X Pictures

STEP TWO: Go under the Image menu, under Adjustments, and choose Hue/Saturation. When the dialog appears, increase the Saturation to 50 (as shown here) and click OK to make your photo's colors more vivid.

STEP THREE: Go under the Filter menu and choose Filter Gallery. In the Filter Gallery dialog, click on the Distort set, and then click on the Glass thumbnail (as shown). Set the Distortion amount to 3, the Smoothness to 3, choose Canvas from the Texture pop-up menu, and set the Scaling to 79% (as shown here). Don't click OK yet.

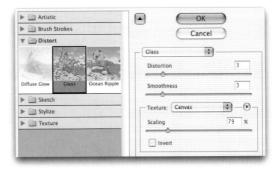

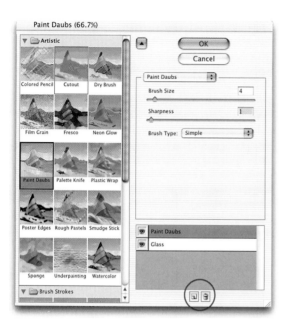

STEP FOUR: Click on the New Effect Layer icon at the bottom of the dialog (right next to the Trash icon). Click on the Artistic set, and then click on the Paint Daubs thumbnail. Set the Brush Size to 4, Sharpness to 1, and for Brush Type choose Simple (as shown here).

STEP FIVE: Click on the New Effect Layer icon at the bottom of the dialog. Click on the Brush Strokes set, and then click on the Angled Strokes thumbnail. Set the Direction Balance to 46, Stroke Length to 3, and Sharpness to 1.

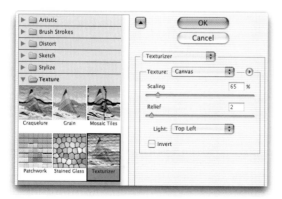

STEP SIX: Click on the New Effect Layer icon at the bottom of the dialog. To add a canvas-like texture, click on the Texture set, then click on the Texturizer thumbnail. For Texture choose Canvas, set the Scaling to 65%, Relief to 2, and for Light choose Top Left. Click OK to apply all four filters to your photo.

Quick Tip:
Loading selections

Numerous times in this book I ask you to put a selection around the contents of a layer by Command-clicking (PC: Control-clicking) on the layer's name in the Layers palette. You can use this same trick for loading Alpha Channels as a selection. Just go to the Channels palette and Command-click (PC: Control-click) on the channel to instantly load it as a selection. An even better trick is just to press Option-Command-4 (PC: Alt-Control-4) to load your first Alpha Channel. If you have other saved Alpha channels, you'd press 5, 6, etc.

continued

STEP SEVEN: Duplicate this layer by pressing Command-J (PC: Control-J). Then, press Shift-Command-U (PC: Shift-Control-U) to desaturate (remove all the color from) this layer. In the Layers palette, change the layer Blend Mode of this layer from Normal to Overlay (as shown here).

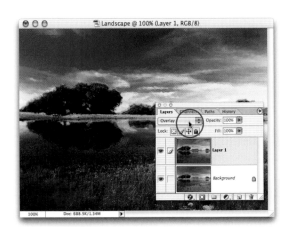

STEP EIGHT: Go under the Filter menu, under Stylize, and choose Emboss. When the Emboss dialog appears, set the Angle to 135°, the Height to 1, and the Amount to 500% (as shown here), and click OK. Lastly, go to the Layers palette and lower the Opacity of this layer to 40%, to give you the oil painting effect shown below.

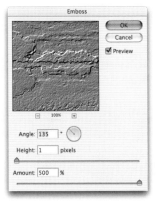

Instant Stock Photo Effect

This "wild color" effect is incredibly popular right now, in fact there are entire collections of royalty-free stock photos that use this technique, and you see it used often in print ads, for photos supporting articles in magazines, and on the Web. It's ideal for taking an otherwise boring image (like the dull phone photo used in this example), and using wild color to make it trendy and interesting.

© Brand X Pictures

STEP ONE: Open the photo you want to apply the effect to. In this case, it's a regular RGB photo that looks kinda, well…boring.

STEP TWO: Go to the Layers palette and from the Create New Adjustment Layer pop-up menu, choose Gradient Map (as shown here). This will bring up the Gradient Map dialog (seen in the next step).

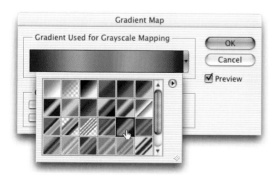

STEP THREE: Click the little down-facing triangle to the right of the current gradient to bring up the Gradient Picker (shown here). From the Picker's pop-down menu (the right-facing arrow), choose "Color Harmonies 2" (then click Append) to load this set of gradients. Choose the "Purple, Green, Gold" gradient (as shown here).

continued

If you've made a selection in Photoshop, there are a wide range of things you can do with that selection (besides dragging it around): you can feather it, save it, copy it to a layer, transform it, etc. Well, you can access a list of the things that you're most likely to do with your selection by holding the Control key and clicking-and-holding inside your selected area (PC: Right-click your mouse). A pop-up contextual menu will appear with a list of commands that you can apply to your selection. This is a huge timesaver and keeps you from digging through menus while you work.

STEP FOUR: Click OK and this applies a Gradient Map over your photo. This Gradient Map is usually too intense, and pretty much trashes your photo. To fix that, go to the Layers palette and change the Blend Mode of this layer from Normal to Color. Now the color of the Gradient Map blends in more smoothly, and replicates the wild color effect that's so popular with stock photo collections.

STEP FIVE: Make sure your Foreground color is black, then press "b" to get the Brush tool. Up in the Options Bar, lower the Opacity for your brush to 50%, then choose a large, soft-edged brush from the Brush Picker (up in the Options Bar) and paint over areas that you want to have more detail. As you paint, some of the original color will start to reappear. That way the background (not the product) gets most of the gradient as shown here.

STEP SIX: Press Command-E (PC: Control-E) to merge the Gradient Map layer with your Background layer, and then press the letter "v" to switch to the Move tool. Drag your photo into the document you want to use it in and it will create its own layer. In the sample layout shown here, I made only one change: I added a black border around the photo by choosing Stroke from the Add a Layer Styles pop-up menu at the bottom of the Layers palette. When the Stroke dialog appears, set the Size to 6, for Position choose Inside (to keep the corners from becoming rounded), and choose black for your Stroke Color. That's it!

tech talk
By Jordan Kelby

Customer Service:
ONLINE VS. ON THE PHONE?

Getting your new customers the help they need is critical in keeping them as your customer. ◆ But the way today's companies offer direct contact with their customer service staff is changing. ◆ Thanks to evolution of the Internet and the customer's willness to use

This is just placeholder copy to look like the text of an article, but it really isn't. It's actually just a copy of an editors' note I wrote for PhotoshopUser magazine. Here's goes: Another Photoshop-World is in the history books, and history was definitely made there. For the first time ever, Adobe chose our annual convention to make a major announcement, as Bryan Lamkin, Adobe Senior President of Digital Imaging and Video, took the stage during the Big Opening Night Photoshop Show! to announce Adobe's new Camera Raw Photoshop plug-in.

This amazing new plug-in (written by Thomas Knoll, the man who originally wrote Photoshop) gives professional and mid-range digital camera users a fast, easy, and flexible way to open and manipulate uncompressed Raw digital camera images from directly within Photoshop. This new plug-in wowed the audience and drew excited crowds at Adobe's booth on the PhotoshopWorld Expo floor.

Check for our coverage of the Camera Raw announcement on page 134. It was really quite an honor to have Mister Bryan Lamkin and the Photoshop team at the conference, and we couldn't have been more excited to have Adobe help kick-off PhotoshopWorld West. As for PhotoshopWorld East, the official dates and location have been set, as we to trendy South Beach to bring our East Coast convention to the Miami Beach Convention Center on Sept. 0-0, 2003.

Check out our web site for all details. Once again this year, one of the most popular sessions at PhotoshopWorld is Ben Willmore's Mastering Channels class. Ben has a real gift for making even the most complex Photoshop techniques accessible and understandable. So much so, that you might even

Real Ripped Edges

For years now we've all been doing the "cheesy Quick Mask with Diffuse filter version" to create edge effects, but generally the pros don't use it—instead they use third-party frame plug-ins, and other stock photo sources for a more realistic edge effect. Well, I came up with a way to get edges that look like the ones the pros use, and although it takes a little more effort than the "Quick Mask w/Diffuse cheesy version," it looks vastly better.

STEP ONE: Open the photo you want to use in this effect. Press Command-A (PC: Control-A) to select the entire photo, then press Shift-Command-J (PC: Shift-Control-J) to cut the photo from the Background layer and copy it on its own separate layer (as shown here).

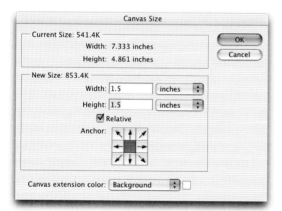

STEP TWO: To create an edge, you'll need to add a little breathing room around your photo, so go under the Image menu and choose Canvas Size. When the dialog appears, click on the Relative checkbox. Then for Width enter 1.5 inches, for Height enter 1.5 inches, and click OK to add some white space around your photo.

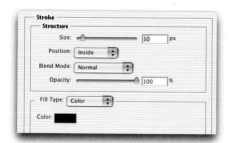

STEP THREE: Now that you've got that white space, you'll need to add a thick black stroke around your photo. Choose Stroke from the Add a Layer Style pop-up menu at the bottom of the Layers palette. Set the Size to 10, set the Position to Inside (to give your stroke straight corners rather than the default rounded corners), and choose black for your Stroke Color.

© Brand X Pictures

Quick Tip:
Cool trick for eliminating backgrounds

You can stroke a path with the Brush tool by going to the Paths palette and choosing Stroke Path from the pop-down menu. When the Stroke Path dialog appears, just choose Brush from the Tool pop-up menu. You can use that same technique to help you remove an object from its background. Just draw a loose path (with the Pen tool) around the object you want to remove from its background (don't let it touch the edge of the object, just get close). Then, instead of choosing the Brush tool in the Stroke Path dialog, choose the Background Eraser tool, then click OK. You'll be amazed because it traces around the edge of your image, erasing all the way around in about two seconds. Plus, it's fun to watch. Note: Make sure you choose a hard-edged brush for your Background Eraser tool before you try this trick.

continued

STEP FOUR: Click OK to apply
the black stroke around your
photo (as shown).

STEP FIVE: Open a photo that
you'd like to use for one of your
four torn edges. Photos that
have a visible edge in them (such
as the closeup of a wall) work
best. The line doesn't have to be
perfectly horizontal or vertical
because you can always rotate it
once it's in place.

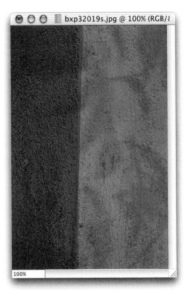

STEP SIX: Press Shift-Command-U (PC: Shift-Control-U)
to remove the color from your
photo. Then, go under the
Image menu, under Adjust-
ments, and choose Brightness/
Contrast. You're going to adjust
the Contrast to create an ultra-
high-contrast image that's just
short of looking bitmapped
(as shown here). In this instance,
moving the Contrast slider over
to +92 gives us a good messy
edge right down the middle.
Click OK.

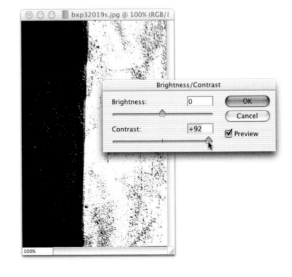

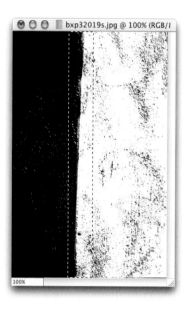

STEP SEVEN: Press the letter "m" to get the Rectangular Marquee tool and drag out a vertical selection that encompasses the center edge (as shown here). Press "v" to switch to the Move tool. Click within your selection and drag it over into your original photo document.

STEP EIGHT: Use the Move tool to position the edge over the right side of your photo (as shown here). In the Layers palette, change the layer Blend Mode from Normal to Darken (this makes it easier to align the edge and blends it in with the black stroke around your photo). If the edge is too large (which in this case—and many cases to come—it is), press Command-T (PC: Control-T) to bring up Free Transform. Hold the Shift key, grab a corner point, and drag inward to scale it down until it fits.

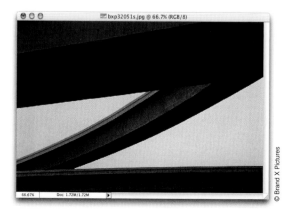

© Brand X Pictures

STEP NINE: Open another photo you want to use for one of the other torn edges. This one looks like an ideal candidate because of the horizontal bar at the bottom of the photo. Again, it doesn't have to be horizontal, but if it is, it's just that much easier because you won't have to rotate it to make it fit as an edge (unless you use it as a side edge, of course).

continued

Quick Tip:
Creating one layer with the contents of all your layers

There's a little trick you can use that takes the layer you're on and converts it into a new layer that is a flattened version of all your layers. It doesn't actually flatten your layers; it gives you one single layer that looks the way your image would look if you flattened it at that point. To do this, start by creating a new blank layer, hold down the Option key (PC: Alt key), go under the Layers palette's drop-down menu, and choose Merge Visible. A new "merged contents" image will appear in the new layer you created in your palette. Why would you need this? I have no earthly idea, but hey, you might need it one day, and now you know. However, you'll never remember which page this tip was on, and it'll take you hours to go through every tip in this book to find it, so maybe you're better off just forgetting this tip now, while you're still sane.

STEP TEN: Press Shift-Command-U (PC: Shift-Control-U) to remove the color from the photo. Go under the Image menu, under Adjustments, and choose Brightness/Contrast. This time, it takes a combination of both the Brightness (set to +74) and the Contrast (set to +87) sliders to bring out the harsh edge at the bottom of the image. Click OK.

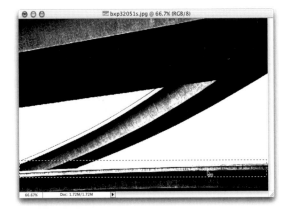

STEP ELEVEN: Get either the Rectangular Marquee tool or the Polygonal Lasso tool and put a selection around the edge area (as shown here). Press "v" to get the Move tool and drag this area over onto your main photo. In the Layers palette, change the layer Blend Mode for this new layer from Normal to Darken.

STEP TWELVE: In this case, the edge is much longer than the top of the photo, so press Command-T (PC: Control-T) to bring up Free Transform again to scale the edge down in size. Also, in this case, there's a black chunk in the top-left corner. To get rid of that (or any other areas that detract from the edge), press the letter "e" to get the Eraser tool, and erase them.

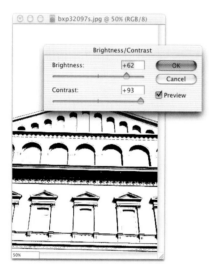

STEP THIRTEEN: Open two other images (with well-defined lines) that you'll convert using the same technique. Remember, you have to remove the color from each photo before you can use Brightness/Contrast. The quickest way is to press Shift-Command-U (PC: Shift-Control-U) which is the shortcut for Desaturate.

STEP FOURTEEN: In both cases, you'll use Brightness/Contrast to find suitable edges. In this case, the lines at the very bottom of the photo look like they'll work. It's angled a bit, so after you drag it into place, you'll have to use Free Transform to rotate it and scale it. The final effect is shown below, with edge chunks from the two photos in the previous step making the left and bottom edges.

Quick Tip:
Layer Style
Angle tip

In the Layer Style dialog box, a number of effects have the Angle control, which gives you control over the angle of your light source. But did you know that if you hold the Shift key while adjusting the Angle, it will snap to 15° increments? You did? Rats!

three

3

Do you have any idea how hard it  is for a type effect to be included in this chapter? Sure, by the time a type

Jealous Type
Cool Type Effects

effect winds up here, with all the glitz and glamour, it's looks like a lot of fun, but believe me, it's a lot of hard work. It all starts with an open audition for type effects, which takes place in Houston, L.A., New York, and Atlanta. In each city, a panel of judges then views each aspiring type effect, and from that group they choose only 30 type effects to go to compete in the regional semifinals. At the semis, the judges then narrow the type effects down to just ten, who will be vying for the title "Coolest American Type Effect." *Cool American Type Effects,* which airs Wednesday nights on FAUX, is hosted by Ryan Seabiscuit, and…. (Do I have to keep this up? Seriously, I was pretty sure that you would've stopped reading back a hundred words or so, and since I was kind of counting on that, I never really developed an ending for this intro. So, I'm just kinda going to end it right here. If you don't tell anyone I didn't have an ending, I won't tell anyone you read this far. Deal? Deal.)

Quick Tip:
Get the "Maximum File Browser Experience"

If you know you're going to be spending some time in the File Browser (sorting, categorizing, etc.), you can get the "Maximum File Browser Experience" by holding the Command key (PC: Control key) before you click on the Toggle File Browser button in the Options Bar. When you do this, it automatically hides the Toolbox and any open palettes, and expands the File Browser to fill your entire screen. Perfect for those times when you're working mostly in the Browser.

Jaguar "X"

When Apple Computer came out with their "gel" look for Mac OS X, that effect quickly became a favorite with designers. When Apple followed up with Mac OS X Jaguar, their Jaguar look became popular, but every tutorial I tried on the Web used Photoshop's Stained Glass filter, and I couldn't find one that really looked like Apple's version; and that's because you can't use that filter. Here's a version I worked out that I hope you'll agree looks much better.

STEP ONE: Open a new document in RGB mode. Click on the Foreground Color Swatch in the Toolbox and set your Foreground color to an orangish-brown in the Color Picker (I used R=255, G=164, B=59). Now, press the letter "t" to switch to the Type tool and type a capital "X" (as shown). I used the typeface Garamond Condensed, which is fairly close to the custom version of Garamond that Apple used.

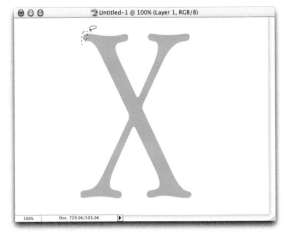

STEP TWO: Create a new blank layer by clicking on the New Layer icon at the bottom of the Layers palette. Press the letter "L" to switch to the Lasso tool, then draw your first jaguar "spot" somewhere near the top of the left side of the letter (as shown here).

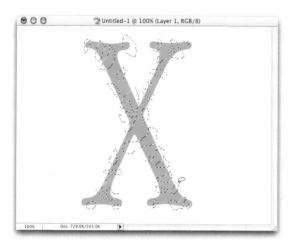

STEP THREE: Once your first "spot" selection is in place, hold the Shift key and draw some more (the Shift key lets you add more selections to your original selection). Make a series of freeform selections in the shape of spots (as shown here). Hint: To make your shapes more like the ones Apple used, make sure some of your selections go from one side of the letter, right through to the other.

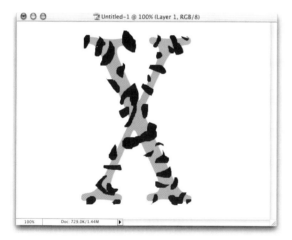

STEP FOUR: Switch your Foreground color to a dark brown (I used R=53, G=32, B=0), and then fill your selected "spots" with this brown color by pressing Option-Delete (PC: Alt-Backspace). Once you've done that, you can then deselect by pressing Command-D (PC: Control-D).

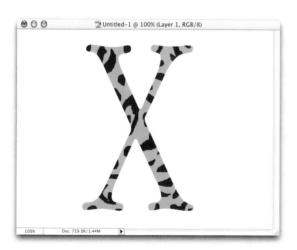

STEP FIVE: To make your spots appear inside the letter "X" only, you can "group" your spots with the letter on the layer beneath it by pressing Command-G (PC: Control-G). When you do this, you're forcing the spots inside the letter and clipping off anything that extends outside the "X." (In Photoshop CS, this is called a "Clipping Mask." Back in Photoshop 7, it was called a "Clipping Group.")

continued

Quick Tip:
Hide everything, and still move your document

You've been able to hide all your palettes and tools and center your photo on a black background for some time now in Photoshop (just press "f," "f," then Tab). The only problem is—once your document is centered on screen—it's stuck there. Well, at least it was until Photoshop CS. Now you can move your image around the screen (while in this Full Screen Mode) by holding the Spacebar and clicking-and-dragging within the black canvas area. Ain't life grand?

STEP SIX: In the Layers palette, you'll see a tiny arrow indicating that the "spot" layer is grouped with the Type layer beneath it (as shown here). This technique is easier if you merge these two layers together, but you can't merge a regular image layer, with a Type layer—unless you know this little secret: Just link them together (by clicking once in the second column of the Type layer), and choose Merge Linked from the Layers palette's pop-down menu (the black, right-facing triangle in the top-right corner) to merge the brown "spots" layer permanently with the Type layer.

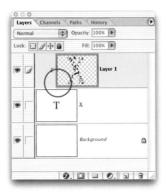

STEP SEVEN: Now, duplicate the merged layer (the "X" with the spots inside) by pressing Command-J (PC: Control-J). You'll need this layer to add color back into the image later, but for now, hide it from view by going to the Layers palette and clicking on the Eye icon in the first column of the layer (as shown). Next, click on the original "X-with-spots" layer in the Layers palette to make it active.

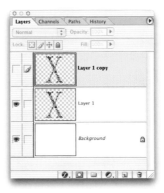

STEP EIGHT: Hold the Command key (PC: Control key), go to the Layers palette, and click once on the "X-with-spots" layer to put a selection around the entire letter (as shown here). Now that the entire letter is selected, you'll have to deselect (or subtract) one "leg" of the letter. That's because you'll have to apply the technique in Steps Ten and Eleven individually to each "leg" for this to look right. Make sure you have the Lasso tool, then move on to the next step.

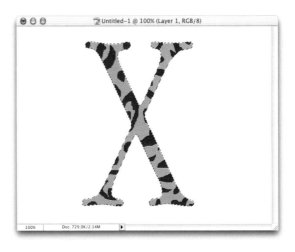

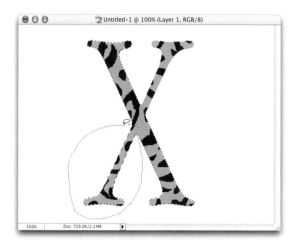

STEP NINE: Hold the Option key (PC: Alt key) and draw a loose selection around the top right side of the letter. The area you select will become "unselected" (if there is such a word). That's because you're holding the Option/Alt key. Do the same thing for the left bottom of the letter (as shown here), leaving just the one "leg" of the letter selected.

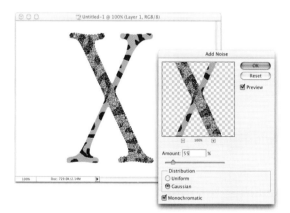

STEP TEN: Go under the Filter menu, under Noise, and choose Add Noise. When the Add Noise filter dialog appears, enter 55% for Amount, choose Gaussian for Distribution, and turn on the Monochromatic checkbox. Click OK, and it fills the selected "leg" of your "X" with noise (as shown). Don't deselect yet.

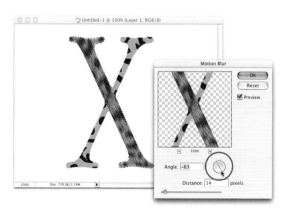

STEP ELEVEN: Go under the Filter menu, under Blur, and choose Motion Blur. When the Motion Blur filter dialog appears, drag the direction of the blur Angle in the circle until it's in the same direction as the letter (as shown here). For Distance, enter 14 pixels, and then click OK to apply the Motion Blur to your letter. This starts to give the letter the "fur" feel. Deselect by pressing Command-D (PC: Control-D).

continued

Quick Tip:
For typography freaks only!

If you're a freak about typography (and I know you are), then you'll be glad to know that Photoshop CS has added a number of high-end type features that only a real typographer could love. Stuff like built-in Titling, Swash, Ordinals, Ornaments, Stylistic Alternates, and a host of other scary-sounding stuff. These puppies are all accessed through the Character palette's pop-down menu.

Quick Tip:
Getting your type quickly back to its defaults

If you've done some major type tweaking to a line of type (such as manually adjusting the tracking, leading, horizontal scale, baseline shift, adding Faux Bold, etc.), those settings stay in the Character palette. So when you go to create a new line of type, you'll often wind up going to each field and resetting everything (changing the leading back to Auto, tracking back to 0, removing Faux Bold, etc.). Well, you can save a ton of time by just going to the Character palette's pop-down menu and choosing Reset Character from the bottom of the menu. This instantly returns the palette to all its default settings. This can really be a HUGE time saver.

STEP TWELVE: Now we're going to do the exact same thing to the other "leg." Start by Command-clicking (PC: Control-clicking) on the visible "X" layer (in the Layers palette) to put a selection around the letter. This time you're going to hold the Option key (PC: Alt key) and use the Lasso tool to re-move the selection from the areas to which you've already added noise and blurred. Be sure to also deselect the area in the middle where the two "legs" intersect, leaving only the un-blurred, noise-free areas selected.

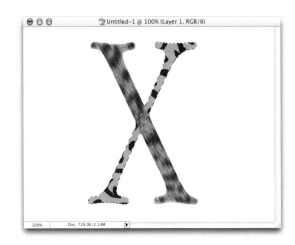

STEP THIRTEEN: Now apply the same amount of Noise and Mo-tion Blur as we did back in Steps Ten and Eleven, but this time change the Angle of the Motion Blur to match the angle of this "leg" (as shown here). For the first side of the letter, we used an Angle of -63°; here we're using +68°. Now deselect by pressing Command-D (PC: Control-D).

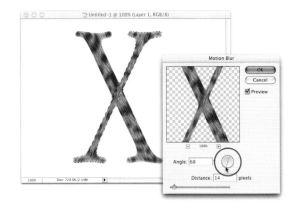

STEP FOURTEEN: Command-click (PC: Control-click) on the layer's name in the Layers palette to select the letter again. Now, switch to the Dodge tool in the Toolbox (shown here); choose a small, soft-edged brush from the Brush Picker in the Options Bar; and paint over the left half of each "leg." As you paint, the area will be lightened (as shown). You'll probably have to paint a few strokes before you can see the effect from the Dodge tool.

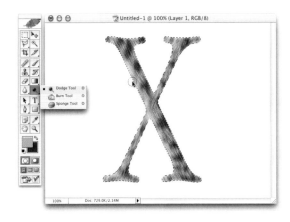

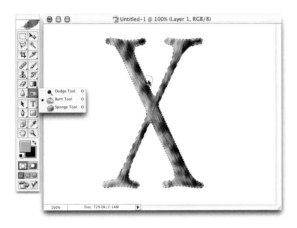

STEP FIFTEEN: Now, switch to the Burn tool (it's in the Dodge tool's flyout menu in the Toolbox), and paint over the right half of each "leg" to darken them a bit. It'll be easier to see the darkened effect as you paint, and luckily, the lightened side will also become more visible (as shown here). Once you're done, deselect by pressing Command-D (PC: Control-D).

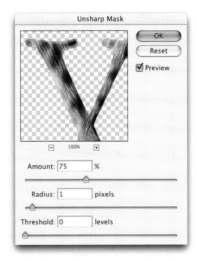

STEP SIXTEEN: Now you'll sharpen the "X" to help accentuate the "fur" look of the effect. Go under the Filter menu, under Sharpen, and choose Unsharp Mask. When the Unsharp Mask dialog appears, enter 75% for Amount, 1 for Radius, and use 0 for Threshold. Click OK to sharpen the fur.

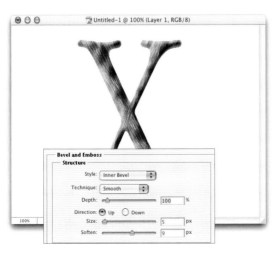

STEP SEVENTEEN: Choose Bevel and Emboss from the Layer Styles pop-up menu at the bottom of the Layers palette (the black circle with an "ƒ"). When the Bevel and Emboss dialog appears, you're only going to change one setting: Increase the Soften setting to 9. Click OK to apply the Bevel and Emboss, which gives the "X" a more rounded 3D look.

Quick Tip:
The File Browser doesn't live in the Palette Well anymore

If you've gone up to the Palette Well searching for the File Browser, you've probably already realized it doesn't live there anymore. Worse than that, you can't even dock it in the Palette Well in Photoshop CS. Instead, Adobe added a button on the right side of the Options Bar (to the left of the Palette Well) for bringing up the File Browser. You can open and close the File Browser using this same button. So it's hello tiny button, goodbye Palette Well tab.

continued

STEP EIGHTEEN: Remember that layer we duplicated and hid all the way back at Step Seven? It's time to bring it "into play." Click on that layer in the Layers palette to make it the active layer (it should be directly above your "X-with-fur" layer as shown here).

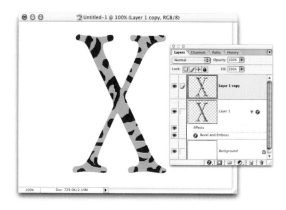

STEP NINETEEN: In the pop-up menu at the top left of the Layers palette, change the Blend Mode of this top layer from Normal to Soft Light (as shown) to bring back the original colors you applied before the Motion Blur and Noise faded them out.

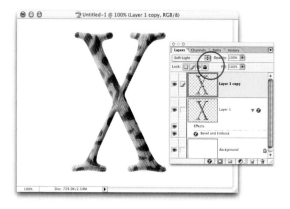

STEP TWENTY: Merge the top layer permanently with the layer directly beneath it by pressing Command-E (PC: Control-E), the keyboard shortcut for Merge Down.

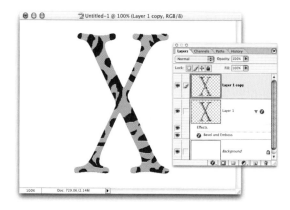

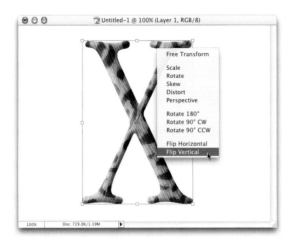

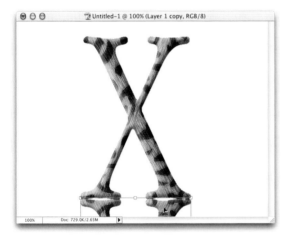

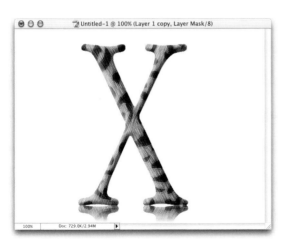

STEP TWENTY-ONE: Duplicate your merged layer by pressing Command-J (PC: Control-J). Now, press Command-T (PC: Control-T) to bring up Photoshop's Free Transform bounding box around the "X" on this duplicate layer. Control-click (PC: Right-click) anywhere within the bounding box to bring up a pop-up list of transformations. Choose Flip Vertical to flip your duplicate "X" vertically. Press Return (PC: Enter).

STEP TWENTY-TWO: Press the letter "v" to switch to the Move tool, and drag this vertically flipped "X" down until it touches the bottom of your original "X" (as shown here). Then press "g" to switch to the Gradient tool. Press "d" to switch your Foreground color to black. Press the Return key (PC: Enter key) and the Gradient Picker will appear at the current location of your cursor. Choose the third gradient in the Picker (by default, it's the Black to White gradient).

STEP TWENTY-THREE: Click on the Add a Layer Mask icon at the bottom of the Layers palette to add a Layer Mask to your flipped layer. Then, click the Gradient tool at the very bottom of your image area and drag upward until you reach the bottom of the original "X." This fades your flipped layer from 100% opacity to 0% opacity at the bottom, giving the impression that the "X" is casting a reflection (as shown here) to complete the effect.

Quick Tip:
The old "clean-filter-preview" trick

When you're working in a Filter dialog box (with the exception of the Filter Gallery filters), most of them give you a large Preview window so you can see how the effect will look before you click OK. However, many of these also have a Preview checkbox, so you not only see the effect in the Preview window, you actually see the effect applied to your entire image, even before you click OK. Well, if you'd like to see what your photo looks like *without* having the filter applied, just click-and-hold within the Filter dialog's preview window, and it will give you the "before" version (your image without the filter). Release the mouse button, and you see the filter-enhanced version. So for a quick "before and after" just click within the preview window.

Quick Tip:
Getting rid of that 01 square in the top-left corner of your image window

If you're one of the millions of Photoshop users who suffer from seeing the number 01, followed by a little rectangular box, you're in luck—there's a simple cure. But what brought this evil little nasty to the top-left corner of your screen in the first place? At some point, you clicked on the Slice tool, or while working with another tool, you pressed the letter "k" to briefly switch to the Slice tool. When you do this (even once), it brings up the dreaded 01 thingy, because it thinks you want to slice the image, and it's showing you the default slice. The bad thing is—when you switch off the Slice tool, the slice stays visible, which can, in turn, drive you insane. To get rid of it, go under the View menu, under Show, and choose Slices to hide the slices and bring sanity back to your world.

Neo Grunge Type Effect

This is a technique I used to create the logo for the band Big Electric Cat, and it makes use of a filter that we don't often get to make use of (the Diffuse Glow filter), primarily because the filter is pretty lame. But luckily, if you apply this filter over white text, it gives it a "sloppy-spray-paint" job that's reminiscent of the neo grunge look. Here's how it's done:

STEP ONE: Open a new document, press the letter "t" to switch to the Type tool, and create your type. In the example shown here, I typed in the word "BIG" using the font Compacta. Then, on a separate layer, I typed "ELECTRIC," and reduced the point size until it was small enough to fit under the word "BIG." Lastly, I duplicated the "BIG" layer (by dragging it to the New Layer icon at the bottom of the Layers palette), and I then highlighted that copy with the Type tool and typed in "CAT." I then used the Move tool to drag it below the word "ELECTRIC."

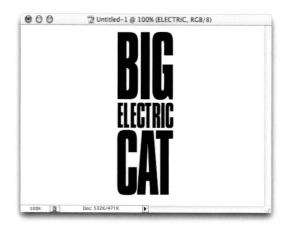

STEP TWO: As you can see by the Layers palette shown here, you'll have three separate Type layers, and as a general rule, you want to keep these layers in their original editable state (just in case). To do that, start by hiding the Background layer from view by clicking on the Eye icon in the first column of the Background layer in the Layers palette. Then, click on the New Layer icon at the bottom of the Layers palette to create a new layer, and drag it to the top of the layer stack. Then, hold Option (PC: Alt) and choose Merge Visible from the palette's pop-down menu (as shown).

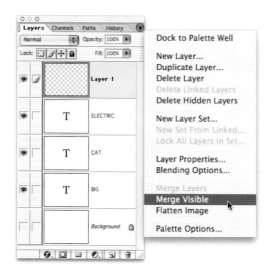

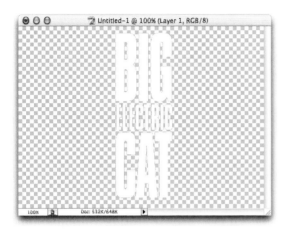

STEP THREE: Holding Option/ Alt creates a merged version from all your Type layers in this top layer with a transparent background. Next, press the letter "d" then "x" to set your Foreground color to white, then press Shift-Option-Delete (PC: Shift-Alt-Backspace) to fill the words "Big Electric Cat" with white (as shown here).

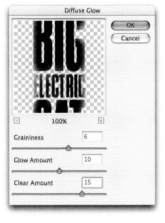

STEP FOUR: Go under the Filter menu, under Distort, and choose Diffuse Glow. When the dialog box appears, set the Graininess to 6, the Glow Amount to 10, and the Clear Amount to 15 (as shown), and click OK. This will turn your text black, and add a sprayed look to the inside edges of your type. (Note: For high-res, 300-ppi images, use a Graininess of 9, a Glow Amount of 17, and a Clear Amount of 19.)

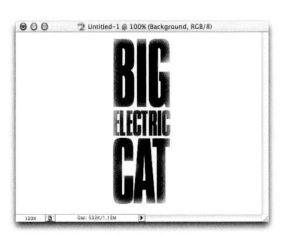

STEP FIVE: When you click OK the effect is applied to your text. Now, go to the Layers palette and click on the Background layer to make it the active layer (which also makes it visible again), giving you the effect shown here. You can stop right here (as the completed effect) or go on to the next page for a variation on the effect.

continued

STEP SIX: Press the letter "d" to set your Foreground color to black, and then make sure you're still on the Background layer in the Layers palette. Press Option-Delete (PC: Alt-Backspace) to fill the Background layer with black. Then, click on your top layer (the type with the effect applied) in the Layers palette, and press Command-I (PC: Control-I) to invert the type, giving you white type on black background (as shown here).

STEP SEVEN: Go under the Filter menu, under Distort, and choose Pinch. When the Pinch dialog appears, lower the Amount to 35%. (Note: For high-res, 300-ppi images, increase the Pinch Amount to 80%.)

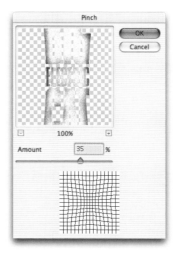

STEP EIGHT: Click OK and the Pinch effect will give your type a perspective look on the top and bottom, completing the effect (as shown here).

Clear Inline Type Effect

It doesn't get any downer or dirtier than this! This is a quick way to create an interesting type effect, where the type remains very readable, but has three levels of depth thanks to the shadows inside and outside the letters. It's that depth that helps it work so well, especially when created on a white background.

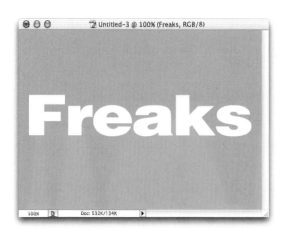

STEP ONE: Open a new document in RGB mode at 72 ppi. Click on the Foreground Color Swatch in the Toolbox and choose a light gray in the Color Picker as your Foreground color. Fill the Background layer with this gray by pressing Option-Delete (PC: Alt-Backspace). Press the letter "d" then "x" to set your Foreground color to white, then press the letter "t" to get the Type tool and create your type. (I used the font Helvetica Black here, with the Horizontal Scaling set to 120% in the Character palette.)

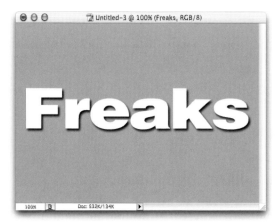

STEP TWO: Choose Drop Shadow from the Add a Layer Style pop-up menu at the bottom of the Layers palette. When the Drop Shadow dialog appears, simply increase the Opacity to 100%. (Note: For high-res, 300-ppi images, increase both the Distance and the Size of the Drop Shadow to 21.) Don't click OK yet because we want to add another Layer Style in the next step.

continued

Quick Tip:
Escape that dialog box!

Almost anytime you're in a dialog box in Photoshop and want to get out of there fast, you can press the Escape key and the box will disappear with no changes made (the same as pressing the Cancel button in the dialog box).

STEP THREE: Next, in the Layer Style dialog, click directly on the name Inner Shadow in the left-hand list of Styles. When the Inner Shadow dialog appears, change the Opacity to 100%. (Note: For high-res, 300-ppi images, increase both the Distance and Size to 21.) Now you can click OK to apply both the Drop Shadow and the Inner Shadow to the type.

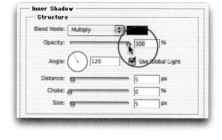

STEP FOUR: For other lines of type, just duplicate this "Freaks" Type layer by pressing Command-J (PC: Control-J). Use the Move tool to reposition this copied type above your main type, then highlight it with the Type tool and type in a new word. Since this is still a Type layer, you can simply highlight it and lower the point size in the Options Bar or Character palette to make it fit between the "F" and the "k."

STEP FIVE: Repeat Step Four to add any additional lines of type. To complete the effect, in the Layers palette click on the Background layer, and press the letter "d" to set your Foreground and Background colors to their defaults. Press Command-A (PC: Control-A) to select the entire gray background, then press Delete (PC: Backspace) to remove the gray, leaving a white background (as shown here).

Gothic Chiseled Type Effect

Sure the Harry Potter movies had some amazing special effects, but did you see that beautifully beveled logo? That thing is a Layer Styles work of art. What may be most amazing about it is that the entire thing is created in just one dialog box (the Layer Styles dialog). So here's a look at how to turn some plain gray type into a gold gothic chiseled effect that is pure gold at the box office.

STEP ONE: Open a new document in RGB mode at 300 ppi. Press "d" to set black as your Foreground color. Fill your Background layer with black by pressing Option-Delete (PC: Alt-Backspace). In the Toolbox, click on the Foreground Color Swatch and set your Foreground color to a medium gray in the Color Picker and click OK.

STEP TWO: Press the letter "t" to get the Type tool and create your type (the font shown here is a freeware font named "Harry Potter"). You can find out how to obtain this font from this book's companion Web site (www.scottkelbybooks.com). To get the font to look right, you'll have to highlight some of the letters and shift them above the Baseline using the Character palette (as shown here, with the letter "n").

STEP THREE: Some letters, like the "n" in "Henry" and the "e" in "Poster," will need a smaller point size, so highlight those letters and reduce the point size in either the Options Bar or the Character palette. (Most of the letters in this example are at 90 point, but I lowered the "n" and "e" to only 60 points.)

Quick Tip:
Gradients

• To bring up the Gradient Editor, switch to the Gradient tool and in the Options Bar at the top, click once on the Gradient thumbnail.

• To add a new Color Stop to your gradient, click anywhere below the Gradient Editor Bar.

• To remove a Color Stop, click-and-drag downward.

• To edit the color of any Color Stop, double-click directly on the Color Stop.

• To change the Opacity setting for the Gradient tool, press the 1–9 number keys on your keyboard (2=20%, 3=30%, etc.) while the Gradient tool is selected.

• To step through the Blend Modes in the Gradient's Options Bar, press Shift-+ while you have the Gradient tool.

• To delete a gradient, hold the Control key (PC: Right mouse button) and in the Gradient Picker or Editor, click-and-hold on the gradient you want to delete, then choose Delete Gradient from the pop-up list.

continued

Quick Tip:
Want some cool metal gradients? You've already got 'em!

If you need a metallic gradient, you don't have to build one from scratch—you've already got a collection of cool preset metallic gradients just waiting for you to load. Fortunately, loading them into your flyout Gradient Picker is a breeze. Here's how: First, switch to the Gradient tool, then in the Options Bar, click on the down-facing triangle right next to the Gradient thumbnail. This brings up the Gradient Picker. In the upper-right corner of this menu is a right-facing triangle, which is a pop-up menu. Click on it, and at the bottom of the menu, you'll see a list of gradient presets you can load just by choosing them from the menu.

To load the metallic gradients, choose the ones named "Metals" from the pop-up list, and Photoshop will ask if you want to replace your current gradients with this set or append (add) them to your current set. It's that easy.

STEP FOUR: Choose Bevel and Emboss from the Layer Style pop-up menu at the bottom of the Layers palette. Choose Chisel Hard for Technique, increase the Depth to 251%, and the Size to 27. (Note: For low-res, 72 ppi images, lower the Size to 6.) Under Shading, set your Angle to 0° and Altitude to 42°. Click the Gloss Contour down arrow to open Contour Picker. Click the arrow at upper right and choose Contours in the pop-up menu. Click OK and choose "Peaks" (as shown). Turn on the Anti-Aliasing checkbox. Change the Highlight Blend Mode from Screen to Color Dodge, and click on the Highlight Color Swatch and change it to orange in the Color Picker (the build shown here is R=224, G=193, B=8).

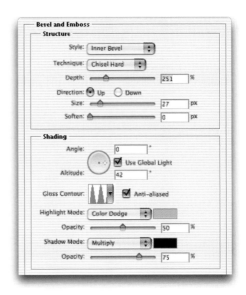

STEP FIVE: In the list of Layer Styles on the left side of the dialog, click directly on the word Color Overlay to make its options visible. Click on the Color Swatch and choose a gold color (the build shown here is R=208, G=119, B=8).

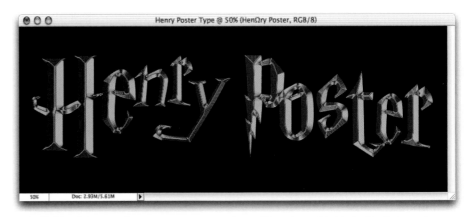

STEP SIX: Click OK and your gray type is transformed into the gold chiseled look shown here.

3D Drop Back Logo

When the UPN TV network introduced their new logo, I just assumed they did it in a 3D program, but you can pretty much get the same effect (where it looks like the logo is dropping back, like a one-point perspective effect) from right within Photoshop, thanks to Photoshop's Free Transform Distort feature.

STEP ONE: Open a new document in RGB mode. Click on the Foreground Color Swatch in the Toolbox and choose a bright red in the Color Picker (similar to the color shown here). Fill the background with this red color by pressing Option-Delete (PC: Alt-Backspace). Next, press "d" then "x" to set your Foreground color to white. Get the Type tool and create your type (the font shown here is Aurora Condensed from Bitstream).

STEP TWO: Create a new blank layer by clicking on the New Layer icon at the bottom of the Layers palette. Press Shift-M until you get the Elliptical Marquee tool. Hold the Shift key and drag out a circular selection that's larger than your type (as shown here).

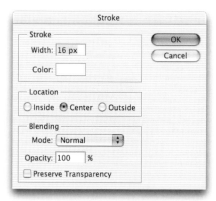

STEP THREE: Go under the Edit menu and choose Stroke. When the Stroke dialog appears, choose 16 for your Width, set the Location to Center, make sure your stroke Color is set to white, and then click OK. This puts a white stroke around your circular selection.

continued

Quick Tip:
Bigger previews in the Filter Gallery

The preview window in the Filter Gallery is pretty large, but you can make it even larger in two ways. First, the dialog itself is resizable—just grab the bottom right-hand corner of the dialog and stretch outward. Secondly, there's an upward-facing black triangle button, just to the left of the OK button. Click on this button, and the list of effects is hidden from view and the Preview area expands into that space. The good thing is, you can still choose different filters, now you just do it from the pop-up menu just below the Cancel button.

Quick Tip:
Changing the
size of selections

Any time you have a
selection in place, you can
make that selection a few
pixels larger or smaller by
going under the Select
menu, under Modify, and
choosing Expand (to make
your selection bigger) or
Contract (to make your
selection smaller). There's
a weird thing about this
function; when you make
a large change either way,
it doesn't keep the edges
sharp and crisp—it tends
to round (Anti-alias) the
edges a bit, so keep this
in mind if you need to
grow your selection by a
large number of pixels. To
see what I mean, draw a
square selection, then go
under the Select menu,
under Modify, and choose
Expand. Enter 15 (the
maximum is 100) and click
OK. Look at the edges of
your selection—they're not
square anymore, they're
sort of rounded off at the
corners. I haven't found
a way around this; I try to
keep my expansions to only
3 or 4 pixels and it works
just fine.

STEP FOUR: Press Command-
D (PC: Control-D) to deselect.
Merge your Type layer and your
white circle layer into a single
layer by going to the Layers palette and clicking in the second
column of the Type layer to link
them together (a tiny link icon
will appear), and then pressing
Command-E (PC: Control-E).
Next, press Command-T (PC:
Control-T) to bring up the
Free Transform bounding box
(shown here).

STEP FIVE: Hold the Command
key (PC: Control key), click on
the top-left corner point of the
Free Transform bounding box,
and drag down and to the right
(you're dragging diagonally
inward), and the logo will tip
back (as shown here).

STEP SIX: Press Return (PC: Enter) to lock in your transformation and to complete the effect
(as shown here).

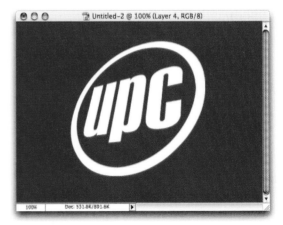

Black Chrome

This is a different style of chrome technique that I developed for my "Down & Dirty Tricks" column in *Photoshop User* magazine. I call it "Black Chrome," but the chrome part is really the bevel around the black shiny letters. Again, this is another technique that works best if you create it at a large size or high resolution first, and then resize it down to the final size you'll need.

STEP ONE: Open a new document in RGB mode (the one shown here is a 7" x 5" at a resolution of 150). Click on the Foreground Color Swatch in the Toolbox and choose a medium gray for your Foreground color in the Color Picker. Press the letter "t" to get the Type tool and create some very large-sized type (the font I used here is Bullet from House Industries, set at 185 points). Next, you'll need to put a selection around your type.

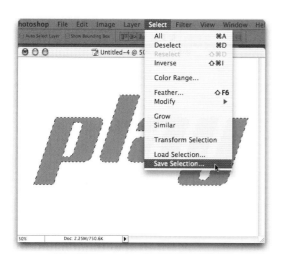

STEP TWO: Hold the Command key (PC: Control key), go to the Layers palette, and click once on the Type layer (this loads a selection around your type, as shown here). Go under the Select menu and choose Save Selection. When the Save Selection dialog appears, click OK.

continued

Quick Tip:
Using the Clouds filter

The Clouds filter renders a random cloud pattern based on your current Foreground color. The clouds generated by the Clouds filter are usually pretty light in density, so if you want darker clouds, instead of choosing the Clouds filter, choose the Difference Clouds filter.

Quick Tip:
Why doesn't my Color Picker look like that?

If you click on the Foreground or Background Color Swatch (at the bottom of the Toolbox) and it doesn't look like it normally does, you may have inadvertently switched your Color Picker. Press Command-K (PC: Control-K) to bring up Photoshop's General Preferences dialog. Under the Color Picker pop-up menu, make sure the chosen Picker is "Adobe." That'll get you back to the right one.

STEP THREE: Deselect by pressing Command-D (PC: Control-D). Hide your Type layer by clicking on the Eye icon in the first column beside it in the Layers palette. Now, go to the Channels palette and click on the channel named Alpha 1 (that's your saved selection). Go under the Filter menu, under Blur, and choose Gaussian Blur. When the dialog appears, enter 5 pixels and click OK to blur the channel.

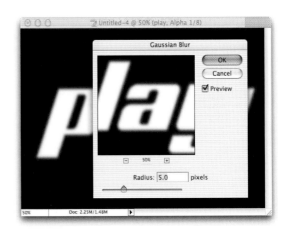

STEP FOUR: Back in the Layers palette, click on the Background layer to make it active. Then go under the Filter menu, under Render, and choose Lighting Effects. You're only going to make one small change in this dialog. At the bottom, choose Alpha 1 in the Texture Channel pop-up menu (as shown here), then click OK.

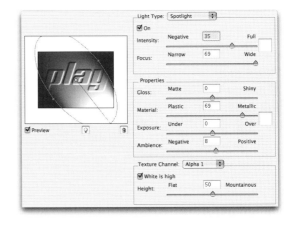

STEP FIVE: When you click OK, an embossed version of your type is applied to the Background layer. Next, press Command-M (PC: Control-M) to bring up the Curves dialog. You're going to create a curve that looks like the one shown here (don't worry—it's easy). Just click on the lower left side of the diagonal line to add a point, click on that point, and drag upward. Click to add another point near the top right, and then drag it down to add a chrome effect to your Background layer. Click OK.

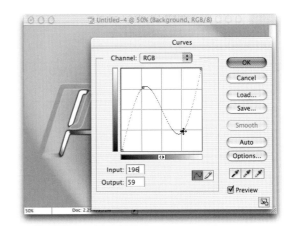

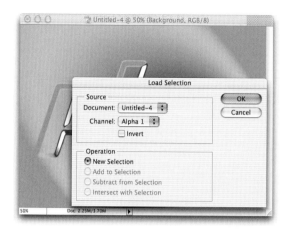

STEP SIX: Go under the Select menu and choose Load Selection. When the Load Selection dialog appears, Alpha 1 will already be chosen as your source channel (as shown here), but if for some reason it's not, choose it from the Channel pop-up menu. Click OK, and your saved selection will appear on your Background layer.

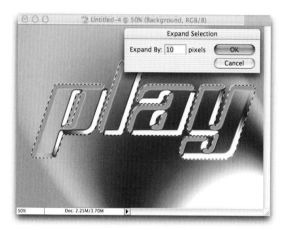

STEP SEVEN: In this step, you'll need to expand your selection to include the thick bevel you created with the Lighting Effects filter. To do that, go under the Select menu, under Modify, and choose Expand. When the Expand Selection dialog box appears, choose to expand by 10 (as shown here), then click OK to expand your selection, encompassing your bevel (as shown).

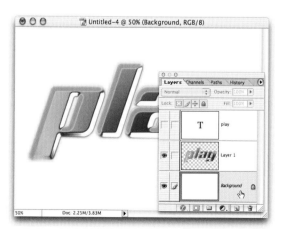

STEP EIGHT: Press Command-J (PC: Control-J) to take your selected area (your type and the full bevel) and copy them up to their own separate layer. In the Layers palette, click on the Background layer. Press Command-A (PC: Control-A) to select the entire Background layer, then press Delete (PC: Backspace) to remove the excess gray area created by the Lighting Effects filter. This leaves you with just your chrome type on its own layer (as shown here).

continued

Quick Tip:
Lighting Effects tips

We use the Lighting Effects filter quite a bit when we're creating interfaces and interface elements. Here are a few tips that will make using the Lighting Effects dialog even easier:

• Think of the Style pop-up menu at the top as a list of "presets," because that's exactly what they are.

• You can create your own styles (presets) by configuring the Lighting Effects the way you want and clicking on the Save button at the top of the dialog, just below the Style pop-up.

• To add another light, click-and-drag the Light icon into the preview, or hold the Option key (PC: Alt key) and click-and-drag a copy of your existing light.

• Press Option-Tab (PC: Alt-Tab) to jump from one light to the next.

• To delete any light, click on it and press Option-Delete (PC: Alt-Backspace).

Quick Tip:
Getting back
your last
selection

If you make a selection, deselect it, then go on about your business and later realize that you forgot to save that selection, you can get your last selection back, as long as you haven't made another selection. Just go under the Select menu, choose Reselect, and the last selection you made will reappear.

STEP NINE: In the Layers palette, click on your original Type layer. Choose Bevel and Emboss from the Add a Layer Style pop-up menu at the bottom of the Layers palette. In the Bevel and Emboss dialog, increase the Depth to 400%, the Size to 21, and Soften to 16. In the Shading section, turn on Anti-aliased, then click on the down-facing arrow next to Gloss Contour to bring up the Contour Picker. Choose the contour named "Ring" (as shown). Don't click OK yet.

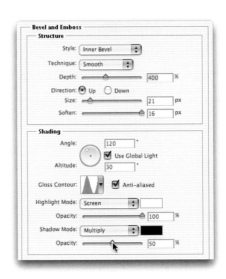

STEP TEN: Increase the Highlight Opacity to 100%, and lower the Shadow Opacity to 50%). Click OK to apply the bevel. (At this point, the effect will look like the one shown here.)

STEP ELEVEN: In the Layers palette, change the layer Blend Mode of this layer from Normal to Color Burn (as shown). Next, click on the beveled chrome layer in the Layers palette to make it active. Choose Drop Shadow from the Add a Layer Style pop-up menu at the bottom of the Layers palette. Increase the Size to 16 and click OK.

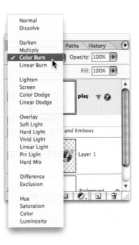

STEP TWELVE: When you click OK, the drop shadow is applied behind your bevel and the effect is complete. (In the example shown here, I just added another line of type, using the same font, in all lowercase.)

Untitled-5 @ 50% (game gear, RGB/8)

50%   Doc: 2.25M/4.13M

Quick Tip:
See RGB and CMYK at the same time

If you're working on an RGB document that you know will be converted to a CMYK document for press, there's a way you can see both RGB and CMYK versions of your document while you're working. That way, you can see how changes you make in the RGB image will actually look in your CMYK image—all in real time. Here's how: While your image is open onscreen, go under the Window menu, under Arrange, and choose New Window. This opens another view of your existing document. Press Command-Y (PC: Control-Y) to show a CMYK preview of your image, then return to your original document and edit as normal. You'll see your changes updated in the CMYK version as you work. Pretty slick!

Quick Tip:
Layer Effects and Global Light

When you use the Layer Effects Drop Shadow to apply a shadow to a layer, Photoshop notes the angle of that shadow, and it makes every shadow on every layer go in that exact same angle. This feature is called Global Light, and by tying all your light sources together, you can adjust the position of this Global Light source on any layer, and all the other shadows will automatically follow suit.

This comes in handy if you've created a file with multiple Layer Effects and your client decides to change the angle of the sun (hey, it happens). Rather than going to every individual layer and changing the angle of every drop shadow, you can just go under the Layer menu, under Layer Style, and choose Global Light. When you change the angle here, all the other layers will change at the same time. You can also do the same thing by simply changing the angle of any shadow on any layer. If you want to have one layer with a shadow going a different direction, just uncheck the Use Global Light checkbox in the Drop Shadow dialog box.

Metal Beveled Type Effect

This is a type effect made popular by EA Sports in the titles for their video games. It stands alone as just a great beveled metallic effect, but EA Sports takes it one better by combining it with a 3D perspective effect that really makes it unique. Here's how to create a similar effect.

STEP ONE: Open a new document in RGB mode (7" x 5" at 200 ppi). Click on the Foreground Color Swatch and choose a grayish blue. Fill the Background layer with this color by pressing Option-Delete (PC: Alt-Back-space). Create a new blank layer. Switch to the Elliptical Marquee tool, hold the Shift key, then drag out a circular selection (like the one shown here). Press "d" then "x' to set your Foreground color to white, then press Option-Delete (PC: Alt-Backspace) to fill your selection with white.

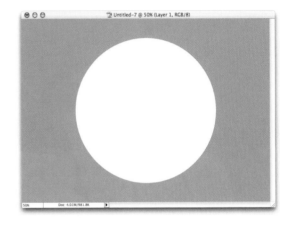

STEP TWO: Choose Gradient Overlay from the Add a Layer Style pop-up menu at the bottom of the Layers palette. Click on the down-facing triangle to the right of the current Gradient thumbnail to bring up the Gradient Picker (shown here). From the Picker's pop-down menu, load the Metals set. Click Append when the dialog appears, then choose the "Silver" gradient shown here. Click OK.

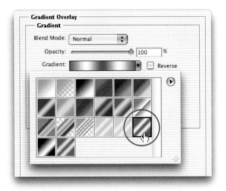

STEP THREE: You should still have a selection around your circle, so go under the Select menu, under Modify, and choose Contract. When the Contract Selection dialog appears, enter 20 pixels (as shown here) and click OK to shrink your selection by 20 pixels.

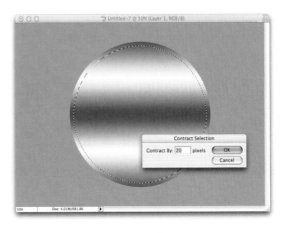

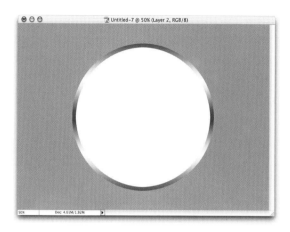

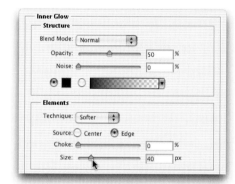

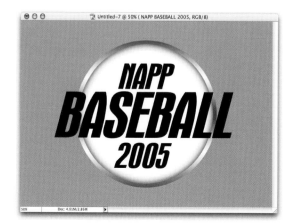

STEP FOUR: Go to the Layers palette and click on the New Layer icon at the bottom of the Layers palette to create a new layer. Fill your selection with white by pressing Option-Delete (PC: Alt-Backspace). Deselect by pressing Command-D (PC: Control-D).

STEP FIVE: Choose Inner Glow from the Add a Layer Style pop-up menu at the bottom of the Layers palette. When the dialog appears, change the Blend Mode from Screen to Normal and lower the Opacity to 50%. Click on the beige Color Swatch and change your glow color to black in the Color Picker. Increase the Size to 40.

STEP SIX: Click OK and a shadow is applied inside the edge of your white circle (as shown here). Now, on to the type effect. Press the letter "t" to switch to the Type tool and the letter "d" to set your Foreground color to black, and then create your type. (For the text shown here I used the font Aurora Condensed from Bitstream. The Horizontal Scaling has been increased to 150% in the Character palette to make the letters look thicker. Also, I didn't have the Italic version of this font installed, so I highlighted the text and chose "Faux Italic" from the Character palette's pop-down menu to create an italic look.)

continued

STEP SEVEN: You're going to add a gradient to your type, so choose Gradient Overlay from the Add a Layer Style pop-up menu at the bottom of the Layers palette. Choose the same metal gradient that you used earlier for the circle in Step Two.

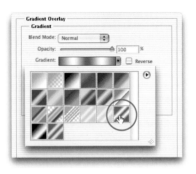

STEP EIGHT: When you click OK, the metal gradient is applied to your type (as shown here).

STEP NINE: Next, you'll need to bevel your type, so choose Bevel and Emboss from the Add a Layer Style pop-up menu. Increase the Depth to 1000 and the Size to 10. In the Shading section, increase the Highlight Opacity to 100%, and lower the Shadow Opacity to 50%.

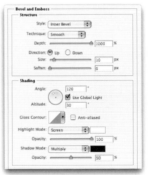

STEP TEN: Click OK and the beveled edge is applied to your text. Hold the Command key (PC: Control key), go to the Layers palette, and click on the Type layer to put a selection around your beveled text. Then, go under the Select menu, under Modify, and choose Contract. When the Contract Selection dialog appears, enter 6 pixels, and click OK (as shown).

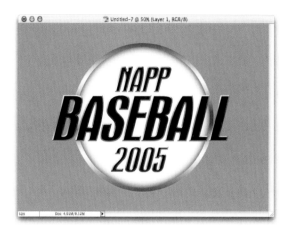

STEP ELEVEN: Create a new blank layer by clicking on the New Layer icon at the bottom of the Layers palette. Press "d" to set your Foreground color to black, then fill your contracted selection with black by pressing Option-Delete (PC: Alt-Backspace). Deselect by pressing Command-D (PC: Control-D) and the effect is complete. However, if you want to make the logo look 3D, continue to the next step.

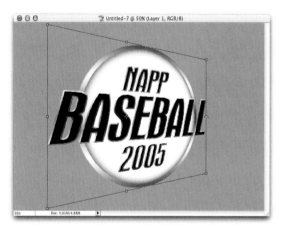

STEP TWELVE: In the Layers palette, hide your Background layer from view by clicking on the Eye icon in the first column beside it. Then, click on the right-facing triangle in the top-right corner of the Layers palette and choose Merge Visible from the palette's pop-down menu to merge all your logo layers into one layer. Press Command-T (PC: Control-T) to bring up Free Transform. Hold Shift-Option-Command (PC: Shift-Alt-Control), grab the bottom-right control point, and drag upward to create a perspective effect.

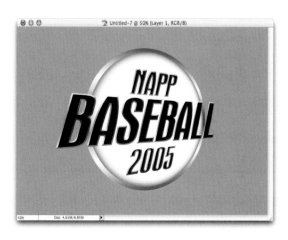

STEP THIRTEEN: With the modifier keys still pressed, grab the bottom-left corner point and drag downward to increase the effect. This perspective effect usually makes the logo look stretched, so release all the keys, grab the right center point and drag to the left until the logo doesn't look stretched. Press Return (PC: Enter) to lock in your transformation, and complete the effect (as shown here).

Quick Tip:
Filter Gallery magnification quick change
Want to see the Preview at 100%, 200%, or even 1,600% with just one click? Then Control-click (PC: Right-click) within the Preview area and a pop-up list will appear, where you can choose the magnification you want.

Quick Tip:
**Clipping Groups
are now
Clipping Masks**

Adobe realized that the
name Clipping Group
wasn't a really accurate
description of what a Clipping Group does (which
is a mask on the image on
the top layer, with the text,
shape, or photo on the
layer beneath it); so in its
ongoing effort to make all
the commands make sense,
they changed the name of
Clipping Groups to Clipping
Masks, and the command
(under the Layer menu)
that creates a Clipping
Group has been changed
to Create Clipping Mask.
See, now you won't freak
out looking for a Clipping
Group that isn't there.

Type on a Path and Curled Ribbons

Photoshop CS did add one of the most long-time requested features—type on a path; and we
attach type to a circular path while building this logo, but I think the star of this technique is later
on in the process, when you create a curved ribbon banner (like you'd normally do with the Pen
tool in Adobe Illustrator) from right within Photoshop. It's so easy you may never go back to the
old Illustrator way again.

STEP ONE: Open a new document in RGB mode. Create a
new layer by clicking on the
New Layer icon at the bottom
of the Layers palette. Press "d"
to set your Foreground color to
black. Get the Custom Shape
tool from the Toolbox. In the
Options Bar click on the third
icon from the left (to create
pixel-based shapes), and then
click on the Shape thumbnail
to bring up the Shape Picker.
From the Picker's pop-down
menu, choose Symbols and
click Append to load that set.
Choose the Yin Yang symbol,
hold the Shift key, and drag out
the shape.

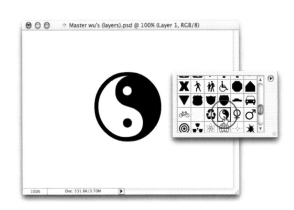

STEP TWO: Hold the Command
key (PC: Control key) and click
the New Layer icon at the bottom
of the Layers palette to create a
new layer under your Yin Yang
layer. Get the Elliptical Marquee
tool from the Toolbox, hold the
Shift key, and drag out a circular
selection that's larger than your
Yin Yang symbol. Press "x" to set
your Foreground color to white,
then press Option-Delete (PC: Alt-
Backspace) to fill your selection
with white. Press "d" to set your
Foreground back to black. Go
under the Edit menu and choose
Stroke. When the Stroke dialog
appears, choose 1 pixel for Width,
Center for Location, and click OK.
Press Command-D (PC: Control-D)
to deselect.

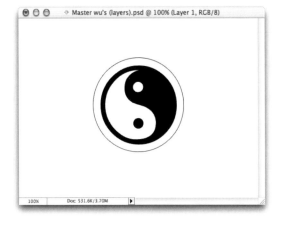

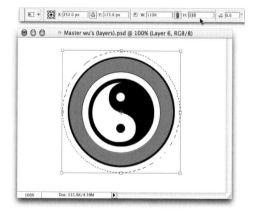

STEP THREE: Command-click (PC: Control-click) the New Layer icon again to create another new blank layer. Click on the Foreground Color Swatch and choose red, then use the Elliptical Marquee tool to create a significantly larger circular selection. Fill this selection with red by pressing Option-Delete (PC: Alt-Backspace).

STEP FOUR: Press "d" to set your Foreground color back to black. With your selection still in place around the red circle, choose Stroke from the Edit menu. Choose 4 pixels for Width, Center for Location, and click OK to put a black stroke around your red circle (as shown).

STEP FIVE: While your selection is still in place, go under the Select menu and choose Transform Selection. Then, go up in the Options Bar and increase both the W (width) and H (height) to 110%, and press Return (PC: Enter) to expand the selection outward by 10% (as shown).

STEP SIX: Hold the Command key (PC: Control key) and click the New Layer icon at the bottom of the Layers palette to create a new layer under your red circle layer. Then, choose Stroke from the Edit menu. This time, set the Width to 1 pixel, leave Location at Center, and click OK to add a thin stroke to your selection (as shown). Press Command-D (PC: Control-D) to deselect.

Quick Tip:
Getting your image down to size

When you're dragging Photoshop layers between documents, have you noticed that if part of your layer extends outside the edge of your document window, Photoshop doesn't delete those areas? Yep, it's still there. For example, if you drag an image of a car over to a new document and position it so that only the front half is showing, the back half (even though you can't see it) is still there. If you decide later that you want to show the whole car, you can simply drag the car further into your image window and the parts hidden off screen will appear. That's good, right? Well, sometimes. Actually, it's only good if you think that at some point you might need those parts. Otherwise, you're eating up memory storing stuff that you don't need. Want to get rid of all that excess image data? Press Command-A (PC: Control-A) to Select All, then go under the Edit menu and choose Crop. Everything outside your image window gets cropped off, shrinking your file size in the process.

continued

Quick Tip:
Don't drag to the Trash in the Filter Gallery

If you want to delete a filter from your Filter Stack, you don't have to drag it down to the Trash icon. If the filter is already selected, just click the Trash icon and it's gone! Good news: if you make a mistake and delete the wrong filter, just press Command-Z (PC: Control-Z) immediately to undo your mistake.

STEP SEVEN: Now you're going to create a ribbon to add to the logo. Create a new document in RGB mode. Press Shift-L until you get the Polygonal Lasso tool, and draw a selection of straight lines like the ones shown here. Hold the Shift key the whole time, and just click once, move to the next spot, and click again; the Polygonal Lasso will connect the straight lines for you.

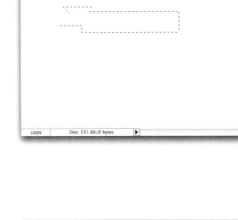

STEP EIGHT: Create a new blank layer by clicking on the New Layer icon at the bottom of the Layers palette. Fill your selection with black (as shown here) by pressing Option-Delete (PC: Alt-Backspace). Deselect by pressing Command-D (PC: Control-D).

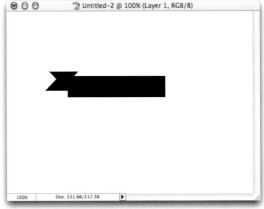

STEP NINE: You're going to apply a filter that will make this ribbon bend, but before you do that, you'll have to rotate it vertically (like the one you see here). So press Command-T (PC: Control-T) to bring up Free Transform. Then go under the Edit menu, under Transform, and choose Rotate 90° CCW. Press Return (PC: Enter), then switch to the Rectangular Marquee tool and draw a rectangular selection that's a bit larger than your ribbon (as shown here).

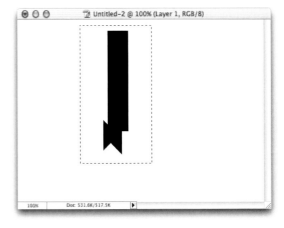

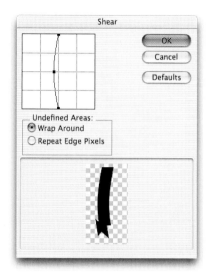

STEP TEN: Go under the Filter menu, under Distort, and choose Shear. When the Shear dialog appears, click in the center of the grid line to add a point. Click on this point and drag it to the left to bend the ribbon. You can see a preview of your bend at the bottom of the filter dialog. When it looks right, click OK to apply the bend. Deselect by pressing Command-D (PC: Control-D).

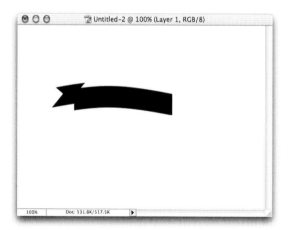

STEP ELEVEN: Press Command-T (PC: Control-T) to bring up Free Transform so you can rotate the ribbon back to its original orientation. Go under the Edit menu, under Transform, and choose Rotate 90° CW, then press Return (PC: Enter) to lock in your Transformation.

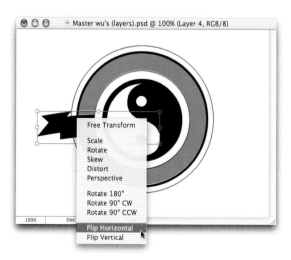

STEP TWELVE: Press the letter "v" to get the Move tool, click on your ribbon, and drag it over to your red circle document. Position it on the left (as shown here). This makes the left side of the ribbon. To make the right side, press Option-Command-T (PC: Alt-Control-T) to bring up a version of Free Transform that duplicates when it transforms. Control-click (PC: Right-click) within the bounding box, and when the menu appears, choose Flip Horizontal.

Quick Tip:
Match another open image's size

If you have an image already open and you want it to be the same size as another open document, here's a quick trick to have Photoshop do all the work for you. While the image is open onscreen, go under the Image menu and choose Image Size. When the dialog box appears, go under the Window menu and choose the name of the open image you want it to match at the bottom of the menu. It will enter all the appropriate information in the Image Size dialog box for you, and as long as you have the Resample Image checkbox turned on, you can click OK and your image will jump to those new specs. Make sure, however, that you resample the image down in size and not up, because you'll wind up pixelating the image.

continued

Quick Tip:
Put your guides right where you want 'em

If you know the exact position where you want a guide placed, you can have Photoshop place it for you by going under the View menu and choosing New Guide. In the dialog box, enter the position you want, click OK, and you're in business.

STEP THIRTEEN: Press Return (PC: Enter) to lock in your transformation, and use the Move tool to drag this flipped duplicate ribbon to the right side. Position it like the one shown here. The ends of the ribbon should be behind the white circle in the middle. If they're not, go to the Layers palette and click-and-drag these ribbon layers beneath the white circle layer.

STEP FOURTEEN: Press Shift-U until you get the Ellipse Shape tool from the Toolbox. Go up in the Options Bar and click on the center of the three small icons on the far left of the bar (as shown here). By choosing this, when you create a shape, it will appear as a path (as if you drew it with the Pen tool). Hold the Shift key and click-and-drag out a circular shape like the one shown here.

STEP FIFTEEN: Press the letter "x" to switch your Foreground color to white, and then get the Type tool. Up in the Options Bar, make sure the justification is set to Center Text (as shown here). Then place your cursor at the top of the circular path (as shown), and the cursor will change slightly to indicate that you're about to attach type to the circular path.

STEP SIXTEEN: Click on the path and enter your type. (Note: the type shown here is Mata Bold from T-26.) As you type, because you chose Center Text in the Type Options Bar in the previous step, the type will be centered on the top of the circle (as shown here).

STEP SEVENTEEN: Duplicate this "type-on-a-path" layer by pressing Command-J (PC: Control-J). Press the letter "a" to switch to the Path Selection tool (it's the black solid arrow to the left of the Type tool), click directly on the first letter of your type on a path, and drag it downward along the path. It will appear upside-down. Just click-and-drag upward, and it will flip in the right direction. To enter new text, go to the Layers palette, and double-click directly on the "T" thumbnail to highlight your type, then type in the word "taekwondo."

STEP EIGHTEEN: If your type seems too high, or to low, along the path (in other words, it's not centered within the red circle area), you can highlight the text (double-click on the "T" thumb-nail in the Layers palette), then use the Baseline Shift amount in the Character palette (shown here) to raise or lower the text until it looks right.

continued

Quick Tip:
Want to bend the top or bottom? Make it vertical first.

If you want to put a bend in the top or bottom of an object (or rasterized type for that matter), here's a quick way to do it. Start by using Free Transform and rotate the image 90° CCW. This enables you to use the Shear filter (found under the Filter menu, under Distort) to bend the object to the left or right; but then after running the filter, you'll need to rotate it back 90° CW to make it upright again.

Quick Tip:
Getting rid of white- or black-edged pixels

If you're collaging and an image you added to your collage was selected from a solid white or solid black background, there's a pretty good chance that a few stray white- or black-edged pixels will appear around your image. To get rid of those annoying white/black pixels, try going under the Layer menu, under Matting, and choosing either Remove White Matte, or Remove Black Matte (again, depending on which color background the image was originally from). In many cases, this can really work wonders.

STEP NINETEEN: It's time to add type on a slight arc to the ribbons. Press "p" to get the Pen tool, then click on the bottom-left corner of the left ribbon. Then, move your cursor to the bottom-right corner of the left ribbon where it meets the white circle, click-and-hold to add a point, and drag to bend the path segment to match the curve of the ribbon (as shown).

STEP TWENTY: Click on the New Layer icon at the bottom of the Layers palette to create a new layer. Switch to the Type tool, then go up to the Options Bar, and click the Left Align Text button. Click your Type cursor on the left side of the path and begin typing, and your type will follow the path. The font used here is Papyrus. Once your type is in place, switch to the Move tool and drag it up into the center of the ribbon (as shown). Do the same for the right side.

STEP TWENTY-ONE: Here's the text "1993" added to the right side of the ribbon. The reason you align the path to the bottom of the ribbon, is so the amount of bend in your curve is perfectly aligned to the bend in your ribbon. At this point, the logo is basically done, but we just can't help tweaking things a bit. So...

STEP TWENTY-TWO: Go to the Layers palette and click on the original Yin Yang layer. Then, choose Bevel and Emboss from the Add a Layer Style pop-up menu at the bottom of the Layers palette. When the dialog box appears, just click OK to apply the standard beveled effect to your Yin Yang symbol.

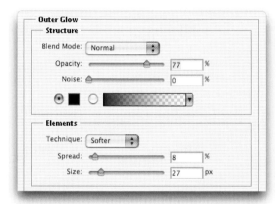

STEP TWENTY-THREE: In the Layers palette, click on the thin black outer ring layer. Press the letter "w" to get the Magic Wand tool, and click in the white area inside the ring to select it. Press "d" then "x" to set white as your Foreground color, and then fill this circle with white by pressing Option-Delete (PC: Alt-Backspace). Choose Outer Glow from the Add a Layer Style pop-up menu. When the dialog appears, change the Blend Mode from Screen to Normal, increase the Spread to 8% and the Size to 27, and click on the beige Color Swatch and change the Glow color to black. Click OK.

STEP TWENTY-FOUR: Here's the final logo, with a black outer glow, and beveled Yin Yang symbol. Again, it didn't need those extra effects, but I just couldn't help myself. It's a sickness.

Quick Tip:
Accurate Unsharp Masking
When applying the Unsharp Mask filter, make sure that your image size is at 100% view, or what you see onscreen will probably be much different than what prints out. Because of the way Photoshop displays your image at smaller views, you might not see little spots and other annoying artifacts that you might be introducing into your document. Therefore, always make sure to apply it at a 100% view and you'll avoid a major case of the "spots."

Quick Tip:
Creating new layers

There are a number of ways to create new layers. The quickest way is to click on the New Layer icon at the bottom of the Layers palette. No dialog box pops up to slow you down—you immediately get a new blank layer.

You can use the keyboard shortcut Shift-Command-N (PC: Shift-Control-N) to create a new layer and bring up the New Layer dialog box (so you can name your layer as you create it), but that's a bit slower.

If you're looking for the absolute slowest way to create a layer (if you're charging by the hour), you can go under the Layer menu, under New, and choose Layer.

You can also choose New Layer from the Layers palette's pop-down menu if you're charging by the hour, but still have a deadline to meet.

Hollywood Grunge Effect

I originally saw a great tutorial that showed me the basis of how to do this effect on the Web site www.dreaminfinity.com. It opened my eyes to a whole new way of creating these trendy "neo" grunge effects that are so popular in movie titles, CD covers, and ads targeting young consumers. Here's my take on how to create this popular effect.

STEP ONE: Open a new blank document in RGB mode. Press the letter "t" to get the Type tool and create some type. (In the example shown here, I used the font Trajan from Adobe.)

STEP TWO: The grunge effect is created using a photo. Any photo with well-defined lines seems to work well, including photos of buildings, cities, walls, and stairs. So, choose a photo with lots of objects that have straight or angled lines (rather than curves).

STEP THREE: Press "v" to get the Move tool, hold the Shift key, and drag this photo over to your Type document (the photo should appear above your Type layer in the Layers stack, and it should be centered because you held the Shift key). Press Shift-Command-U (PC: Shift-Control-U) to remove the color from your photo (as shown here).

© Brand X Pictures

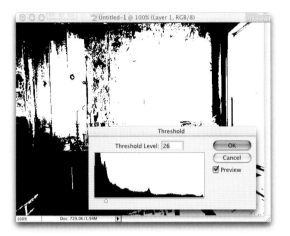

STEP FOUR: Go under the Image menu, under Adjustments, and choose Threshold. When the Threshold dialog appears, drag the Threshold slider (under the Histogram) to the left until the Threshold Level (at the top of the dialog) reads 26 (as shown here). This increases the contrast of the photo, and gives it a noisy, dirty look. Click OK.

Quick Tip:
Hiding the marching ants

If you're working on a project, there are times where you need to have something selected, but it would help if you didn't have to see the "marching ants" selection border on the screen. To keep your selection in place, but to hide those annoying marching ants, press Command-H (PC: Control-H). Adobe now calls this command just "Extras," but it probably should be called "Hide Selection" or "Hide Marching Ants"; but if they did name commands with such obvious names, then you wouldn't need this book, so now that I think of it, I really like that name, Extras. Yep, that works for me.

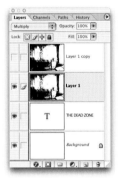

STEP FIVE: Duplicate this layer by pressing Command-J (PC: Control-J). Then, in the Layers palette, hide this duplicate layer (by clicking on the Eye icon beside it) and click on the original photo layer (as shown). Then, change the Blend Mode of this layer from Normal to Multiply in the Layers palette, so you can see through to your text on the layer beneath it (as shown here).

STEP SIX: Press the letter "m" to get the Rectangular Marquee tool and drag a rectangular selection around your type (like the one shown here). Remember, you're still on the photo layer—you're just seeing the type layer beneath it.

continued

STEP SEVEN: Go under the Select menu and choose Inverse (this selects everything except the area you just selected) and press Delete (PC: Backspace) to erase the top and bottom chunks of your photo layer (as shown here). Deselect by pressing Command-D (PC: Control-D).

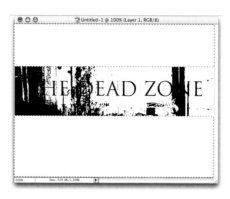

STEP EIGHT: Press "e" to get the Eraser tool. In the Option Bar, click on the down-facing arrow next to the Brush thumbnail to get the Brush Picker. Choose a Spatter brush (any Spatter brush will do: 24, 27, 39, etc.). Use the Master Diameter slider in the Picker to increase your brush size to 65.

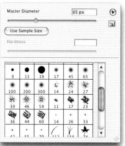

STEP NINE: Take the Eraser tool (with this Spatter brush) and starting clicking your way across the word, erasing as you click. Basically, you're erasing away the grunge that obscures the type. This will take hundreds of clicks as you work your way from left to right (don't worry, it only takes a minute or so). Then start clicking over other areas, erasing away (remember—no paint strokes— only clicks).

STEP TEN: Spend another minute or two erasing other areas until you basically have a mess (like the one shown here). Yours won't necessarily look just like the one shown here, and that's perfectly fine—just erase the areas that annoy you, and leave some grunge around your type area. How much grunge is enough? It's your call.

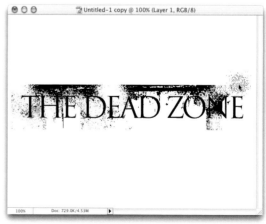

STEP ELEVEN: Now make the duplicate photo layer visible and active by clicking on it in the Layers palette. In the Layers palette, change the Blend Mode of this layer from Normal to Multiply (so you can see through it). Switch to the Move tool and drag this layer around (down, left, etc.) to find an area of this layer that looks cool over your existing type and grunge. Again, where you stop is up to you (I went down a little and to the left in this example).

STEP TWELVE: Once your duplicate photo layer is in place, get the Rectangular Marquee tool, drag a large rectangular selection around the top half of your image area, and press Delete (PC: Backspace). Then do the same for the bottom, starting ½ inch or so under your type (like the one shown here) and press Delete (PC: Backspace) to delete this excess area. Get the Eraser tool again, and click away over any areas that look too distracting or cover up your type too much.

STEP THIRTEEN: Here's the finished effect, with a line of text added underneath it (I used the standard font Helvetica). This technique is fun to experiment with, either using different photos, or using the same photo and trying different Blend Modes (other than Multiply) and erasing different parts of your photo.

Quick Tip:
Zooming around the Layers palette

You can jump to the layer directly below your current layer in the Layers palette by pressing Option-Left Bracket (PC: Alt-Left Bracket), or you can move to the layer above your current layer by pressing Option-Right Bracket (PC: Alt-Right Bracket). Using these keyboard shortcuts, you can quickly step up and down through your Layers palette.

Quick Tip:
Moving your image when in Full Screen Mode

If you're in Full Screen Mode (no menus, no palettes, no tools, and your photo is centered on a black background) in Photoshop CS, you can now drag your photo around within the black canvas area. Just hold the Spacebar and your cursor will change from the Move tool to the Hand tool. Now you can click-and-drag the entire image around. Freaky. I know.

Diamond Effect

I originally saw the technique for creating diamonds in a book I bought in Japan. But it was still a little bit tricky figuring it out, because (a) the book used the Japanese language version of Photoshop, and (b) I don't read Japanese. Since then, I've seen the effect used numerous times in ads and on CD covers, and here we're using it as part of a fictitious hip-hop radio station logo.

STEP ONE: This particular effect requires you to create the original image at a very large physical size (like at least 11" x 8" at 72 ppi) in RGB mode. Press the letter "t" to get the Type tool and create your type (the font shown here is Serpentine Bold Oblique, from Adobe).

STEP TWO: You're going to apply a filter to your type, so you'll need to convert your Type layer into a regular image layer by Control-clicking (PC: Right-clicking) on the Type layer and choosing Rasterize Layer (as shown here).

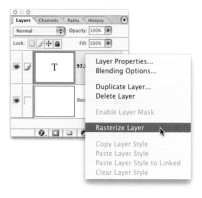

STEP THREE: Go under the Filter menu, under Distort, and choose Glass. When the Glass dialog appears, increase the Distortion to 20, set the Smoothness to 1, choose Tiny Lens for Texture, and set the Scaling at 85% (as shown here). Click OK to apply a diamond pattern to your type (as shown in the filter preview window here). Next, you'll add a shadow inside your text.

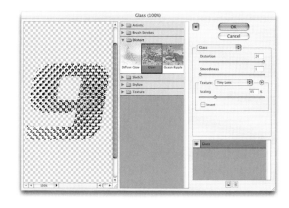

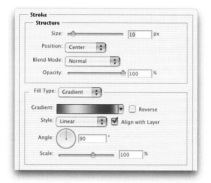

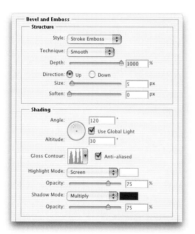

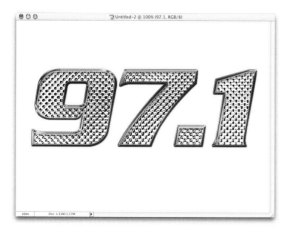

STEP FOUR: Choose Inner Shadow from the Layer Styles pop-up menu at the bottom of the Layers palette. Increase the Opacity to 100% and increase the Size to 13. Don't click OK yet.

STEP FIVE: From the list of Styles on the left side of the dialog, click directly on the word Stroke. Increase the Size to 10, and Position to Center. For Fill Type choose Gradient. Click on the down-facing arrow next to the Gradient thumbnail, then choose the default Copper Gradient (as shown) from the Gradient Picker.

STEP SIX: Go to the list of Styles again, but this time choose Bevel and Emboss. Change the Style to Stroke Emboss, and increase the Depth to 1000%. In the Shading section, turn on Anti-aliased, set the Altitude at 30°, then click on the down-facing arrow next to Gloss Contour to bring up the Picker. From the Picker's pop-down menu load the set named "Contours" (then click Append). Choose the Contour named "Ring-Triple" as shown here.

STEP SEVEN: Click OK and the inner shadow (added for depth), copper gradient stroke, and the bevel effect on that stroke will all be applied simultaneously (as shown here). Now, you could stop right here (okay, you'd probably add a drop shadow, but that's all it needs). But to show the effect in action, you can continue and create a logo using this type.

continued

Quick Tip:
Opening 16-bit images

Back in Photoshop 7, the only way to directly open 16-bit raw images from high-end digital cameras was to buy Adobe's Camera Raw plug-in (or you could process the raw photos in a separate application to make them readable in Photoshop). But in Photoshop CS, you bypass all that, and now you can open 16-bit directly from within the File Browser, just like you would any regular 8-bit image—just double-click the 16-bit image that appears as a thumbnail and it will open directly in the Raw dialog.

Quick Tip:
Choose the size for your custom thumbnails

Photoshop CS's File Browser lets you set your own custom size for viewing your thumbnails (which is really great, because I've always felt the "Large Thumbnail" setting was never really large enough). But finding out where to set your own custom size is a bit trickier. To set your size, go to the File Browser, and in the File Browser's own "mini-menubar" in the top left corner, go under the Edit menu and choose Preferences. In the field named "Custom Thumbnail Size" enter the width you'd like for your custom thumbnails (up to 1024 pixels wide). Once you click OK in your Preferences, go under the View menu and choose Custom Thumbnail Size.

STEP EIGHT: Create a new document (at a smaller size, like 7"x5") in RGB mode. Press "d" to set your Foreground color to black, then press Option-Delete (PC: Alt-Backspace) to fill the Background layer with black. Create a new blank layer, then get the Elliptical Marquee tool and draw an oval-shaped selection (like the one shown here). Click on the Foreground Color Swatch, and choose a red, then fill your selection with red by pressing Option-Delete (PC: Alt-Backspace).

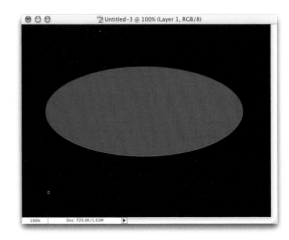

STEP NINE: Press Command-D (PC: Control-D) to deselect. Choose Stroke from the Add a Layer Style pop-up menu at the bottom of the Layers palette. Set the Size to 10, the Position to Inside, click on the Color swatch, then choose a bright yellow (like the one shown here) as your stroke Color. From the list of Styles on the left side of the dialog, click on Inner Shadow. Increase the Distance to 15 and the size to 13, then click OK to apply a shadow inside your red oval, and the yellow stroke around the outside.

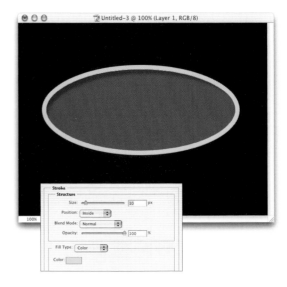

STEP TEN: Hold the Command key (PC: Control key), go to the Layers palette, and click on the oval layer to put a selection around your oval. Go under the Select menu and choose Transform Selection. Once the bounding box appears, go up to the Options Bar, and for Width enter 90%, for Height enter 80%, then press Enter to shrink your selection.

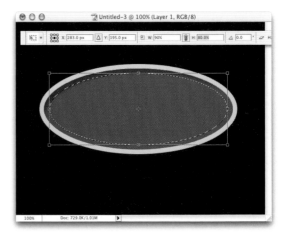

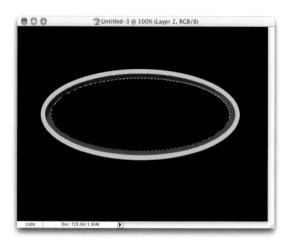

STEP ELEVEN: Create a new layer, press "d" to set your Foreground color to black, then fill your smaller oval-shaped selection with black by pressing Option-Delete (PC: Alt-Backspace).

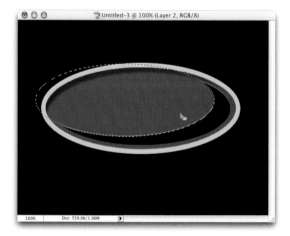

STEP TWELVE: Click your Elliptical Marquee tool inside the black oval-shaped selection and drag the selection up and to the left (as shown here). Then press Delete (PC: Backspace), which knocks a hole out of your black oval, revealing the red oval on the layer below it. When you do this, it creates a Nike-like swoosh out of your once-black oval. Deselect by pressing Command-D (PC: Control-D).

STEP THIRTEEN: Go back to your diamond text document. Press "v" to get the Move tool, and click-and-drag your diamond text over onto your red, black, and yellow oval document. Your text will be too big, so press Command-T (PC: Control-T) to bring up Free Transform. Hold the Shift key, grab a corner point, and drag inward to scale the text down to size (as shown here). Press Return (PC: Enter) to lock in your transformation.

continued

STEP FOURTEEN: Choose Drop
Shadow from the Add a Layer
Style pop-up menu. Turn off
Use Global Light then set the
Angle to 138°, Distance to 12,
and click OK to apply a soft drop
shadow to your diamond text
(as shown). For the tag line,
create your type using the same
font, then choose Stroke from
the Add a Layer Style pop-up
menu. Set your Stroke color to
yellow, and click OK.

STEP FIFTEEN: Now you'll add
the station's call letters. Type in
"KJAM" right above the number
"9" in the logo, then set your
Foreground color to yellow and
your Background color to red.
Then, choose Gradient Overlay
from the Add a Layer Style pop-
up menu. In the Gradient Picker
in the dialog, make sure the
very first gradient (Foreground
to Background) is selected. Set
the Angle to -90°. Then choose
Stroke from the list of Styles.
Change the Stroke Color to
black and click OK.

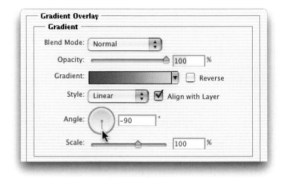

STEP SIXTEEN: In the Layers
palette, click on your diamond
type layer. Although the copper
gradient looked fine when the
diamond type was on white, it
looks all wrong when put over
this black, red, and yellow logo.
So, double-click on the word
Stroke on your diamond text
layer. Click on the down-
facing arrow next to the Gradient thumbnail, then from the
Gradient Picker's pop-down
menu, choose Metals to load
that set of gradients. Click on
the Silver gradient shown here.

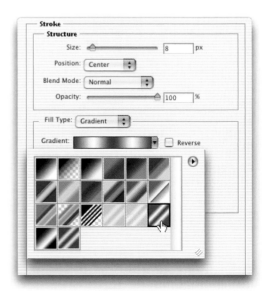

STEP SEVENTEEN: Click OK and your stroke gradient is changed to the silver metal (as shown here). If the call letters don't stand out enough, click on the call letters layer in the Layer palette, then choose Outer Glow from the Add a Layer Style pop-up menu. Set the Glow Color to white, Blend Mode to Normal, and increase the Spread to 38, Size to 15, and click OK

STEP EIGHTEEN: The final step is to scale the size of the Layer Styles down on your diamond text layer. Even though you scaled the dialog text down earlier, the effects you applied stay at the same size, so go under the Layer menu, under Layer Style, and choose Scale Effects. Lower the scale to 84% and click OK. The final effect is shown below.

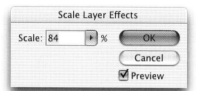

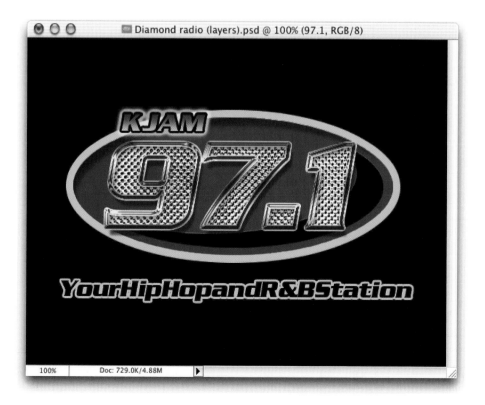

Quick Tip:
**Creating type
on a path**

The secret to creating type on a path is (are you ready for this) there is no Type on a Path tool. That's right, there's no special Type tool—it uses the standard Type tool. Just draw your Path (using a custom shape or the Pen tool), then get the standard Type tool, and when you move the cursor near the path, the cursor will change, indicating that if you click and start typing, your text will adhere to the path. Pretty slick stuff.

Movie Poster Type

This is probably the most popular effect in Hollywood movie titles, and it's used in a dozen other places as well (I saw it in a Levi's print ad just this evening). It uses the technique of grunging a photo (which is used in another tutorial here in the book), but it uses it in a different way. Also, after you've created the effect, you'll drop it into a movie poster layout (you'll have to do a little work there, mostly formatting type, but it's easy).

STEP ONE: Open a new document in RGB mode. Click on the Foreground Color Swatch and set your Foreground color to red. Press the letter "t" to get the Type tool and create your type (the type shown here is in Compacta Bold, from Bitstream, with the Horizontal Scaling set to 85% in the Character palette).

STEP TWO: Open the photo that you'll use to create your grunge. Photos with lots of vertical lines seem to work best; photos that have lots of rounded objects (like palm trees) don't work nearly as well (I know from experience). I had to test the effect on about eight photos before I found this one.

STEP THREE: Go under the Image menu, under Adjustments, and choose Threshold. Drag the slider nearly all the way to the left, to remove the color and detail, leaving just broken lines, spots, and smudges (as shown here). This is the step you'll probably have to try on a number of photos until you find one that looks good. Click OK to apply Threshold.

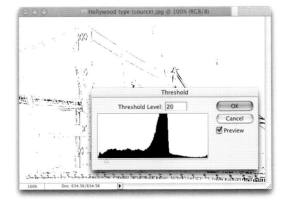

© Brand X Pictures

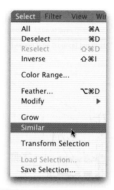

STEP FOUR: Switch to the Magic Wand tool, then click directly inside one black area of your photo (it will probably only select a tiny section of your photo). Then go under the Select menu, and choose Similar (as shown here) to select all the similar black colored areas in your photo

STEP FIVE: Get the Move tool and drag these selected black areas over into your red Type document as one unit. When it comes over, press Command-T (PC: Control-T) to bring up Free Transform. Hold the Shift key, grab a corner point, and drag inward to shrink the photo until it's just slightly larger than your text (as shown here). Then press Return (PC: Enter) to lock in your transformation.

STEP SIX: Press "d" then "x" to set your Foreground color to white. Then press Shift-Option-Delete (PC: Shift-Alt-Backspace) to fill your grunge junk with white (as shown here). Press Command-G (PC: Control-G) to group the white grunge inside your Type. You can now use the Move tool to reposition the grunge that's inside the type. At this point the type portion of this effect is now complete.

EXAMPLE: Here's an example of how this effect was used for the logo of the hit comedy *American Wedding* just so you can see how it would look. However, turn the page, and we'll continue with our "Blackmail" logo and turn it into a complete movie poster.

continued

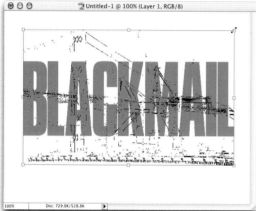

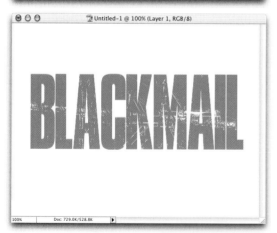

Quick Tip:
Editing type on a path

When you have type on a path, it's still live editable type, so you can change the word, leading, size, font, etc. The easiest way to do this (once your type is on the path) is to go to the Layers palette and double-click directly on the "T" icon beside your Type layer. This puts a selection around your type on a path, and then you can go to Window>Character to bring up the Character palette where you can adjust the attributes of your type.

Quick Tip:
Getting that Welcome Screen back

If you, like most people, got tired of having the Photoshop CS Welcome Screen appear each time you launch Photoshop CS, you probably turned off the checkbox that appears in the lower left-hand corner named "Show this dialog at startup." However, there are times when you might want it back (to see the list of new features, get some tips and tricks, etc.). If that happens (and that's a pretty big "if"), just go under the Help menu and choose Welcome Screen.

STEP SEVEN: Press "d" to set your Foreground color to black. Go to the Layers palette, and click on the grouped layer that has your grunge on it. Then press Shift-Option-Delete (PC: Shift-Alt-Backspace) to fill your grunge with black (instead of the white grunge that was there).

STEP EIGHT: Open the photo you want to use in your movie poster. Here's a typical "stressed guy working late at the office" photo. You'll use this as the main photo for your poster, but it'll need a little editing later on (as you'll see).

STEP NINE: Open another new document, and make it have a vertical orientation (like a 5"x7"). Fill the Background layer with black. Get the Move tool and drag the stressed office guy onto this black background. Position it so just the man is visible, and not the computer. Get the Brush tool, choose a large soft-edge brush, and cover up the desk by painting over it with black paint strokes (as shown).

© Brand X Pictures

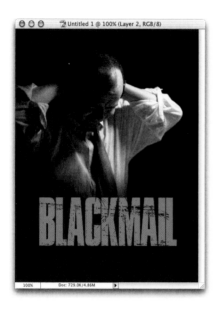

STEP TEN: Go back to your grunge type document. You need to merge the grunge layer and Type layer together but you can't merge Type layers with other layers. The trick is to link the layers first, so click in the second column of the Type layer to link it to the grunge layer, then press Command-E (PC: Control-E) to permanently merge them. Switch to the Move tool and drag this red type over onto your poster document. Scale the type down to size using Free Transform.

STEP ELEVEN: The final step is to add the rest of the movie poster type. The type at the top (in all caps) is set in Trajan (from Adobe). The subhead under the red type is set in Futura Extra Bold (from Adobe) with 220% Horizontal Scaling. The small type at the bottom is in Helvetica Bold Condensed, and the "Coming Soon" at the very bottom (in red) is in the font Impact.

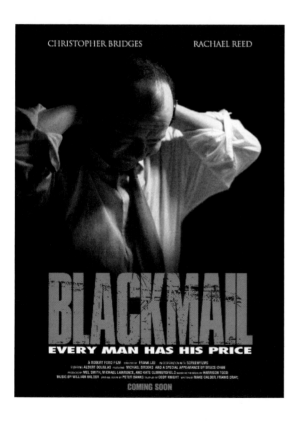

Quick Tip:
Finding the lost 3D Transform filter

In Photoshop CS, Adobe figured that you probably had enough of the lame 3D Transform filter that used to appear under the Filter menu, under Distort, so they yanked it out of Photoshop CS, and stuck it on the install CD as an "Optional Plug-in." If you want this plug-in back again, just drag it from the CD into your Photoshop Plug-ins folder, then restart Photoshop.

I have to 'fess up. There aren't really a dozen special effects in this chapter. The real name of this chapter is

The Dirty Dozen
More Down & Dirty Tricks

"More Down & Dirty Tricks" (which is what this chapter is). The "Dirty Dozen" thing is more like a slogan. I only used it because my editor told me if I found a way to work the word "Dirty" into a chapter title, according to research it would increase sales of the book by as much as 16% (18% in some parts of New Jersey). Hey, I can't argue with him, because in my last book he told me to slip in the word "Naughty" somewhere and it increased sales by over 19%, despite the fact that the chapter was then awkwardly named "Naughty CMYK Prepress Settings." He also said if I casually noted that I know Britney Spears personally (which I do not), it would open a whole new teen market for my books. And if I could somehow slip the words "Tom Clancy" onto the front cover of the book, in all caps, at a large point size, sales would really take off. So far, it's working. Well, gotta run—my next Harry Potter book isn't just going to write itself, ya know.

Quick Tip:
Kerning
shortcuts

Increasing or decreasing the space between two letters is called "kerning," and Photoshop lets you kern your type either numerically or by using a keyboard shortcut (which is much better because kerning should be done by eye). To visually kern tighter (remove space between two letters), click your cursor between the two letters that you want to kern (just click, don't highlight), then press Option-Left Arrow (PC: Alt-Left Arrow) to tighten. Press Option-Right Arrow (PC: Alt-Right Arrow) to add space between the two letters.

Glassy Reflections

It's funny how certain techniques come into vogue, and this one is everywhere, from the Ford logo to the Land Rover logo to Philadelphia Brand Cream Cheese. It adds a glassy highlight and shadow the easy way.

STEP ONE: Open a new document in RGB mode. Press "d" to set your Foreground color to black, and then Option-Delete (PC: Alt-Backspace) to fill the Background with black. Create a new blank layer by clicking on the New Layer Icon at the bottom of the Layers palette. Set your Foreground to a dark red. Use the Elliptical Marquee tool to draw an oval-shaped selection. Fill your selection with red by pressing Option-Delete (PC: Alt-Backspace).

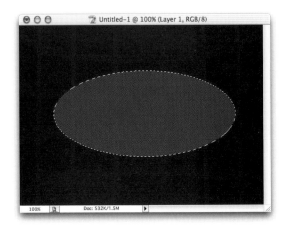

STEP TWO: Deselect by pressing Command-D (PC: Control-D). Next you're going to add a stroke around your red oval. Choose Stroke from the Add a Layer Style pop-up menu at the bottom of the Layers palette. When the Stroke dialog appears (shown here), enter 6 for Size, then click on the Color Swatch and choose a mustard yellow .

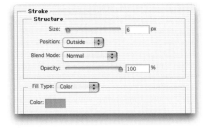

STEP THREE: When you click OK, a yellow stroke is added around your red oval (as shown here).

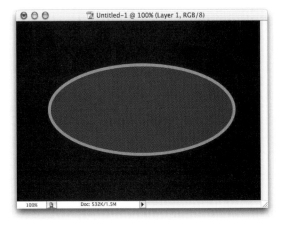

STEP FOUR: To add some depth, choose Inner Shadow from the Add a Layer Style pop-up menu at the bottom of the Layers palette. Set the Distance to 10 and the Size to 9.

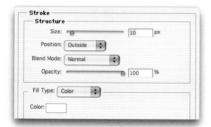

STEP FIVE: When you click OK, a shadow is added to the top and left side of your oval, inside the red area (as shown here).

STEP SIX: Press Command-J (PC: Control-J) to duplicate your red oval layer. Then, double-click on the word Stroke below your original red oval layer. When the Stroke Layer Style dialog appears, click on the Color Swatch and change the stroke Color to white, and then increase the Size to 10.

STEP SEVEN: Click OK to make a white stroke appear outside your yellow stroke (as shown here). Click on the red oval copy layer to make it active in the Layers palette. Press the letter "t" to get the Type tool, set your Foreground to a gold color, and create some type for the logo. I used the font Copperplate Gothic (from Adobe) for the word "Authentic" and the font Papyrus (also from Adobe) for the words "Hawaiian Surf Gear."

Quick Tip:
Using the Radial Blur in Best mode means "Coffee Break" time

When using Zoom set to Best as the Blur Method for a Radial Blur on a low-resolution image (for example, 72-ppi), it'll take a minute or two, maybe less. However, if you run a Radial Zoom Blur on a high-res, 300-ppi image, you have time to grab a cup of coffee. In fact, depending on your computer, you may have time to run out for lunch. This is one slooooooooow filter. It's doing a lot of that "Mr. Science"-type math, so it takes forever (in computer terms, forever is anything more than two minutes. A lifetime is 30 minutes). This filter sometimes takes a lifetime. Sorry 'bout that.

continued

Quick Tip:
Avoiding Type tool confusion

As you've learned by now, I like to switch tools by pressing their keyboard shortcut (rather than traveling all the way over to the Toolbox). It just saves so much time that it doesn't make sense to move your mouse all the way across the screen each time you need a different tool. However, when using Photoshop's Type tool, it can get confusing. That's because when you have the Type tool active and you press a key on your keyboard, Photoshop thinks you want to type (not switch tools), which makes perfect sense. That's why if you want to switch tools when you're using the Type tool, you need to click on the tool in the Toolbox, rather than typing the keyboard shortcut. You'll notice that in some of these tutorials, after you create your type, I ask you to click on the Move tool (rather than press the letter "v") so that you can bring up commands like Free Transform. If I didn't and you had the Type tool chosen and pressed the letter "v," it would just type a letter "v." Makes sense now, eh? Eh? Oh come on, it makes sense.

STEP EIGHT: Our logo is made up of a number of different layers, but you'll want to apply the effect to a flattened version of the logo. Here's a trick that will let you do that without actually flattening the document. Click on your top layer in the layer stack and create a New Layer above that. Hide the Background layer by clicking on the Eye icon in the first column beside it, hold Option (PC: Alt), click on the right-facing triangle at the top right of the Layers palette, and choose Merge Visible from the pop-down menu.

STEP NINE: Now that you have a flattened version of your logo on its own separate layer, make the black Background visible again by clicking where the Eye icon used to be. Next, get the Elliptical Marquee tool and draw an oval selection like the one shown here that's slightly larger than your logo, but don't let the edges extend outside your image area.

STEP TEN: To soften the edges of your selection, go under the Select menu and choose Feather. When the Feather Selection dialog appears, enter 30 pixels (for high-res, 300-ppi photos, enter 60 instead), and click OK to soften the edges of your selection.

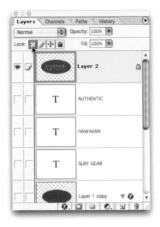

STEP ELEVEN: Now that your oval has soft edges, it needs to be rotated a bit. Go under the Select menu and choose Transform Selection. When the Transform Selection bounding box appears, move your cursor below the bounding box and click-and-drag to the right to rotate the oval selection counterclockwise (as shown). Click Return (PC: Enter) to lock in your transformation.

Quick Tip:
Faster duplicating

To duplicate an entire image in Photoshop, you go under the Image menu and choose Duplicate (seems easy enough). But if you want to bypass the annoying dialog box that asks you to name the new document, just hold the Option key (PC: Alt key) when choosing Duplicate. This way, the duplicate will appear immediately rather than making you stop to dismiss the dialog.

STEP TWELVE: You'll need to position the selection to where it covers the top-left corner of your logo (as shown). As long as you still have the Elliptical Marquee tool, you can reposition the oval without moving anything under the selected area. Just move your cursor within the oval, and click-and-drag it up and to the left (as shown).

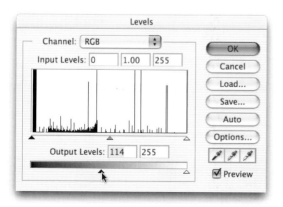

STEP THIRTEEN: To create the highlight for your glassy reflection, go under the Image menu, under Adjustments, and choose Levels. Drag the bottom-Left Output Levels slider to the right to add a highlight to your logo.

continued

Quick Tip:
Alternatives to the Type Mask tool

The Type Mask tool creates selections in the shape of type, rather than type itself (like the regular Type tool). If you prefer to use the regular Type tool to create a type-shaped selection, you can. In fact, I prefer it because you can really see what your type is going to look like.

Just create your type as usual, hold the Command key (PC: Control key), and click once on the Type layer's name in the Layers palette. This puts a selection around your type. Now you can drag your Type layer into the Trash icon at the bottom of the Layers palette. So what are you left with? That's right, a selection in the shape of your type—exactly like what the Type Mask tool would've done.

STEP FOURTEEN: You can see the highlight appear as you drag the output slider. When it looks about right, click OK in the Levels dialog box. Don't deselect yet.

STEP FIFTEEN: Click your Elliptical Marquee tool within the oval selection again, but this time drag it down to the bottom-right corner (as shown here).

STEP SIXTEEN: Go under the Image menu, under Adjustments, and choose Levels again. This time, grab the bottom-*right* Output Levels slider and drag it to the left to darken the selected area, creating the shadowed part of the logo.

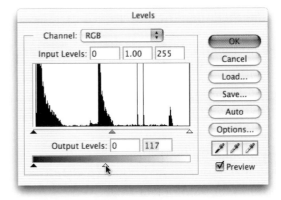

STEP SEVENTEEN: Click OK in the Levels dialog, then deselect by pressing Command-D (PC: Control-D) to see the final effect.

Quick Tip:
A faster way to rasterize your Type layer

Tired of digging through the Layer menu to rasterize your type? Here's a shortcut: Go to the Layers palette, hold the Control key (PC: Right-click), and click-and-hold on your Type layer. A contextual pop-up menu will appear where you can choose Rasterize Layer. No more digging!

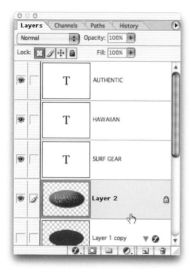

STEP EIGHTEEN: As I'm sure you've realized, the highlights and shadows you just added were applied right over your type (since we flattened the layer), but if you want your type to stand out more—it's easy! Just go to the Layers palette and drag this flattened layer beneath your Type layers (as shown here), which puts your type in front of your highlights and shadows.

STEP NINETEEN: Here's the final logo, with the type in front (which makes the type look cleaner) and the glassy reflection on the oval itself.

Quick Tip:
Ruler guide trick

Any time that you're dragging out a guide from your ruler, you can change its orientation as you drag it (just in case you meant to grab a horizontal guide and instead you accidentally grabbed a vertical guide. Hey, it could happen). To change the guide from vertical to horizontal (or vice versa), press the Option key (PC: Alt key) while you're dragging, and it'll switch to the other orientation. Release the key and it switches back. That way you can position it exactly how you like before releasing the mouse button.

New 3D Curved Video Wall

I've done video wall techniques dating back to the original 5.0 version of this book, and in my "Down & Dirty Tricks" column in *Photoshop User* magazine, but this version (which I saw used in the contents page of *Entertainment Weekly*) is the best I've seen yet. It has a number of steps, but it's not hard to do, and it looks pretty darn cool when complete.

STEP ONE: Open a new blank document that's about an inch larger than you'll want your final document size. Create a new blank layer by clicking on the New Layer icon at the bottom of the Layers palette. Press "m" to get the Rectangular Marquee tool and draw a horizontal rectangular selection. Press "d" to set your Foreground color to black, then Option-Delete (PC: Alt-Backspace) to fill your selection with black (as shown).

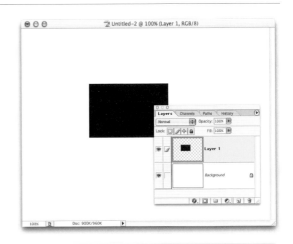

STEP TWO: Press Shift-M to switch to the Elliptical Marquee tool (Shift-M toggles between the Elliptical and Rectangular Marquee tools). Drag out a large oval-shaped selection (like the one shown here). Move your cursor inside the oval and click-and-drag to position the top edge near the top of the black rectangle (as shown here).

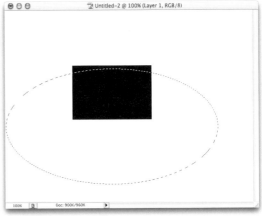

STEP THREE: Press Delete (PC: Backspace) to knock out the bottom section of the black rectangle, then deselect by pressing Command-D (PC: Control-D). This leaves the shape you see here (straight on the top and sides, and curved inward on the bottom).

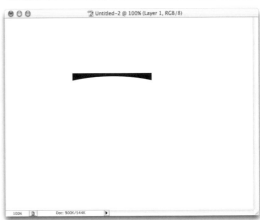

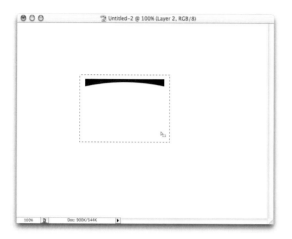

STEP FOUR: Create a new blank layer by clicking on the New Layer icon at the bottom of the Layers palette. Press Shift-M to switch back to the Rectangular Marquee tool, and draw a rectangular selection that's a little wider and quite a bit higher than the black shape (as shown here). This will become the frame of your video monitor.

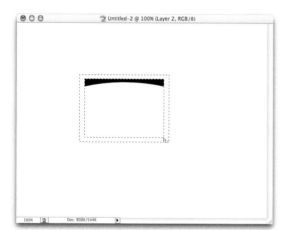

STEP FIVE: Hold the Option key (PC: Alt key), which lets you subtract from the current selection when using the Marquee tools. Then, draw a smaller selection that starts at the top-left corner of the thin black shape and extends down and to the right edge of the shape, forming a smaller rectangle (as shown here). This removes that area from the selected area, leaving you with a narrow border.

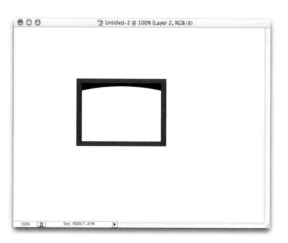

STEP SIX: In the Toolbox, click on the Foreground Color Swatch to bring up the Color Picker. When the Color Picker appears, choose a dark gray color, then click OK. To fill your selected border with this gray, press Option-Delete (PC: Alt-Backspace). Then, deselect by pressing Command-D (PC: Control-D).

Quick Tip:
The automated way to turn all of your layers into separate documents

Photoshop CS comes with some built-in scripts for some handy tasks. One of my favorites is a script that you'd run on a multi-layered document, to take each layer and duplicate it out to its own separate document, and it's all done automatically. To use this built-in script, just go under the File menu, under Scripts, and choose Export Layers to Files.

continued

Quick Tip:
Free Transform: The keyboard shortcut brain teaser

Most of the time when we use the Free Transform function, we Control-click (PC: Right-click) inside the Free Transform bounding box and choose our desired transformation from the handy pop-up menu. This way we only have to remember one keyboard shortcut—Control-click (PC: Right-click). But in actuality, there are keyboard shortcuts for almost every Free Transform function (except for rotate—just move your pointer outside the bounding box then move your mouse to rotate). Here's the list just in case you feel like learning them:

• Hold the Command key (PC: Control key) and drag a corner square handle to distort your object.

• Hold Shift and drag a square handle on any corner for proportional scaling of your object.

• Hold Shift-Option-Command (PC: Shift-Alt-Control) and grab a top or bottom corner square handle and drag outward to add a perspective effect.

• Hold Shift-Command (PC: Shift-Control), grab either the top or bottom center handle, and drag right or left to skew.

STEP SEVEN: Choose Bevel and Emboss from the Add a Layer Style pop-up menu at the bottom of the Layers palette. When the dialog appears, increase the Depth to 400%, lower the Size to 1, then click OK to apply a beveled edge to your gray area.

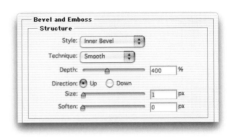

STEP EIGHT: Now you need to merge this rectangle layer with the thin black shape layer directly beneath it. To do this, just press Command-E (PC: Control-E) to merge the two layers into one (as shown here). Although it doesn't look like one at this stage, the first video monitor is complete, but it's too large; so you'll use Free Transform to scale it down in the next step.

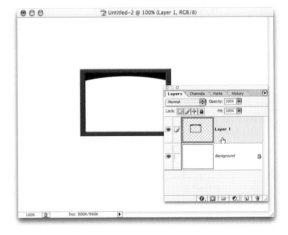

STEP NINE: Press Command-T (PC: Control-T) to bring up Free Transform. Hold the Shift key, grab a corner point, and drag inward to shrink the size of the video monitor similar to the one shown here. Once you've scaled it down, move your cursor inside the bounding box and click-and-drag the video monitor down to the bottom of the image area (as shown). Press Return (PC: Enter) to lock in your transformation.

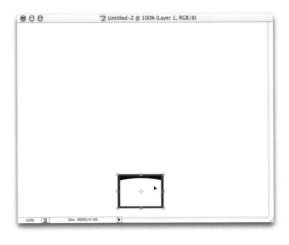

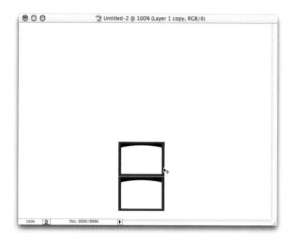

STEP TEN: Now you're going to make an exact copy of the video monitor, without duplicating the layer first. To do that, switch to the Move tool, hold Shift-Option-Command (PC: Shift-Alt-Control), click directly on the video monitor, and drag straight upward (as shown here). What you're doing is "dragging a copy."

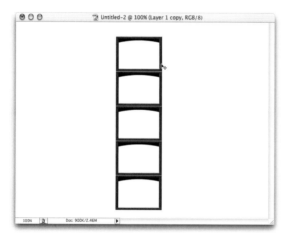

STEP ELEVEN: Once you've got one copy (and you've got the hang of "drag-copying"), drag out a few more. Just remember to hold Shift-Option-Command (PC: Shift-Alt-Control). By the way, the reason we add the Shift key is to keep the monitors perfectly aligned; it keeps your dragged copies snapped to an invisible vertical grid.

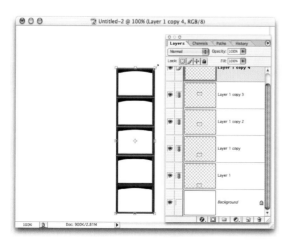

STEP TWELVE: Five monitors filled the screen from top to bottom, but we need seven for the effect, so we need to scale them all down as one unit. To do that, go to the Layers palette and click in the second column of each monitor layer to link them together. Press Command-T (PC: Control-T) to bring up Free Transform. Hold the Shift key, and click-and-drag a corner point to scale all five down at once (as if they were one unit). When it looks right, press Return (PC: Enter).

continued

Quick Tip:
Getting out of a transformation

While you're using the Free Transform function, if you suddenly decide you don't want to transform your object after all, just press the Escape key on your keyboard to leave Free Transform. If you've made a transformation you don't like, you can undo your last step by pressing Command-Z (PC: Control-Z) while you're still in Free Transform.

Also, while you're in Free Transform, you can move your object by placing your pointer inside the bounding box (your pointer changes to an arrow) and clicking-and-dragging the box to a new location.

When you're transforming your object, you can lock in your transformation by either pressing Return (PC: Enter) or double-clicking within the bounding box.

COOL TIP: If you want to transform an object *and* put a copy of it on its own layer at the same time, add the Option key (PC: Alt key) to the Free Transform keyboard shortcut, making it Option-Command-T (PC: Alt-Control-T).

In this book, we often make
a selection and put the selected area on its own layer
by pressing Shift-Com-
mand-J (PC: Shift-Control-
J). This performs the same
function as going under the
Layer menu, under New,
and choosing Layer via Cut.

Layer via Cut cuts out
your selection from the
currently active layer and
moves it to its own layer
(leaving a big white space
in the layer below). If you
want to move your selec-
tion to its own layer *without*
cutting (and leaving a
knockout where you cut),
leave out the Shift key and
just press Command-J (PC:
Control-J). This is the same
as going under the Layer
menu, under New, and
choosing Layer via Copy
(which leaves your original
selected area intact on the
layer below and places an
exact duplicate of your selection on the layer above).

STEP THIRTEEN: Now, unlink all
the layers by clicking on the Link
icon, and "drag-copy" two more
monitors. Once you've gotten
all your screens in place, link the
monitor layers again and position them so they extend off the
top and bottom of the image
area as shown here (you can use
Free Transform again if necessary). Next, you'll want to get all
your video monitors on just one
layer, so go to the Layers palette,
click on the bottom video monitor layer, and press Command-E
(PC: Control-E). This will merge
all seven linked monitor layers
into just one layer.

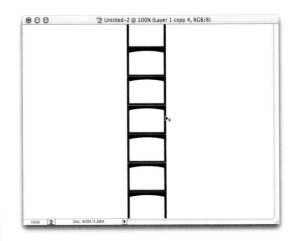

STEP FOURTEEN: Duplicate this
one layer (containing all seven
video monitors) by pressing
Command-J (PC: Control-J).
Hold the Shift key, and with the
Move tool, drag this duplicate
layer straight over to the right
(as shown here), creating a second vertical stack that touches
the right edge of the first stack.

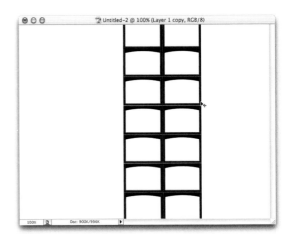

STEP FIFTEEN: Press Command-
T (PC: Control-T) to bring up
Free Transform. You won't be
able to see the top or bottom
Free Transform handles, so
press Command-0 (zero),
(PC: Control-0) and your image
window will resize so you can
reach them. Now, hold Shift-
Option-Command (PC: Shift-
Alt-Control), grab the top right
corner point and drag upward
to add a perspective effect to
your second stack (as shown).

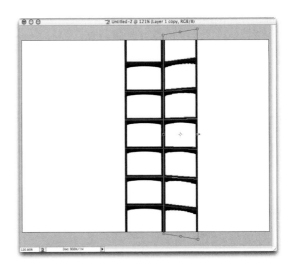

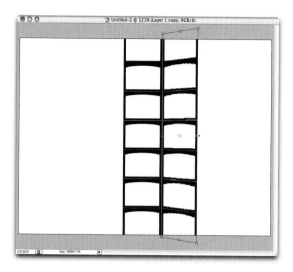

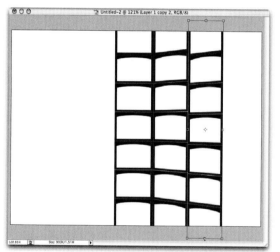

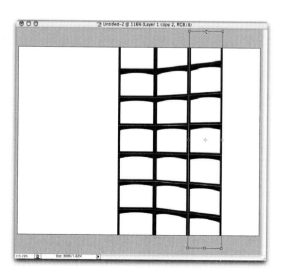

STEP SIXTEEN: Adding this perspective effect tends to stretch out the width of the monitors. You can fix that while you're still in Free Transform by releasing the keys on your keyboard, clicking on the right center point (as shown here), and dragging inward (to the left) just a little until the monitors don't look stretched anymore. Press Return (PC: Enter) when it looks about right. In the next step, you'll create a third stack.

STEP SEVENTEEN: Hold Shift-Option-Command again (PC: Shift-Alt-Control), click on the second stack of monitors, and drag to the right to create a third stack (as shown here). The lines separating each monitor won't line up with the previous stack, so you'll have to press Command-T (PC: Control-T) to bring up Free Transform. Press Command-0 (PC: Control-0) to reach the handles, and then drag the bottom center point downward until the lines between the bottom monitors begin to align.

STEP EIGHTEEN: Next, grab the top center point (as shown here) and drag upward to make the lines between the top monitors align. Don't press Return (PC: Enter) yet, because you still have to add the perspective effect to this stack of monitors.

Quick Tip:
Making your Actions palette less cluttered

Once you've created a number of Actions, your Actions palette can start to look a bit cluttered (and confusing). That's why Adobe created Button Mode, which hides all of the Actions controls, nested folders, and annoying stuff like that and puts all your Actions just one button-click away. You can access Button Mode in the Actions palette's pop-down menu.

You can also visually organize your Actions by color. Just Option-Double-click (PC: Alt-Double-click) on any Action and you'll see a pop-up list of Colors in the Action Options dialog that you can use to visually group your Actions. When you're in Button Mode each button takes on the color of its Action. You could, for example, make all your prepress Actions one color, drop shadow Actions another, and so on to group your Actions by color for easy access.

continued

Quick Tip:
Making copies of layers

We often make a copy of a layer by dragging it (in the Layers palette) to the New Layer icon at the bottom of the Layers palette. But there are other ways of creating copies of layers. The fastest is probably to press Command-J (PC: Control-J). This makes an instant duplicate of your current layer.

Another way is to take the Move tool, hold the Option key (PC: Alt key), click within your image on the layer you want to copy, and drag. When you release the mouse button, you'll see that a new layer copy has been created in the Layers palette.

Another method is to go under the Layer menu and choose Duplicate Layer. A dialog box will appear that enables you to name your newly copied layer and to choose whether you want it to appear in your current document, in another open document, or to become a new document.

As a shortcut, you can Control-click (PC: Right-click) on your layer (in the Layers palette) and a pop-up menu will appear where you can choose Duplicate Layer.

STEP NINETEEN: If you've lost sight of the top transform handles, press Command-0 (zero) (PC: Control-0) again to reach them. Hold Shift-Option-Command (PC: Shift-Alt-Control), grab the top right corner point and drag upward, dragging a bit farther than you did for your second stack to add a more pronounced perspective effect (as shown). Release the keys, then grab the right center point and drag inward so it doesn't look too stretched.

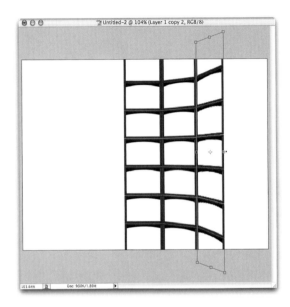

STEP TWENTY: Press Return (PC: Enter) to lock in your transformation. Now you're going to repeat the whole process one more time to create one more row: "drag-copy" the layer, use Free Transform to align the monitor lines, use the Perspective transformation (pulling it upward even farther than the previous row), then release the keys and tuck in the right side center point (as shown).

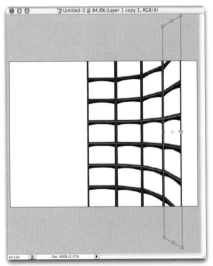

STEP TWENTY-ONE: Now that your right side is complete, you can save a lot of time by using it to create the left side. To do that, go to the Layers palette, click on the top layer of monitors, then press Command-E (PC: Control-E) three times to merge all the monitor layers into just one layer (as shown).

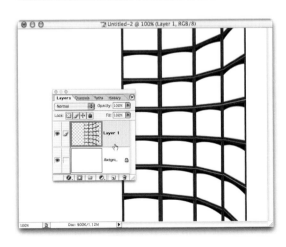

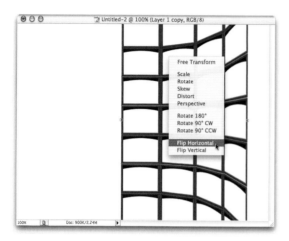

STEP TWENTY-TWO: Now duplicate this right side wall of monitors layer by pressing Command-J (PC: Control-J). Now press Command-T (PC: Control-T) to bring up Free Transform again. Control-click (PC: Right-click) within the bounding box and a pop-up menu will appear. Choose Flip Horizontal from the menu, and it will flip your duplicate layer, making a mirror image (the left side).

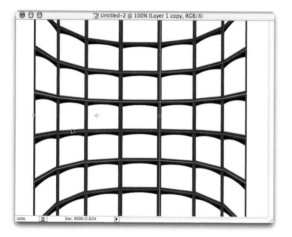

STEP TWENTY-THREE: Once you've flipped the layer, click your cursor within the bounding box, hold the Shift key, and drag to the left until the center stack of monitors on the left side is positioned exactly over the center stack of monitors on the right side, as shown here (this leaves a center stack, with three stacks to the left of it, and three to the right). Press Return (PC: Enter) to lock in your transformation.

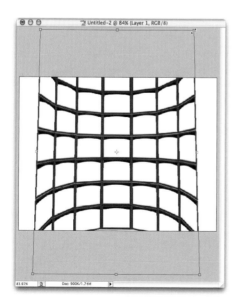

STEP TWENTY-FOUR: Merge these two layers into one layer by pressing Command-E (PC: Control-E). Press Command-T (PC: Control-T) to bring up Free Transform again. Press Command-0 (PC: Control-0) to reach the top transform handles. Press Shift-Option-Command (Shift-Alt-Control) and drag the top right corner point inward to the left to add a perspective effect, making the monitors seem to be leaning back a bit. Press Return (PC: Enter to lock in your Transformation).

continued

Quick Tip:
Making selections in a straight line

If you need to draw a selection that includes straight lines but is not a rectangle or a square, you can use the Polygonal Lasso. It draws straight lines from point to point as you click. To access the Polygonal Lasso tool while using the regular Lasso tool, click-and-hold in the document where you want your selection to start, press the Option key (PC: Alt key), and then release the mouse to switch temporarily to the Polygonal Lasso. Just click in your document where you want to create a straight line. As long as you hold the Option/Alt key, it remains the Polygonal tool. When you release the Option/Alt key, it turns into an active selection. If you want to continue drawing with the regular Lasso tool without closing the selection, click-and-hold before releasing the Option/Alt key.

Quick Tip:
Easy background transparency in Photoshop

Remember back in the old days when you wanted a background color to be transparent in a GIF Web graphic, you'd use GIF89a and click on the color you wanted transparent? Well, those good ol' days returned in Photoshop 7, but in Photoshop CS you don't have to suffer through GIF89a because you can choose a background color to be transparent right from within the Save for Web dialog box. Just use the Eyedropper tool to click on the color you want to appear transparent, then at the bottom of the Color Table, click on the first icon from the left to make that color transparent. See, good things have a way of coming back.

STEP TWENTY-FIVE: It's now time to crop the video wall image down to size (remember in Step One, I mentioned to make your document a little larger than you'd need for your final photo? This is why). Press the letter "c" to get the Crop tool, then drag out a cropping border around the area you want to keep (you want your video wall to appear as if it extends outside of the document on all sides). Press Return (PC: Enter) to crop your photo down to size.

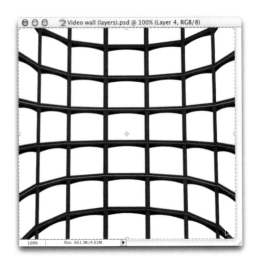

STEP TWENTY-SIX: Now open the photo you'd like to appear inside your video wall. Get the Move tool, click on this photo, and drag it over into your video wall document.

STEP TWENTY-SEVEN: When the photo appears in your document, it will probably appear in front of your video wall, so go to the Layers palette, click on your photo layer, and drag it below the video wall layer (as shown here) to put it behind the wall.

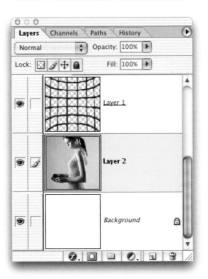

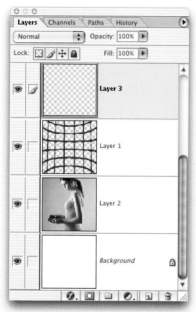

STEP TWENTY-EIGHT: In the Layers palette, click on the video wall layer, then add a new blank layer by clicking on the New Layer icon at the bottom of the Layers palette. We'll use this layer to add some shading to the video wall so it looks more rounded. We'll add a highlight in the center, and shadows on both sides. Press "b" to get the Brush tool, then Control-click (PC: Right-click) in the image to bring up the Brush Picker. Choose a very large, soft-edged brush (I chose a 300-pixel brush).

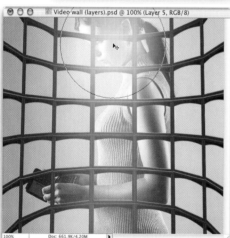

STEP TWENTY-NINE: Up in the Options Bar, lower the Opacity setting for the Brush tool to 45%. Then press "x" to set your Foreground color to white, and paint a stroke from the bottom center of your image up to the top (as shown here). It doesn't really matter whether you start at the top or the bottom, just paint a stroke through the center.

STEP THIRTY: Press "d" to set your Foreground color to black, then paint a stroke down the left side, and a stroke down the right side (as shown). Adding these strokes helps to give the rows of monitors more dimension by adding highlights and shadows.

continued

Quick Tip:
Don't confuse Clipping Mask with Clipping Paths

The layer term Clipping Group (now known in Photoshop CS as Clipping Mask) is often confused with the well-known path term Clipping Path, but the two are entirely different. Okay, they're not entirely different in what they do: a clipping mask puts your image inside type (or anything black) on the layer beneath it, so you could say it clips off everything outside the type. A clipping path is created with the Pen tool and you can choose to save this path with your document, so when you import your image into another application (such as QuarkXPress, Adobe InDesign, Adobe Illustrator, etc.), everything outside the path is clipped off. This is most often used for clipping off the white backgrounds that appear behind objects.

In short, it'll help if you remember that a clipping group is a layer technique, while a clipping path is a path created with the Pen tool that's used mostly in print for silhouetting images against their backgrounds.

Quick Tip:
Easy-to-remember keyboard shortcuts

In the technique shown on this page, you have the option to Create a Clipping Mask (otherwise known as Group with Previous in prior versions) to keep your highlights and shadows within the layer directly beneath them (the monitor layer in this case). The keyboard shortcut is easy to remember because it uses the same keyboard shortcut almost all other Adobe products use to "Group" objects together. It's Command-G (PC: Control-G). Adobe has gone to great lengths to keep you from having to learn a new set of keyboard shortcuts for each Adobe application, so once you learn one application's shortcuts, chances are you can apply them to other Adobe applications. Many of Photoshop's shortcuts are based on Adobe Illustrator shortcuts, so if you know those, you're well on your way. So keep that in mind when working in Photoshop. If you don't know the keyboard shortcut, ask yourself what that shortcut would be in Illustrator, and chances are you'll be right. However, if you're used to CorelDRAW … you're about out of luck.

STEP THIRTY-ONE: To get this paint-stroke layer to blend in with the rest of the image, go to the Layers palette and change the layer Blend Mode from Normal to Color Dodge (as shown here). Next, to make these highlights and shadows only appear on the monitors themselves (and not over the photo), press Command-G (PC: Control-G) to create a clipping mask and group them into the monitor frames.

STEP THIRTY-TWO: Once you apply your clipping mask, you can see the highlights appear in the center of your video wall (as shown here). If the highlights are too intense, lower the Opacity of the paintstroke layer in the Layers palette.

STEP THIRTY-THREE: To get some sense of scale, it's a good idea to add an object (in this case a person) to the photo to create the idea that it's a pretty large wall of monitors. In the example shown here, I opened the photo of a woman, selected her with the Lasso tool, then dragged her over onto the image.

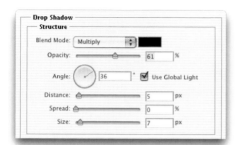

STEP THIRTY-FOUR: Add a Drop Shadow from the Add a Layer Style pop-up menu at the bottom of the Layers palette. Lower the Opacity to around 60%, and increase the Size of the shadow to 7 to complete the effect.

Quick Tip:
Getting rid of white edge pixels in collaged images

In the technique shown on these pages, when I brought the girl into the image, she had a tiny white halo around her arms and hair. This leftover fringe came with the original image that I took her from, which had a white background. When I selected her, it brought some of the fringe along too.

I was able to quickly get rid of that white fringe around the edge by going under the Layer menu, under Matting, and choosing Defringe. I used the default 1-pixel setting, clicked OK, and it immediately removed the white edge fringe. It does this by creating a new edge pixel that is a combination of the background and the edge of your object. If you try a 1-pixel Defringe and it's not enough, undo it, and try a 2-pixel Defringe.

DVD Disc

This is a simple version of how to create a DVD disc. I've seen different gradients used for this effect, but the rainbow one I'm showing here seems to be the most popular. At the end of this technique I show how to make the disc appear as if it's protruding from some DVD packaging because that's what everybody seems to be doing these days to make it clear that the package contains a DVD, not a VHS tape. If you want to learn how to create the DVD packaging from a flat photo, flip to Chapter 6, "Portfolio Effects."

STEP ONE: Open a new document with the same resolution and color mode as the DVD packaging image that you'll use at the end of this technique. Create a new blank layer by clicking on the New Layer icon at the bottom of the Layers palette. Press Shift-M until you get the Elliptical Marquee tool, hold the Shift key, and drag out a circular selection like the one shown here.

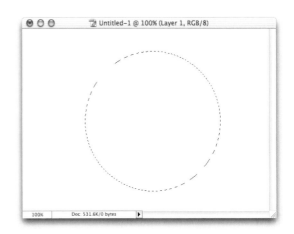

STEP TWO: Press "g" to get the Gradient tool, then up in the Options Bar click directly on the Gradient thumbnail to bring up the Gradient Editor. When the Gradient Editor appears, create a gradient that goes from a medium gray to white to medium gray, and click OK. (Note: to change the color of a Color Stop [those little house-looking things under the Gradient Bar] just double-click on them and it brings up the Color Picker. To add another stop, just click directly under the Bar.)

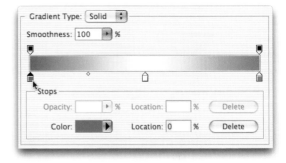

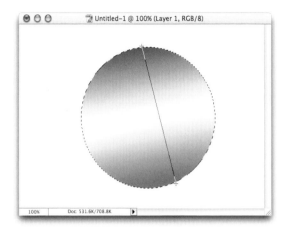

STEP THREE: Drag the Gradient tool through the circular selection starting at the top of the selection and drag downward at an angle (as shown here). Don't deselect yet. Create a new blank layer, then go under the Select menu, under Modify, and choose Contract. When the Contract dialog appears, enter 4 and click OK to shrink your selection by four pixels.

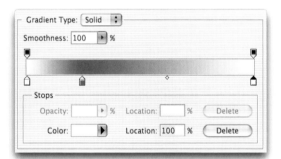

STEP FOUR: You'll build a different gradient for this layer, so get the Gradient tool again and click on the Gradient thumbnail in the Options Bar to bring up the Gradient Editor. Just edit the existing gradient by changing the far left Color Stop to white, the center Stop to dark gray, and the far right Stop to white. Drag the center Stop over closer to the left white Stop (as shown here) and click OK.

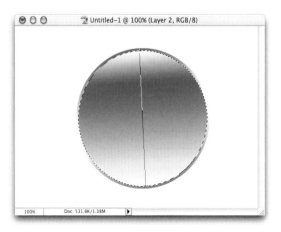

STEP FIVE: Take the Gradient tool and drag from the top of the selection downward at a slight angle (as shown here). Since you contracted the selection by four pixels, it only affects the area within the selected area, and you can see the original gradient behind your new gradient.

Quick Tip:
Jump to Overlay mode shortcut
In many cases, you have to change the Blend Mode of a layer from Normal to Overlay. I usually show you how to do that by choosing Overlay from the pop-up menu in the Layers palette, but actually, there's a way to change to Overlay mode without going to the Layers palette at all. Just use the keyboard shortcut Shift-Option-O (PC: Shift-Alt-O), and your active layer will switch to Overlay mode. Before you do this keyboard shortcut, make sure you have the Move tool selected (press the letter "v"). The reason is that if you have one of the paint tools selected, you'll end up changing the Blend Mode for that tool instead in the Options Bar, because just like layers, paint tools have Blend Modes, and they share the same keyboard shortcuts.

continued

Quick Tip:
Scan lines
filter trick

If you want a quick way to create scan lines, believe it or not there's a filter you can apply that does a pretty good job at creating them. Here's how to use it:

(1) Open the image to which you want to apply scan lines, then create a new blank layer above it.

(2) Press "d" then "x" to set your Foreground color to white, then press Option-Delete (PC: Alt-Backspace) to fill the layer with white.

(3) Go under the Filter menu, under Sketch, and choose Halftone Pattern. In the dialog box, set the Size to 2, Contrast to 50, and Pattern Type to Line. Click OK to apply vertical black-and-white lines to your layer.

(4) Change the Blend Mode of this layer from Normal to Overlay and lower the Opacity to taste.

Give this method a try and see how you like it compared to other techniques.

STEP SIX: Choose Stroke from the Add a Layer Style pop-up menu at the bottom of the Layers palette. When the Stroke dialog appears, lower the Size to 1, leave the position set at Outside, click on the Color Swatch and choose black in the Color Picker, lower the Opacity to 50%, and then click OK to put a thin black stroke around your inner circle gradient.

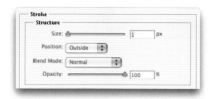

STEP SEVEN: In the Layers palette, you can copy this stroke, with all its settings, and apply it to the original, larger gradient circle layer. Click directly on the word "Effects" on the smaller circle layer, then drag-and-drop it right onto the larger circle layer (the one below it in the layer stack) to apply the same stroke.

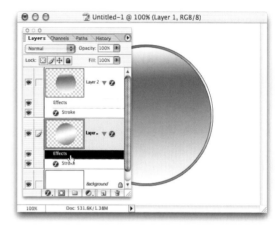

STEP EIGHT: With your selection still in place around the smaller circle layer, create a new blank layer, and in the Layers palette drag it to the top, making it the topmost layer. Get the Gradient tool, and press Return (PC: Enter) to bring up the Gradient Picker. Choose the Transparent Rainbow gradient (as shown here).

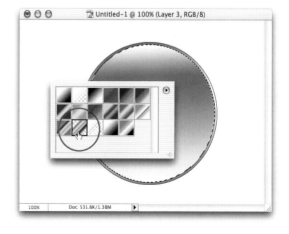

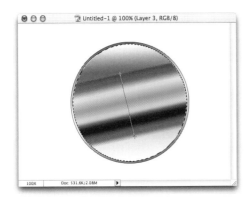

STEP NINE: Click-and-drag this rainbow gradient through the center of your selection (as shown). Don't drag from the top of the selection to the bottom—start just above the middle and drag downward just below the middle (as shown here).

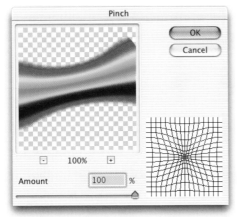

STEP TEN: Go under the Filter menu, under Distort, and choose Pinch. Enter 100% for Amount and click OK. Now, go under the Filter menu again, under Blur, and choose Radial Blur. Enter 40 for Amount, choose Spin for Blur Method, Good for Quality, and click OK.

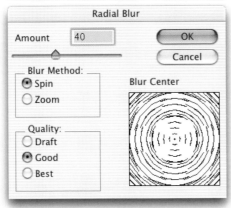

STEP ELEVEN: Go under the Select menu and choose Transform Selection. Go to the Options Bar and enter 50% for both Height and Width. Press Enter twice to apply the transformation.

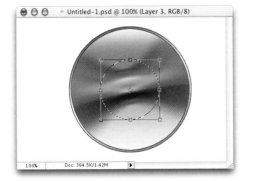

Quick Tip:
Rounding corners

If you use the Rounded Rectangle Shape tool with its default settings, you'll probably think the corners aren't rounded enough, so it's helpful to know that the roundness of the corners is controlled in the Options Bar. Increase the Radius size to make them more round and decrease the Radius to make them less round. While we're talking rounded corners, there's a selection tool in ImageReady that I wish Adobe would move over to Photoshop—it's the Rounded Rectangle Marquee tool, that makes, well…do I even have to describe it?

continued

Quick Tip:
Makin' copies

Once you've created a
Web tab or button (or
almost anything else on a
layer such as the DVD we
created in these pages),
you can make duplicate
copies super-fast by using
this shortcut: First, hold the
Command key (PC: Control
key) and click on the layer
you want to duplicate (this
puts a selection around
everything on the layer).
Then, hold Option-Com-
mand (PC: Alt-Control) and
drag off copies as you need
them. Yeah, baby!

STEP TWELVE: Go under the Select menu, and choose Feather. Enter 20 and click OK. Press Delete (PC: Backspace) to soften the center of the rainbow effect. Press Command-D (PC: Control-D) to deselect.

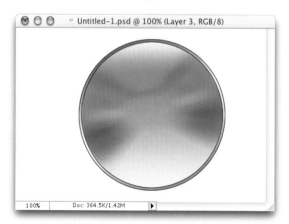

STEP THIRTEEN: Choose the Elliptical Marquee tool from the Toolbox, hold the Shift key, and create a small circle in the center of your DVD. Press Delete (PC: Backspace) to knock out the Rainbow gradient.

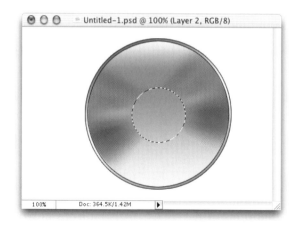

STEP FOURTEEN: Go under the Select menu and choose Transform Selection. Go to the Options Bar and Enter 90% for both Height and Width. Press Return (PC: Enter) twice to apply the transformation. Now, click on Layer 2 (the smaller circle layer) in the Layers palette and press Delete (PC: Backspace). Then, click on Layer 1 (the larger circle layer) and press Delete (PC: Backspace). This will knock out a hole to the Background layer. Press Command-D (PC: Control-D) to deselect. Click on the top layer in the Layers palette and press Command-E (PC: Control-E) twice to merge the three layers down into one layer.

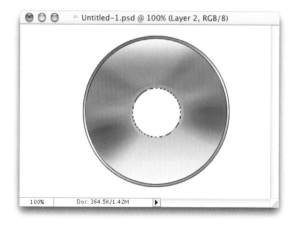

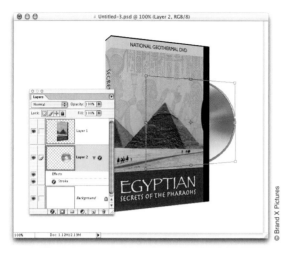

© Brand X Pictures

STEP FIFTEEN: Get the Move tool and drag this one layer (the full circular disc) over onto your DVD box document (check out Chapter 6 to see how to create your own DVD packaging). In the Layers palette, drag the DVD behind the box layer. Press Command-T (PC: Control-T) to bring up Free Transform. Control-click (PC: Right-click) in the bounding box and choose Perspective from the pop-up menu. Grab the bottom-left corner point and drag downward (as shown) to give the disc a similar perspective effect as the box.

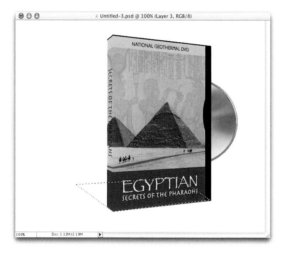

STEP SIXTEEN: In the Layers palette, create a new blank layer and drag this layer down in the layer stack until it appears directly beneath the DVD box layer. Get the Polygonal Lasso tool (from the Lasso tool flyout menu) and draw a selection where you want the shadow for the DVD box to appear (use the selection shown here as a guide).

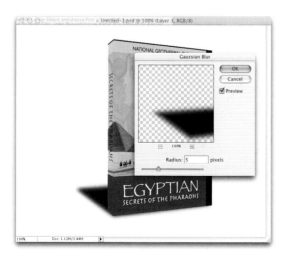

STEP SEVENTEEN: Press "d" to set your Foreground color to black, then press Option-Delete (PC: Alt-Backspace) to fill your selection with black, then de-select by pressing Command-D (PC: Control-D). Next, to soften the shadow, go under the Filter menu, under Blur, and choose Gaussian Blur. When the Gaussian Blur dialog appears (shown here), drag the Radius slider until the shadow looks soft. Try around 5 for low-res images, 20 for high-res, and click OK.

continued

When using the Free
Transform tool, don't let
it freak you out that the
preview you're seeing while
manipulating your image is
horribly pixelated—that's
just a low-res preview
Photoshop displays while
you're transforming so
things keep moving as
fast as possible. When you
finally hit Return (PC: Enter),
it then redraws your image
at its full resolution and the
pixelation should disappear
(unless of course, you did
something that actually
increases pixelation, such
as scaling up a 72-ppi document by 300%, but I know
you wouldn't do that).

STEP EIGHTEEN: To make the
shadow less prominent, go to
the Layers palette and lower
the Opacity of this layer to
around 20%, to give you the
lighter effect shown here.

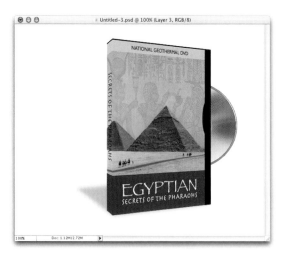

STEP NINETEEN: Here's the
completed image with the DVD
that we created in this technique and the DVD packaging
from Chapter 6.

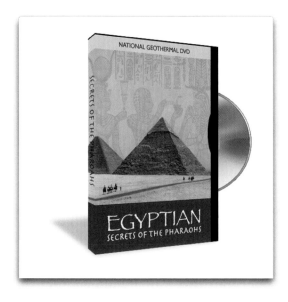

Attaching a Note to a Photo

If you need to add a caption to a photo, don't just backscreen an area, or create some reverse type, because with this effect you can create some real visual interest for your caption, drawing the reader's eye right where you want it to go.

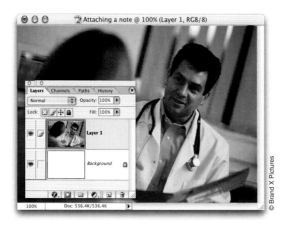

STEP ONE: Open the photo you want to use in the effect. Press Command-A (PC: Control-A) to select the entire photo, then press Shift-Command-J (PC: Shift-Control-J) to cut the photo from the Background layer and copy it on its own separate layer (as shown here).

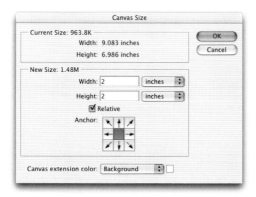

STEP TWO: Go under the Image menu and choose Canvas Size. When the dialog appears, click on the Relative checkbox, and then for Width enter 2 inches and for Height enter 2 inches. Click OK to add some white space around your photo.

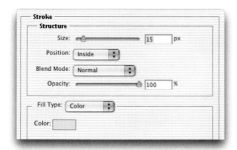

STEP THREE: Choose Stroke from the Add a Layer Style pop-up menu at the bottom of the Layers palette. Set the Size to 15 (30 for high-res, 300-ppi images), set the Position to Inside (to give your stroke straight corners rather than the default rounded corners), and choose a light gray (like the one shown here) for your stroke Color. Don't click OK yet.

continued

Quick Tip:
Saving time in the Fill Dialog box

In Photoshop 7 (and even earlier) if you wanted to fill a selection, or a layer, with a color like bright red, you'd have to set bright red as your Foreground color before you opened the Fill dialog box. If you forgot to do that first, you'd have to cancel out of your fill, set the color, and then open the Fill dialog again. Luckily, now in Photoshop CS you'll never have to do that again, because now you can choose any fill color from right within the Fill dialog box. Where it says "Use" just choose "Color" from the pop-up menu, which brings up the Color Picker right within the Fill dialog. It's the little things, isn't it?

Quick Tip:
Layer Set
nesting season

If you're into using Layer Sets (to organize documents with lots of layers), then you're going to love the fact that in Photoshop CS you can go Layer Set crazy. That's because you can now nest Layer Sets within other Layer Sets and go up to five sets deep. It boggles the mind!

STEP FOUR: Click directly on the name Drop Shadow in the list of Styles on the left side of the Layer Style dialog box to reveal the Drop Shadow options. Lower the Opacity to 50%, turn off Use Global Light, and increase the Distance and Size to 10. Click OK and it adds a border around your photo, with a soft drop shadow (as shown here). Next, create a new layer by clicking on the New Layer icon on the bottom of the Layers palette.

STEP FIVE: Press the letter "m" to get the Rectangular Marquee tool, and make a rectangular selection (like the one shown here). In the Toolbox, click on the Foreground Color Swatch and choose a "Post-it-like" yellow color in the Color Picker (I used R=255, G=255, B=161). Fill your selection with this yellow by pressing Option-Delete (PC: Alt-Backspace), then deselect by pressing Command-D (PC: Control-D).

STEP SIX: Press Shift-U until you get the Custom Shape tool from the Toolbox. Go up to the Options Bar and choose the third icon from the left so the Custom Shape tool will create pixel-based shapes. Press the Return key (PC: Enter key) to bring up the Custom Shape Picker (as shown here). From the Picker's pop-down menu, choose Objects to load a new set of custom Shapes (click Append in the resulting dialog). Scroll down and click on the paperclip shape (as shown).

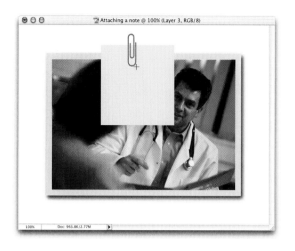

STEP SEVEN: Create a new blank layer, and set your Foreground color to gray. Hold the Shift key, and then use the Custom Shape tool to create a paperclip. Position it at the top of your yellow note (as shown here).

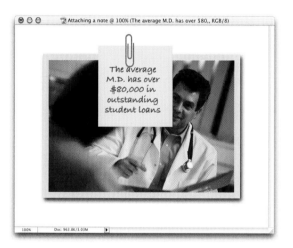

STEP EIGHT: Change your Foreground color to a dark blue, and press the letter "t" to get the Type tool. Add your message to the note. (The text here is in the font ITC Bradley Hand.)

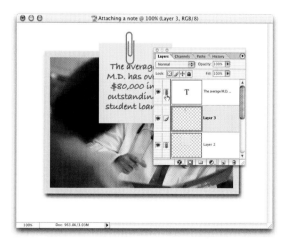

STEP NINE: Go to the Layers palette and link the paperclip, note, and Type layers together by clicking in the second column (as shown here) of each layer so you can move all three layers as one group.

continued

Quick Tip:
Turn your Layer Comps into their own documents

Photoshop CS has a very slick new feature called Layer Comps that lets you save a version of your document, complete with all the layer attributes (like Opacity, position, Blend Mode, Layer Styles, etc.) within the Layer Comps palette. That way, you can create a layout, save it as a comp (right within your same document), then keep experimenting with different layers. Every time you come up with a layout you like, just save it as a Layer Comp. Then you can compare entirely different layouts with just one click (and when you change layouts, the layers all change back too, so you can pick up right where you left off). But the cool tip here is that there's a built-in Script you can run that will take all your Layer Comps and turn them into separate PDFs (great for e-mailing to clients for proofing). Just go under the File menu, under Scripts, and choose Layer Comps to PDFs.

Quick Tip:
Replacing color by numeric value

If you use the Replace Color command to select an area of color, and then replace the color in that area with another color, there's a new feature (added in Photoshop CS) that will let you enter a numeric value for the color you want to edit (rather than just clicking around with the Eyedropper). When you open Replace Color (under Adjustments in the Image menu), you'll find a Color Swatch in the Selection section. Click on it, and the standard Color Picker appears, where you can type in numeric values in the RGB, CMYK, etc. fields, or even choose Custom colors as your color to replace. Not too shabby!

STEP TEN: Press Command-T (PC: Control-T) to bring up Free Transform. Move your cursor outside the bounding box and click-and-drag upward to rotate the note (like the note shown here). You can click-and-drag inside the bounding box to reposition the note. Press Return (PC: Enter) when it looks about right.

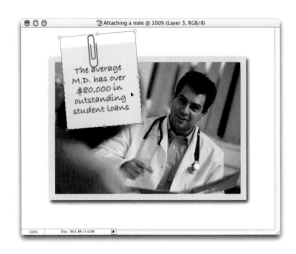

STEP ELEVEN: Next, you'll add a metallic look to the paperclip. Make sure you're still on the paperclip layer, then choose Bevel and Emboss from the Add a Layer Style pop-up menu at the bottom of the Layers palette. Increase the Depth to around 300%, and lower the Size to 2. In the Shading section, turn on Anti-aliased, then click on the down-facing arrow next to the Gloss Contour thumbnail to bring up the Contour Picker, and choose the Contour named "Ring" (as shown). Also, lower the Shadow Opacity to 50%, and then click OK.

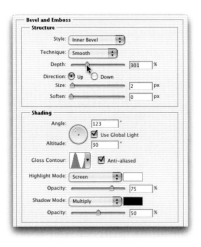

STEP TWELVE: Press the letter "e" to get the Eraser tool. Choose a small, hard-edged brush and erase the inside of the paperclip to make it appear that it's behind the note and photo. To complete the effect, click on the yellow note layer, then choose Drop Shadow from the Add a Layer Style pop-up menu. When the dialog appears, decrease the Size to 4 and click OK to apply a drop shadow behind the note.

3D Hardcover Book Effect

This technique, from my "Down & Dirty Tricks" column from *Photoshop User* magazine, makes great use of what is perhaps the lamest filter in all of Photoshop—3D Transform—to create the pages and spine for a hardcover book. In fact 3D Transform was so lame, it no longer automatically in-stalls with Photoshop CS. You'll have to look for it on the install CD and drag it over to your Photo-shop Plug-ins folder. Any technique that manages to use this filter has got to be worth something.

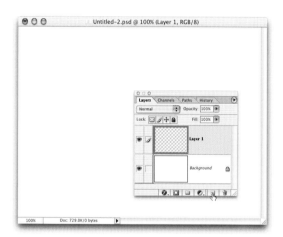

STEP ONE: Create a new document in RGB mode. Create a new layer by clicking on the New Layer icon at the bottom of the Layers palette.

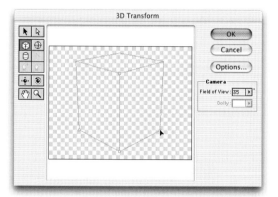

STEP TWO: Go under the Filter menu, under Render, and choose 3D Transform. Click the Cube tool, and drag out a cube (in the preview window) as shown here.

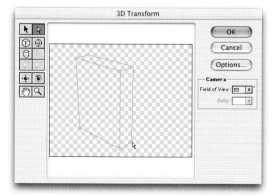

STEP THREE: Switch to the Direct Selection tool (the hollow arrow), click on the bottom-right corner (as shown), and drag down and to the left to shrink the width of your cube, making it look more like a cereal box (as shown here).

continued

Quick Tip:
Quick Mask preferences

When you enter Quick Mask mode (by making a selection and pressing the letter "q"), the color red can display either what's masked or what's selected. By default, the color red shows the masked area. For some odd reason, I prefer having red show what's selected, so if what you see on your screen in Quick Mask is the opposite of what you'd like, all you have to do is change a simple preference setting. To find the Quick Mask preferences, double-click on the Quick Mask icon (located in the Toolbox, directly below the Foreground and Background Color Swatches).

STEP FOUR: Take the Direct Selection tool, click on the top center point (as shown) and drag to the right to tip the box back a bit (don't worry—it'll tip—it's in 3D).

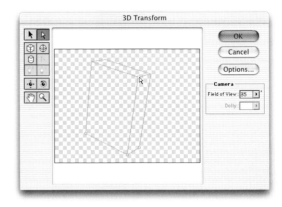

STEP FIVE: Get the Trackball tool (it's right above the Zoom tool), click on the left side of the preview window, and drag to the right. Keep dragging until your shape rotates all the way around to reveal the back side of your shape (which is shaded). When it looks like the one shown here, click OK.

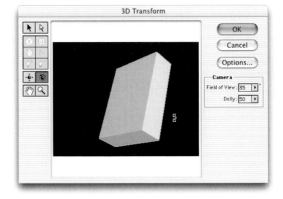

STEP SIX: In many cases, the edges of your cube will have some fringe, or look somewhat jaggy, but that's easy to fix. Hold the Command key (PC: Control key), go to the Layers palette, and click on the cube layer to put a selection around your cube. Then go under the Select menu, under Modify, and choose Contract. Enter 1 and click OK to shrink your selection inward by 1 pixel.

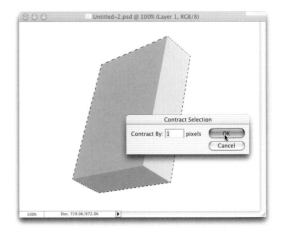

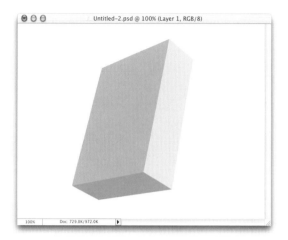

STEP SEVEN: To get rid of that fringe, go under the Select menu and choose Inverse (so now the only thing that is selected on this layer is that 1 pixel, all the way around your cube shape). Then, press Delete (PC: Backspace) to remove this 1-pixel edge fringe. Now you can deselect by pressing Command-D (PC: Control-D).

STEP EIGHT: Open the cover you want to use for your hard-cover book. Here's a fictitious book cover you can download from this book's companion site to practice with. Press "v" to switch to the Move tool, click on this book cover, and drag it over into your cube document. Go to the Layers palette and drag this layer up/down until it appears directly above the cube layer in the stack of layers.

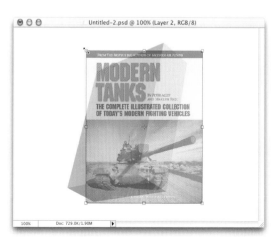

STEP NINE: In the Layers palette, lower the Opacity of this layer to 50% so you can see the cube through the cover. Press Command-T (PC: Control-T) to bring up Free Transform. If you can't see the Free Transform handles, press Command-0 (PC: Control-0) to zoom your image out. Then, hold the Shift key and scale the photo down by dragging one of the corner points until it's just a little larger than the cube (as shown).

Quick Tip:
Wacom tablet users rejoice!

If you used a Wacom tablet with the old Photoshop 7, chances are the Brushes palette drove you crazy. That's because if you went to the Brushes palette, chose a Brush Preset, and then turned on a Pen attribute like Pen Pressure controls Opacity, or Pen Pressure controls Size, that attribute only worked for that particular brush. If you changed brushes, it turned the Pen sensitivity off. This made tablet users just short of suicidal. Now, in Photoshop CS, when you set a brush to respond to Pen Pressure in the Brushes palette, you'll see a little "lock" icon you can click to tell Photoshop to leave pressure sensitivity turned on, even if you switch brush presets. This calls for a major celebration throughout the kingdom.

continued

Quick Tip:
Levels tip

If you need to lighten or darken the overall image, the Output Levels sliders at the bottom of the Levels dialog box can help. Dragging the left slider to the right will lighten the overall image. Dragging the right Output Levels slider to the left will darken the overall image. Since this change is so global (affecting the entire image across the board), it's generally used for special effects rather than for image correction, in which case you would use the Input Levels sliders up at the top instead.

STEP TEN: While Free Transform is still active, hold the Command key (PC: Control key), grab the top-left corner of the cover, and drag it over until it aligns with the top-left corner of the cube (as shown here).

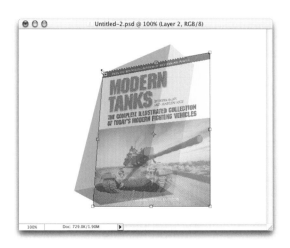

STEP ELEVEN: Keep holding the Command key (PC: Control key), grab the bottom-left corner of the cover and do the same thing—stretch that corner down to match the bottom-left corner of the cube. When you're close, drag it down just a tiny bit past the bottom of the cube, because you want this fake cover to hang below the pages just a bit.

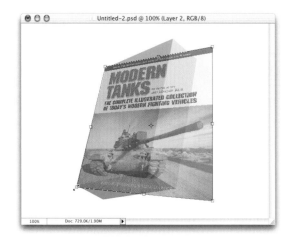

STEP TWELVE: Now grab the top-right corner and align it, but let it extend a little over the edge as well (you can see that tiny bit in the capture shown here), and do the same thing for the bottom-right corner—let a little hang over the edge (like a cover would on a real book). When it looks right, press Return (PC: Enter) to lock in your transformation.

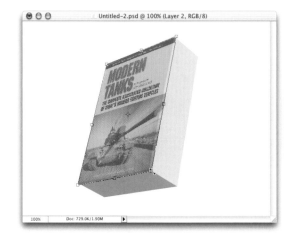

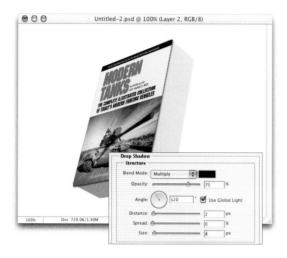

STEP THIRTEEN: Go to the Layers palette, and raise the Opacity of your cover layer back up to 100%. Now you're going to need a tiny drop shadow between your cover and the pages (your cube) so choose Drop Shadow from the Add a Layer Style pop-up menu at the bottom of the Layers palette. Decrease the Distance to 2 and lower the Size to 4 to create a subtle shadow along the edge (as shown).

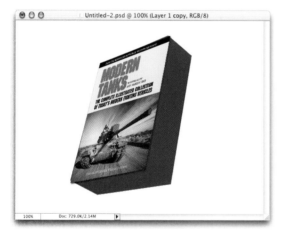

STEP FOURTEEN: In the Layers palette, click on your pages layer (the cube layer) and press Command-J (PC: Control-J) to duplicate it. Press the letter "i" to get the Eyedropper tool and click on a color within your book cover (this will become the color of your spine and back cover). In this example, click on the dark blue in the sky to set it as your Foreground color, then press Shift-Option-Delete (PC: Shift-Alt-Backspace) to fill your duplicate cube with blue (as shown).

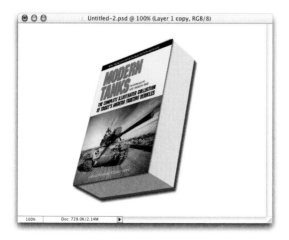

STEP FIFTEEN: Go to the Layers palette and drag this layer under the cube layer. Press "v" to get the Move tool. Then, press the Down Arrow key (on your keyboard) two or three times, and the Right Arrow key two or three times, to reveal the blue cube, which forms the spine and back cover (as shown here). Last, choose Drop Shadow from the Add a Layer Style pop-up menu and click OK to add a soft drop shadow, completing the effect.

Quick Tip:
Adjust those Options on the fly

Want to quickly change the Tolerance setting for a tool (say the Magic Wand tool, for example)? You don't have to go up into the Options Bar, just press "w" to get the Magic Wand tool, then press the Return key (PC: Enter key) and the first field in the Options Bar will automatically become highlighted. All you have to do is type in your setting and you're set.

So what makes this Photoshop iCandy chapter different than the "Special Effects" chapter? Do the effects

I Want Candy
Photoshop iCandy

in this chapter use Alien Skin's Eye Candy effects plug-in? Nope. It's "iCandy" not "EyeCandy." What sets these two apart is that iCandy only has six letters and Special Effects has 14 letters and is two words. What I'm trying to tell you is there is no real difference between the style of effects here and the ones in Special Effects, or even the Down & Dirty tricks chapter. The simple fact is, to make a book like this digestible, you have to divide it into chapters. If not, you've got just one big honkin' chapter (book publishers have spent millions on research that shows pretty convincingly that nobody wants to buy a book with just one big honkin' chapter). Look, this whole book is Photoshop special effects. I was darn lucky to be able to separate some effects into chapters for type, advertising, portfolio effects, and two photographics effects chapters. So, if you're looking at an effect in the iCandy chapter and think, "Shouldn't this have been in the Special Effects chapter?" Rest assured that nobody can prove you wrong.

Photo Pin-On Buttons

When I turned the page and saw this effect (used in a full-page ad for CMT's [Country Music Television] Flameworthy 2003 Video Awards), I just had to figure it out. It does a great job of looking like those pin-on election campaign buttons, but the way they added the photos in a cutout on the button is what really sold me. It takes a few steps, but once you've created one, you can use it as a template so the rest are easy!

STEP ONE: Open a new document in RGB mode. Click on the Foreground Color Swatch (in the Toolbox) and when the Color Picker appears, choose a red color like the one shown here. Press Option-Delete (PC: Alt-Backspace) to fill your Background layer with this red. Press Shift-M until you switch to the Elliptical Marquee tool, hold the Shift key, then drag out a circular selection.

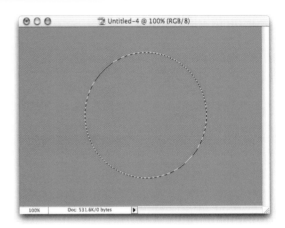

STEP TWO: Open the photo that you want to appear at the top of your button. Once it's open, press Command-A (PC: Control-A) to select the entire photo. Then, press Command-C (PC: Control-C) to copy that photo into memory. Now switch back to your red circle document.

STEP THREE: Go under the Edit menu and choose Paste Into, and the photo in memory will be pasted into the circular selection (as shown here). Don't worry about the size or position of the photo for now—we'll fix that later.

© Brand X Pictures

STEP FOUR: Hold the Command key (PC: Control key), go to the Layers palette, and click directly on the black Layer Mask thumbnail (as shown here) to put a circular selection back around your photo.

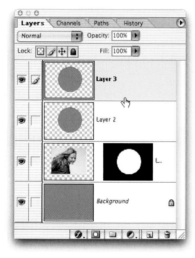

STEP FIVE: Click the New Layer icon at the bottom of the Layers palette. Fill your circular selection with red by pressing Option-Delete (PC: Alt-Backspace). Now, make a duplicate of this red circle layer by pressing Command-J (PC: Control-J) to give you two red circles, aligned one on top of the other (as shown here in the Layers palette).

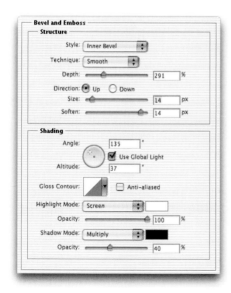

STEP SIX: Choose Bevel and Emboss from the Add a Layer Style pop-up menu at the bottom of the Layers palette. Increase the Depth to 291 and set both Size and Soften to 14. In the Shading section in the lower half of the dialog, set your Angle to 135°, the Altitude to 37°, increase the Opacity of the Highlight to 100%, and then lower the Opacity of the Shadow to 40% (as shown).

Quick Tip:
Pasting Layer Styles to multiple layers

Once you've applied a Layer Style to a particular layer, you can copy that effect, link as many layers as you want to your original layer, and make that same effect appear on every single linked layer with just one click. The feature is called "Paste Layer Style to Linked." To use it, hold the Control key (PC: Right-click) and click on the layer that contains the effect you want to copy. When the pop-up menu appears, choose Copy Layer Style, then start linking the layers you want to affect by clicking in the center column next to them in the Layers palette. To apply your copied style to every linked layer, hold the Control key (PC: Right-click), click on your current layer, and when the pop-up menu appears, choose Paste Layer Style to Linked, and you're done!

continued

Quick Tip:
Changing Image Size? Let Photoshop do the math.

In Photoshop's Image Size dialog box, there's a button that most people ignore. It's called Auto, and here's how it works: You tell Photoshop what line screen you need to output your file at and what level of quality you're looking for (Draft, Good, or Best), and it will do the math, calculating the proper resolution for you based on your choices.

Here's what it does: If you enter 133 line screen and choose Best quality, it doubles that figure and sets your resolution at 266. At Good quality, it gives you 1.5 times the line screen, and at Draft it gives you 72 ppi.

When using this feature, be careful to start with a 300-dpi scan or higher. If you start with a 72-dpi scan, and choose 133 line with Best quality, it'll jump you up to 266 ppi; but it doesn't warn you that your image will look so pixelated when printed that it will trash your whole project, because you can't add resolution that's not really there to begin with.

STEP SEVEN: When you click OK, it applies a soft highlight and shadow to the circle on the top layer, and makes the button look rounded (as shown here). Command-click (PC: Control-click) on the top red circle layer (Layer 3) in the Layers palette to put a selection around your beveled circle.

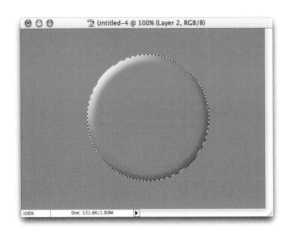

STEP EIGHT: Go under the Select menu, under Modify, and choose Contract. When the Contract Selection dialog appears, enter 12 pixels (as shown) to shrink your selection by 12 pixels (for high-res, 300-ppi images, use 44 pixels).

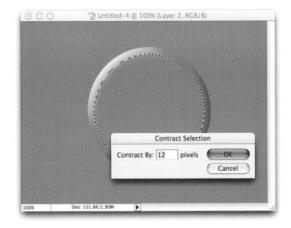

STEP NINE: Press Shift-M until you get the Rectangular Marquee tool, hold the Option key (PC: Alt key), and drag out a rectangular selection across the bottom ¾ of your circular selection. When you release the mouse, that rectangular area will be removed from the circular selection, leaving you with just the top ¼ still selected (as shown here). This is where your photo will appear.

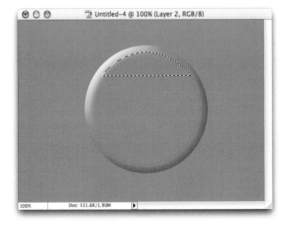

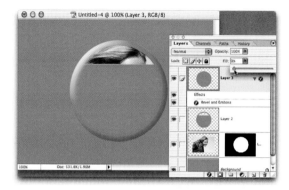

STEP TEN: Go to the Layers palette and click on the red circle layer (Layer 2) just below your top beveled circle layer. Press Delete (PC: Backspace), then Command-D (PC: Control-D) to deselect. You won't see your photo quite yet. Now click on the top layer, and lower the Fill amount to 0% in the Layers palette (as shown), and now you'll be able to see the photo. (Lowering the Fill leaves the bevel effect visible, but hides the red fill.)

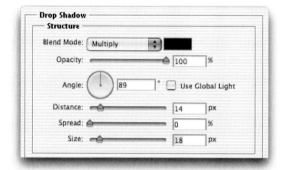

STEP ELEVEN: While the top layer is still active, choose Drop Shadow from the Add a Layer Style pop-up menu at the bottom of the Layers palette. Increase the Opacity to 100%, turn off the Use Global Light checkbox, then set your Angle to around 90°. Increase the Distance to 14 and the Size to 18.

STEP TWELVE: Click OK to apply a black soft shadow to your button. Now you can add some type. (In the example shown here, I used the font Compacta with the tracking set at -25.)

Quick Tip:
Don't open that huge layered file! Instead…

Sometimes you just need a quick look at a file, but if your layered file is 200MB, 300MB, etc. in total size, it's not going to be a quick look. That is, unless you know this little trick that lets you open a flattened version of that very same file, which will be dramatically smaller in file size (which means it will open much faster). Just hold Shift-Option (PC: Shift-Alt) before you open the file (using Photoshop's Open command) and it will bring up a dialog asking you if you want to open just "the composite data." Click OK and a flattened version will open instead (leaving your layered version untouched).

continued

You're probably already familiar with Photoshop's History feature, which by default, lets you undo your last 20 steps. Unfortunately, when you close Photoshop, those undos go away. But there is a way to undo color or tonal corrections days, weeks, or months later. Here's how: The next time you're going to apply a tonal change of some sort (using either Levels, Brightness/Contrast, Curves, Hue/Saturation, Color Balance, or a few others), don't just choose them from the menus. Instead, go to the bottom of the Layers palette and click on the New Fill or Adjustment Layer icon. It's the little circle that is half black and half white. A pop-up menu will appear and you can choose which tonal change (or fill) you want to apply. A special layer will appear in your Layers palette with the name of your tonal change (e.g., Color Balance). After you save your layered document, when you reopen it, the Color Balance layer will still be there. To edit your original Color balance adjustment, double-click on it. To undo your color balance change, drag the Color Balance layer into the Trash icon at the bottom of the Layers palette.

STEP THIRTEEN: In the Layers palette, click on the photo layer. Press "v" to switch to the Move tool, then position the photo so the person's face is visible in the cutout (as shown here). If you need to resize the photo, press Command-T (PC: Control-T) to bring up Free Transform. Hold the Shift key, grab a corner point, and drag to resize the photo within the cutout area. This will be your template for making multiple buttons, so Save this document now as a layered Photoshop file.

STEP FOURTEEN: Go to the Layers palette and hide the Background layer by clicking on the Eye icon in the first column. Click on the top layer, and create a new blank layer by clicking on the New Layer icon at the bottom of the Layers palette. Hold the Option key (PC: Alt key) and choose Merge Visible from the palette's pop-down menu (as shown here). This turns your new layer into a flattened version of all your visible layers.

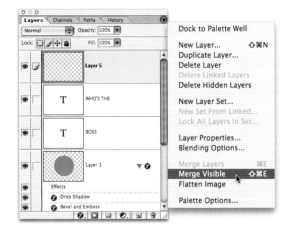

STEP FIFTEEN: Create the document you want to use for your poster, ad, Web page, etc. Press "v" to switch to the Move tool, then just drag the top layer from your button document (the merged button with a transparent background) onto your final document. Press Command-T (PC: Control-T) to bring up Free Transform, and scale the button down to size. Move your cursor outside the bounding box and click-and-drag to rotate (as shown).

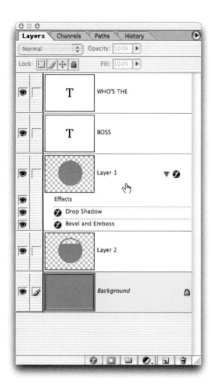

STEP SIXTEEN: Now back to your button template document. Delete the top layer (the merged full button layer) by dragging it to the Trash icon at the bottom of the Layers palette. Drag your photo layer into the Trash as well. Click on the Background layer to make it active and visible again. Command-click (PC: Control-click) on the top circle layer to make a circular selection appear on your Background layer. Now, open the next photo you want in a button. Press Command-A (PC: Control-A) to select the entire photo. Then press Command-C (PC: Control-C) to copy that photo into memory. Switch back to your template document, go under the Edit menu and choose Paste Into.

STEP SEVENTEEN: This pastes the photo into the circular selection, but it appears on a new layer above your Background layer. Use the Move tool and Free Transform to position and scale the photo in the button, and use the Type tool to highlight and change your text. Now you'll repeat Step Fourteen again to create a merged version of the new button, then you'll use the Move tool to drag the merged button into your main document. Go back to Step Sixteen and create as many buttons as you'd like using this method. The example shown here shows five buttons and some type, to give an example of the finished project, which is somewhat similar to the design used in the CMT Flameworthy awards ad.

Quick Tip:
How to view at just the right percentage

If you want to view your document at a specific percentage, you can jump right to that view by highlighting the view percentage (in the lower left-hand corner of your document window), typing in the exact percentage you want, and then pressing the Return (PC: Enter) key.

Quick Tip:
Bending the horizon of the Chrome gradient

One of Photoshop's default gradients, the Chrome gradient, has a "horizon line" that's perfectly straight. Most airbrush artists vary this horizon line slightly to make the gradient look more natural. You can do the same thing in Photoshop (vary the horizon line) by using Photoshop's Wave filter (found under the Distort submenu). Use this filter to create a slight rolling effect along the horizon line. A good place to start is to lower the Number of Generators to 1. Set the Wave Length Min. to 1 and Max to 100. Set the Amplitude to 1 and 6, and click OK. This should add a slight roll to your horizon line.

The Fastest Logo Job in Town

This is another popular method for making a glassy reflection, and it's so quick you can complete the effect in less than 60 seconds (if you stop at Step Six). If you decide to take it further, it could take you as long as a whopping 90 seconds to get through Step Nine. Either way, it's a minute and a half tops that bills more like eight hours. (Kidding. Kind of.)

STEP ONE: Open a new document in RGB mode. Create a new blank layer by clicking on the New Layer icon at the bottom of the Layers palette. Get the Elliptical Marquee tool and draw an oval selection in the middle of your image area (as shown). Click on the Foreground Color Swatch and choose a medium blue as your Foreground color, then fill your oval with blue by pressing Option-Delete (PC: Alt-Backspace).

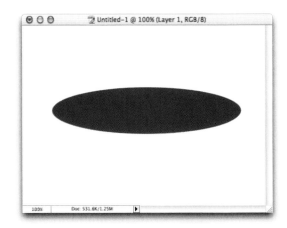

STEP TWO: Deselect by pressing Command-D (PC: Control-D). Press the letter "t" to get the Type tool and create your type. (In the example shown here, I used the font Helvetica Black Oblique, with 120% Horizontal Scaling applied in the Character palette.)

STEP THREE: Go to the Layers palette and Command-click (PC: Control-click) on the oval layer to put a selection around it (as shown). Then go under the Select menu, under Modify, and choose Contract. When the Contract Selection dialog appears (shown here) enter 10 and click OK. (Note: For high-res, 300-ppi images contract by 40 instead.)

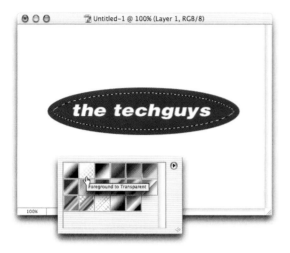

STEP FOUR: Press "d" then "x" to set white as your Foreground color, then press the letter "g" to get the Gradient tool. Move your cursor into your image area and press Return (PC: Enter) to bring up the Gradient Picker (shown here). Choose the second default gradient (Foreground to Transparent) as shown.

STEP FIVE: Create a new blank layer by clicking on the New Layer icon at the bottom of the Layers palette. Then drag your gradient from the top of your selection down about halfway through (as shown here).

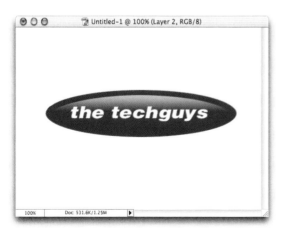

STEP SIX: Deselect by pressing Command-D (PC Control-D). In the Layers palette, lower the Opacity of this layer to 70%. You could stop at this point and consider the effect complete (and I've seen this technique many times that only went this far), but if you want to add a little more detail (by adding a shadow), go on to the next step.

Quick Tip:
Which gradient should you edit?

When you're creating custom gradients, you always have to start with a gradient (by that I mean, when you open the Gradient Editor, it opens with a gradient already loaded into the Editor). This is weird because it works in about exactly the opposite way you'd think it would. You'd imagine you'd click the "New" button, and it would give you some default starting point, but it doesn't. Instead, it works like this—you open the Editor, the last gradient you used is already there waiting to be edited, and when it looks the way you want it to, you put a name in the Name field, and only then do you click the "New" button. (I know, it's weird but that's the way it works.) So which gradient should you use? Who knows for sure, but I always start by clicking on the third default icon in the top row. It's the Black to White gradient, which is easier to edit than the Foreground to Background gradient (the first in the list) for a variety of reasons that I don't have the space to explain here. Just trust me, give the "edit-the-Black-to-White-gradient" thing a try.

continued

A use for the Find Edges filter

One thing I often use the Find Edges filter for is converting a photograph into a line drawing. Just apply the Find Edges filter (Filter>Stylize>Find Edges) and it does a pretty nice job of tracing the edges of your photo. It does create a slight problem in that it often introduces a number of weird colors to the resulting line art, but all you have to do is go under the Image menu, under Adjustments, and choose Desaturate to remove the extra colors and return it to a black and white line drawing.

STEP SEVEN: Create a new blank layer by clicking on the New Layer icon at the bottom of the Layers palette. Next, go to the Layers palette and Command-click (PC: Control-click) on the oval layer to put a selection around it (as shown).

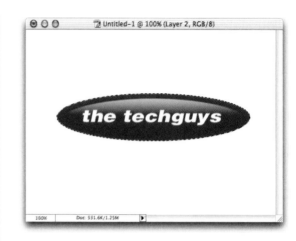

STEP EIGHT: Press "b" to get the Brush tool, then choose a 70-pixel (or larger) soft-edged brush from the Brush Picker in the Options Bar. Press "d" to set your Foreground color to black, then paint a stroke starting at the right side of the oval, and trace along the bottom of your selection, painting down and to the left as you go (as shown here). Deselect by pressing Command-D (PC Control-D).

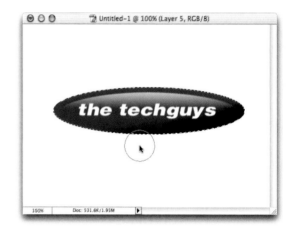

STEP NINE: After your stroke is drawn, go to the Layers palette, and lower the Opacity of this layer to 70% to complete the effect. (Note: This is one of those rare times where I wouldn't add a drop shadow, because what you just painted acts as a shadow on its own.)

The *Star Trek* Look

The TV show *Star Trek* introduced us to a futuristic graphic design look (used in computer panels, onboard signage, etc.) that was so forward thinking that it still looks great today. Here's how to get a similar effect, which will definitely bring a smile when used as a template for slide presentations, signage, and video clip headers, because everybody immediately recognizes its distinctive style.

STEP ONE: Create a new document in RGB mode. Press the letter "d" to set your Foreground color to black, then fill your Background layer with black by pressing Option-Delete (PC: Alt-Backspace). Get the Rounded Rectangle tool from the Toolbox (as shown here). Create a new layer by clicking on the New Layer icon at the bottom of the Layers palette.

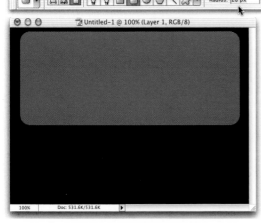

STEP TWO: Up in the Options Bar, click on the third icon from the left (as shown at top) to create pixel-based shapes with this tool. Then set the Radius (the roundness of your corners) to 20. Click on the Foreground Color Swatch and set your Foreground color to bright blue in the Color Picker (the blue shown here is R=87, B=145, G=255). Drag out a rounded rectangle that is approximately the same size and shape as the one shown here.

STEP THREE: Hold the Command key (PC: Control key), go to the Layers palette, and click on your blue rectangle layer to put a selection around it (as shown here).

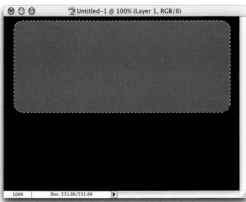

Quick Tip:
Why choose Monochromatic Noise?

Every time we use the Noise filter (Filter>Noise>Add Noise), we also check the Monochromatic box at the bottom of the Add Noise dialog. The reason is that if Monochromatic is not turned on, you get noise that is composed of little red, green, and blue dots, and that can get in the way of colorization that will often take place later on in the tutorial.

continued

STEP FOUR: Press "m" to switch to the Rectangular Marquee tool, then click within your selected area and drag your selection up and to the right (as shown here). The reason you switched to the Rectangular Marquee tool is it enables you to move just the selection, and not the area underneath your selection.

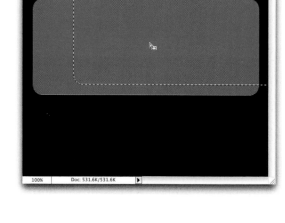

STEP FIVE: Press Delete (PC: Backspace) to knock that selection out of your blue rectangle (as shown here). Deselect by pressing Command-D (PC: Control-D).

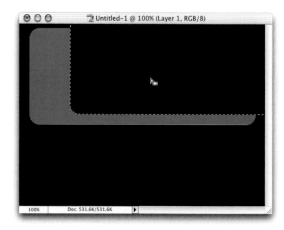

STEP SIX: Use the Rectangular Marquee tool to drag out a rectangular selection over the curved area on the top left side of your shape (as shown here), then press Delete (PC: Back-space) to erase that rounded corner, leaving the top flat (as shown). Do the same thing to the bottom right end where it's rounded: put a selection around it and delete that rounded area.

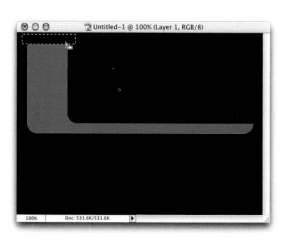

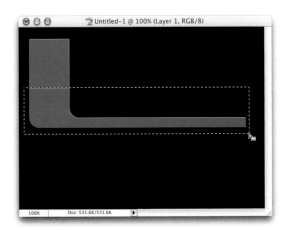

STEP SEVEN: Use the same tool to drag out a large rectangular selection around the bottom half of the shape (as shown here).

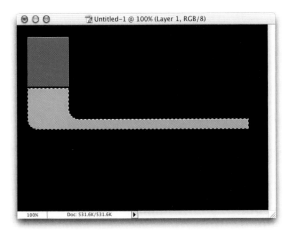

STEP EIGHT: Hold the Command key (PC: Control key), then press the Down Arrow key three times. This selects the bottom half of your shape, and nudges it down, leaving a thin gap between your two segments. While it's still selected, choose a lighter blue for your Foreground color (I used R=173, B=196, G=255) and fill your selected area with this blue by pressing Option-Delete (PC: Alt-Backspace). Deselect by pressing Command-D (PC: Control-D).

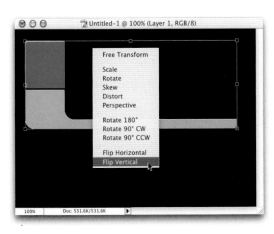

STEP NINE: Press Option-Command-T (PC: Alt-Control-T) to bring up Free Transform in duplicate mode. Control-click (PC: Right-click) within the bounding box, then choose Flip Vertical (as shown), and a flipped duplicate of your shape will appear on its own separate layer. Hold the Shift key, click in the bounding box, and drag the duplicate shape down below your original shape until there is a slight gap between the two.

continued

Quick Tip:
Finding the right gradient

When you have the Gradient tool, you can access the built-in preset gradients (and your own custom gradients) from the Gradient Picker. This is found in the Options Bar by clicking on the down-facing triangle just to the right of the Gradient thumbnail (which shows your currently selected gradient). When you click on this triangle, it reveals the Gradient Picker. By default, the Foreground to Background gradient is the first swatch on the top row in the Gradient Picker. It's a smart thumbnail, because it changes to display your currently selected Foreground and Background colors.

STEP TEN: After you press Return (PC: Enter) to lock in your transformation, press the letter "w" to switch to the Magic Wand tool. Click in the top half of this duplicate shape to put a selection around it. Set your Foreground color to a medium pink (I used R=206, B=156, G=206), and fill this top half selection with pink by pressing Option-Delete (PC: Alt-Backspace). Then select the bottom square (with the Magic Wand tool) and fill with R=126, B=122, G=201. Press Command-D (PC: Control-D) to deselect.

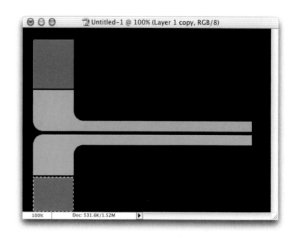

STEP ELEVEN: In the Layers palette, click back on your original (light blue) layer. In the next step, you're going to add some text to the light blue line, but most people like to round the end first. To do that, set your Foreground color to that same light blue color again, then get the Rounded Rectangle tool, and drag out a pill-shaped selection over the right end of the larger shape (like the one shown here). You want the right end of your new pill shape to create the rounded end of your larger shape.

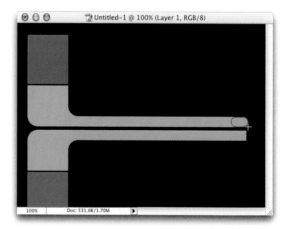

STEP TWELVE: Press the letter "t" to get the Type tool, then "d" then "x" to set your Foreground color to white. Create the type you want to appear within your light blue bar. (The font used here is Compacta from Bitstream.) Position the type within the blue area, then size the type until it's the same height as the bar (as shown here).

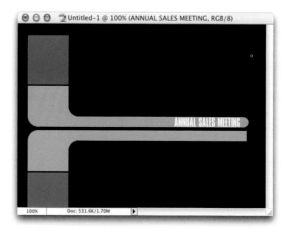

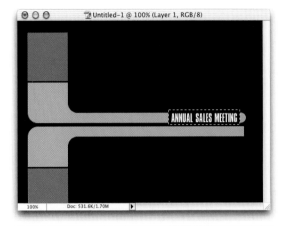

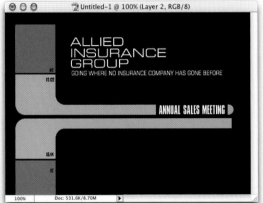

STEP THIRTEEN: Press "m" to switch back to the Rectangular Marquee tool, and drag out a selection around your type (like the one shown here). Click back on your original blue shape layer in the Layers palette to make it active, and then press Delete (PC: Backspace) to knock out a hole in the bar for your type (as shown). Deselect by pressing Command-D (PC: Control-D).

STEP FOURTEEN: Now it's time to set up the rest of your slide. I added some random letters and numbers within the color bars using the font Compacta. Then I added the company name in the font Eurostile Extended (from Adobe). All the rest of the type is also in Eurostile Extended or plain Eurostile. The final slide is shown below.

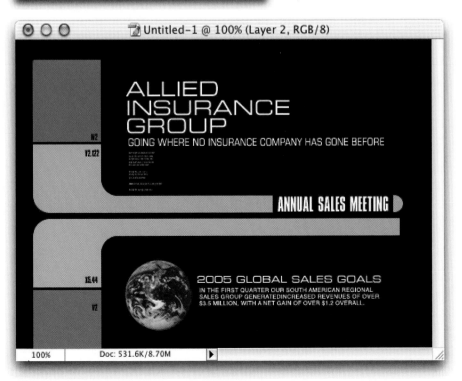

Quick Tip:
Making circular selections

When you draw a circular selection with the Elliptical Marquee tool, by default, it draws from where you first click your mouse button, but if you prefer, you can drag your circular selection from the center outward by holding the Option key (PC: Alt key) while you drag. Don't forget to add the Shift key if you want to keep your circle perfectly round as you drag.

High-Tech Transparent Info Boxes

I wanted to include an effect that was similar to the high-tech transparent info boxes you see used on ESPN, FOX Sports, and other nationally televised sports events for displaying scores, stats, and team info during games. I used this effect myself when creating the interface for a Photoshop training CD-ROM, but it works just as well over video, as a DVD interface, or even simply in print.

STEP ONE: Open the photo you want to use as your CD-ROM interface background. Then open a new document at the size you want for your interface. Create a new blank layer by clicking on the New Layer icon at the bottom of the Layers palette.

STEP TWO: Get the Polygonal Lasso tool and draw a selection that will later become the navigation area (like the one shown here). To build a selection in this shape, hold the Shift key, click once, move to the next spot, then click again. (The Shift key creates perfectly vertical or horizontal lines and exact 45° angles.) Keep clicking these straight line sections until you have the shape shown here.

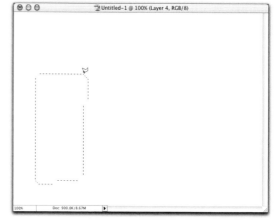

STEP THREE: Press "d" to set your Foreground color to black, then press Option-Delete (PC: Alt-Backspace) to fill the selection with black (as shown here). Deselect by pressing Command-D (PC: Control-D).

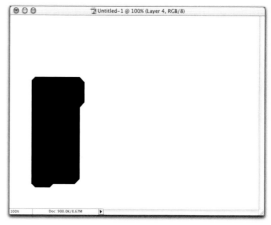

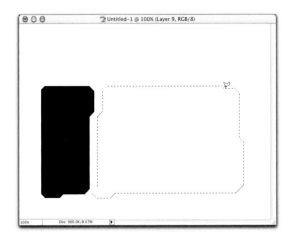

STEP FOUR: On this same layer, draw another shape using the Polygonal Lasso tool (like the one shown here). Again, hold the Shift key to create perfectly vertical or horizontal lines, and exact 45° angles.

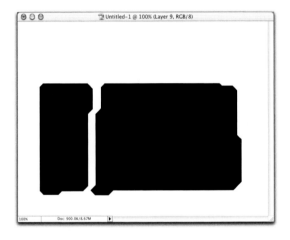

STEP FIVE: When the selection is complete, press Option-Delete (PC: Alt-Backspace) to fill it with black. Deselect by pressing Command-D (PC: Control-D).

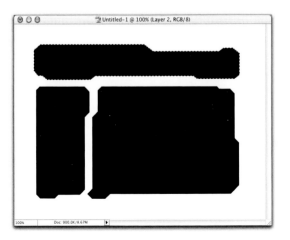

STEP SIX: Use the Polygonal Lasso tool to draw another selection like the shape shown here at the top, and fill it with black as well.

Quick Tip:
Save a trip up to the Gradient Picker

If you have the Gradient tool and need to change gradients, don't travel all the way up to the Options Bar to get the Gradient Picker. Instead, just press the Return key (PC: Enter key) and the Gradient Picker will appear at the current location of your cursor, right within the image area. Then just double-click on the gradient you want, and the Picker will close itself up.

continued

Quick Tip:
Make 'em big

Many designers prefer to create their Web graphics at a much larger physical size (like two or three times bigger) than the final size that the graphic will be on the Web page. This is especially helpful when the final size is very small, like Web buttons—which would be hard to create from scratch at their actual size. If you decide to go this route, you can scale your object down to its final size by using Free Transform (Command-T [PC: Control-T]) and sizing down before you save the file for the Web.

STEP SEVEN: Deselect by pressing Command-D (PC: Control-D). Press the letter "v" to switch to the Move tool, hold the Shift key, and drag-and-drop this shape layer into the photo that you opened in Step One. (Holding the Shift key will center the shapes in the photo.) Now that the main areas of your interface are in place, all you have to do is a little tweaking.

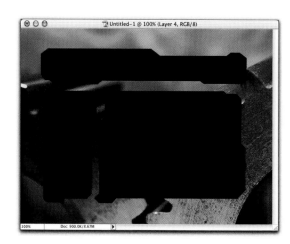

STEP EIGHT: In the Layers palette, lower the Opacity setting for this layer to 60% (as shown here) to let the background show through your shapes. Create a new blank layer by clicking on the New Layer icon at the bottom of the Layers palette.

STEP NINE: Hold the Command key (PC: Control key), go to the Layers palette, and click on your shape layer. This puts a selection around your shapes (as you see here). Go under the Edit menu and choose Stroke. Set the Width to 1 pixel, click on the Color Swatch and change the stroke Color to white in the Color Picker, set the Location to Center, and click OK to put a white stroke around your selection.

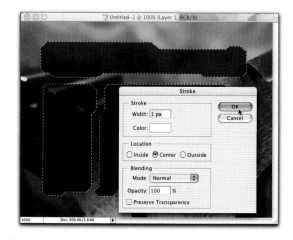

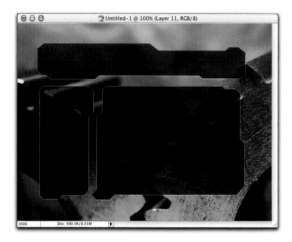

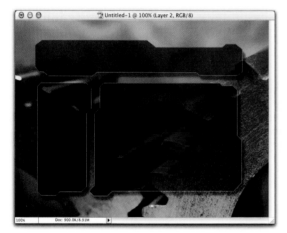

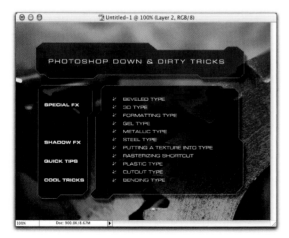

STEP TEN: Deselect by pressing Command-D (PC: Control-D). In the Layers palette, lower the Opacity setting of this white stroke layer to 50%. This makes the stroke appear thinner than its 1-pixel width. Next, in the Layers palette, click back on your shapes layer.

STEP ELEVEN: Choose Drop Shadow from the Add a Layer Style pop-up menu at the bottom of the Layers palette. Increase the Distance to 13, uncheck Use Global Light, then click OK to apply a soft drop shadow to your shapes (as shown here). Now you're ready to add your type. Press the letter "t" to switch to the Type tool and create the text. (Note: all the type shown here uses Eurostile Extended or Extended Bold from Adobe.)

STEP TWELVE: I also added a column of chrome buttons by creating a new layer, drawing a very small circular selection, filling it with a standard black to white gradient, then adding a Bevel and Emboss using the settings shown below.

Quick Tip:
Loading selections

Most of the time in this book we ask you to go under the Select menu and choose Load Selection to load a selection that you've saved as an Alpha Channel. However, you can also load a selection by going to the Channels palette, clicking on the Alpha Channel you want to load as a selection, and dragging it to the Selection icon at the bottom of the Channels palette. (It's the first one from the left.) Click back on the RGB channel to view the entire RGB image again with the loaded selection.

Blurred Backscreen Effect

This effect has really become popular in the past 12 months, and I'm seeing it everywhere, from print to TV. It's a takeoff on the classic backscreened effect (where you darken or lighten an area of your photo so that text can placed over the photo and still be easily read); but what they're doing now is blurring just the area behind the screen, leaving the rest of the photo un-blurred, which helps make the type even more readable.

STEP ONE: Open the photo you want to apply text over. Create a new blank layer by clicking on the New Layer icon at the bottom of the Layers palette.

STEP TWO: Get the Polygonal Lasso tool (it draws selections using straight lines), hold the Shift key, and create a selection like the one shown here. Start by clicking once, and as you move the cursor, a straight line selection is drawn. Click to change directions (but keep the Shift key held the entire time because it creates perfectly horizontal lines and exact 45° angles).

STEP THREE: Press "d" to set your Foreground color to black, then fill your selected area with black by pressing Option-Delete (PC: Alt-Backspace). Lower the Opacity of this layer to 60%, so you can see through it (as shown). This creates a dark backscreened effect. Don't deselect yet.

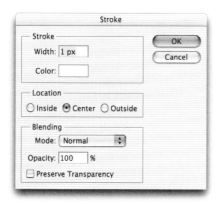

STEP FOUR: Create another new blank layer (click on the New layer icon at the bottom of the Layers palette). Press "x" to switch your Foreground color to white, then go under the Edit menu and choose Stroke. When the dialog appears (shown here), for Width enter 1 pixel and for Location choose Center, then click OK to apply a 1-pixel white stroke around your selection. Lower the Opacity of this white-stroke layer to 50% (this makes the line look thinner).

STEP FIVE: Don't deselect yet. In the Layers palette, click on the Background layer (your selection should still be in place), then go under the Filter menu, under Blur, and choose Gaussian Blur. When the dialog appears, enter 10 pixels (try 40 for high-res, 300-ppi photos) and then click OK to blur the area of the photo that will appear behind your backscreened area. Now you can deselect by pressing Command-D (PC: Control-D).

STEP SIX: In the Layers palette, click back on the black bar layer and lower the Opacity a bit more until the blurring is more visible (I lowered it to 40% in the example shown here), and add text to complete the effect. (Note: The top and bottom text is Eurostile Extended 2 and the words "midtown maggie" are Serpentine Oblique, both from Adobe.)

Quick Tip:
Seeing your full-color image, while editing just one channel

Here's a handy tip that lets you edit an individual color channel (like the Red or Green channel) while seeing the full-color RGB composite as you edit (normally, when you click on a channel, you see just that channel). To do this, just press the tilde key (~) [Note: it's right above your Tab key] and your channel will still be active, but your image will now be displayed in full color.

Photographic Chrome Reflections

It was the new logo for BVD briefs that got me interested in figuring out how to do this effect. In the past, to get a photographic chrome-like look, you'd have to use displacement maps and jump through a lot of hoops, but when I gave that BVD logo a good look I started to wonder if there wasn't an easier way. Luckily, there is, and in this logo project, you'll learn how to get that photo-chrome look the easy way.

STEP ONE: Open a new document at 72 ppi in RGB mode. Create a new layer by clicking on the New Layer icon at the bottom of the Layers palette. Get the Elliptical Marquee tool, hold the Shift key, and drag out a large circular selection in the center of your image area. Press the letter "g" to switch to the Gradient tool, then press Return (PC: Enter) to bring up the Gradient Picker (shown upper left). From the Picker's pop-down menu, choose Metals (then click Append) to load a set of metallic-looking gradients.

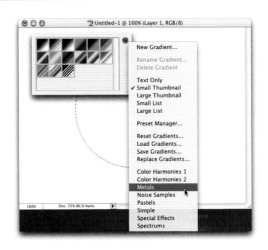

STEP TWO: Once the Metal gradients load, choose the "Silver" gradient—it's gray with two white diagonal stripes (as shown in the inset). Take the Gradient tool, click at the top of your selection and drag downward to the bottom of the selection. Don't deselect yet.

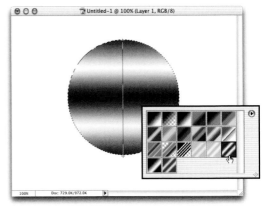

STEP THREE: Go under the Select menu, under Modify, and choose Contract. When the Contract dialog appears, enter 6 and click OK to shrink your selection by six pixels. Then take the gradient tool, click at the bottom of your gradient, and drag upward (the opposite direction of the gradient you drew in the previous step).

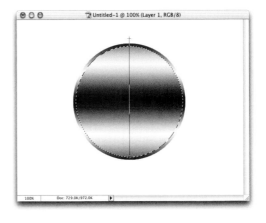

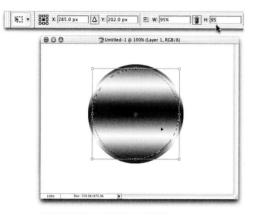

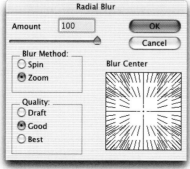

© Brand X Pictures

STEP FOUR: Create a new blank layer in the Layers palette. Go under the Select menu and choose Transform Selection. Then go up in the Options Bar and enter 95% for both Width and Height (as shown at top), then press Enter to shrink your selection. The reason I have you do it this way, rather than contracting the selection like you did in the previous step, is that it helps keep the circle round, whereas continual contracting tends to make your circle look blocky.

STEP FIVE: Click on the Foreground Color Swatch and choose a medium red in the Color Picker (I chose R=97, G=11, B=11) and fill your selection with this red by pressing Option-Delete (PC: Alt-Backspace). Now you can deselect by pressing Command-D (PC: Control-D).

STEP SIX: Open a photo you want to use as your chrome reflection. Landscapes seem to work best for this effect, but try to choose a landscape that has a lot of color variation (of course, you can always download this photo from the book's companion site at www.scottkelbybooks.com/csphotos.html). Press "m" to get the Rectangular Marquee tool and drag out a selection around the center focal point of the photo (as shown here).

STEP SEVEN: Go under the Filter menu, under Blur, and choose Radial Blur. Increase the Amount to 100, set the Blur Method to Zoom, leave the Quality set at Good, and click OK. Apply this filter once more (for a total of two times) by pressing Command-F (PC: Control-F). Don't deselect yet.

continued

Quick Tip:
Reaching the Free Transform handles

Have you ever brought up Free Transform, but you couldn't reach the Free Transform handles (only about 12 times a day, eh?). Then try this—just press Command-0 (zero) (PC: Control-0) and your image window view will scale down, revealing the gray canvas area, and enabling you to reach all the handles. Works like a charm.

Quick Tip:
Photoshop's hidden step and repeat

If you want to copy a layer, and then "step-and-repeat" (creating a row of identical objects, spaced evenly apart, or rotating a series of shapes around a circle, etc.), you can do it by using this sequence: Press Option-Command-T (PC: Alt-Control-T) to bring up Free Transform. Then transform (rotate, move, etc.) your first copy. This doesn't move the original, it moves a copy. Press Return (PC: Enter) to lock in your transformation, then press Shift-Option-Command-T (PC: Shift-Alt-Control-T) which is the shortcut for Step and Repeat. Each time you press this command, another duplicate layer will be created, and the element will be repeated using the same distance, rotation, etc.

STEP EIGHT: Press "v" to get the Move tool, then click within the selected area of your photo and drag-and-drop it onto your gradient circle document. In the Layers palette, drag this photo layer so it's between the red circle and the gradients (in other words, from bottom to top it should be: Background, gradients, photo layer, then red circle layer on top).

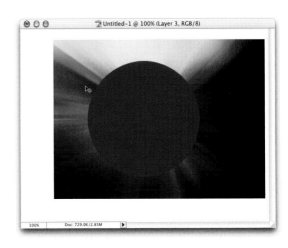

STEP NINE: Press Command-G (PC: Control-G) to put this photo inside your gradient circle (as shown). Then, to get the photo to blend in with the gradient, change the layer Blend Mode of this layer from Normal to Color Burn (as shown here). Next, in the Layers palette, click on the circular gradient layer (Layer 1).

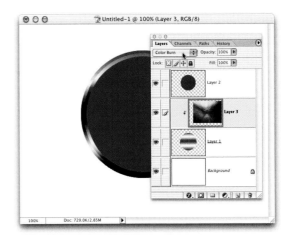

STEP TEN: Choose Bevel and Emboss from the Add a Layer Style pop-up menu at the bottom of the Layers palette. Change the Technique to Chisel Hard, increase the Depth to 341% and Soften to 3. In the Shading section, turn on Anti-aliased, then click on the Gloss Contour down-facing arrow to bring up the Contour Picker. From the Picker's pop-down menu load the set named Contours, then choose the contour with three peaks called "Ring-Triple" (as shown here). Last, lower the Highlight Opacity to 55%. Don't click OK quite yet.

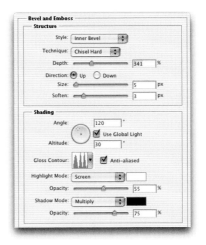

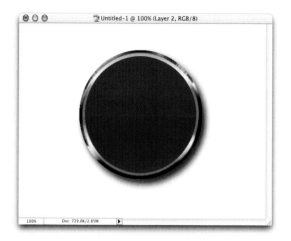

STEP ELEVEN: In the left side of the Bevel and Emboss dialog, click directly on the word "Drop Shadow" in the list of Styles. When the dialog appears, increase the Distance to 13 and the Size to 16, and then click OK to apply a soft drop shadow to your gradient layer (as shown here).

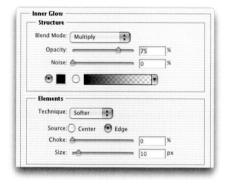

STEP TWELVE: In the Layers palette, click on your red circle layer to make it active. Choose Inner Glow from the Add a Layer Style pop-up menu. Set the Size to 13 (to add a slight shadow inside your red circle) but don't click OK yet.

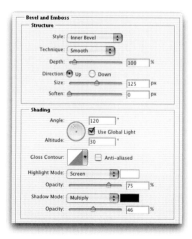

STEP THIRTEEN: From the list of Styles on the left side of the Layer Style dialog, click directly on the words "Bevel and Emboss" to make its options visible. Increase the Size to 125. In the Shading section, lower the Shadow Opacity to 46%.

Quick Tip:
One click and all your open docs are in Full Screen Mode

If you want all your open images to appear in Full Screen Mode (no menu bars, no palettes) just Shift-click on the Full Screen Mode icon (in the Toolbox, second row from the bottom, third icon from the left). Press Tab to hide your palettes; then you can create a slide show from within Photoshop by pressing Control-Tab (PC: Right-click-Tab).

continued

Quick Tip:
Want a larger Canvas area? Crop it.

That's right, if you want more Canvas space, you can skip the Canvas Size dialog box altogether. Just pull out the bottom right corner of your image window (to reveal the gray canvas area), then take the Crop tool, and draw a cropping border that encompasses the entire image area. Then click-and-drag any of the cropping border's control handles out into that gray canvas area that you'd like to add as white Canvas space. When you click Return (PC: Enter) it adds that excess gray canvas area as Canvas space. This is a wonderfully visual way to add Canvas space without using any math.

STEP FOURTEEN: Click OK to apply a wide bevel and the Inner Glow effect to your red circle. These create a rounded glassy look (as shown here).

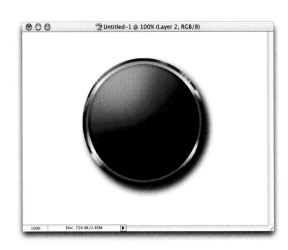

STEP FIFTEEN: Hold the Command key (PC: Control key), go to the Layers palette and click on the red circle layer to put a selection around the red circle (as shown here). Next, switch to the Elliptical Marquee tool.

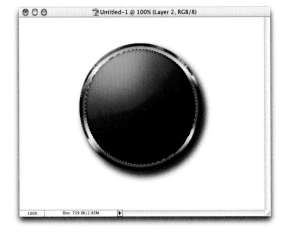

STEP SIXTEEN: Hold the Option key (PC: Alt key) and drag out a large oval-shaped selection that covers all but the top-left area of your circular selection (like the one shown here). Because you're holding the Option (Alt) key, the area that falls within the oval will be subtracted from your existing circular selection. Basically, you're cutting away everything but that little crescent-shaped selection at the upper-left side.

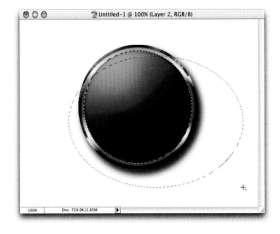

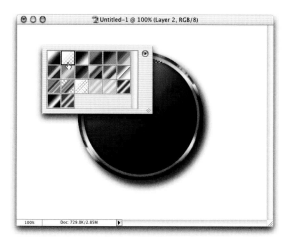

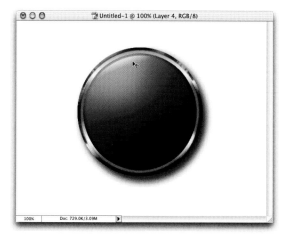

STEP SEVENTEEN: Now you'll build a highlight to help the logo look more glassy. Press "x" to set your Foreground color to white, create a new blank layer in the Layers palette, then get the Gradient tool. Press the Return key (PC: Enter) to bring up the Gradient Picker, then choose the second gradient from the top left (the Foreground to Transparent gradient). Click-and-drag this gradient from the top of your crescent-shaped selection to the bottom.

STEP EIGHTEEN: Deselect by pressing Command-D (PC: Control-D) then press "v" to switch to the Move tool. Drag your crescent-shaped gradient down just a little (as shown here), so it's no longer right against the edge of the red circle. Then in the Layers palette, lower the Opacity of this layer to 72%. This creates the glassy highlight for your logo.

STEP NINETEEN: All that's left to do is add some type to your logo to complete the project. The font for both the large "M" in the middle of the logo and the type beneath it is Mata from House Industries. To make the big "M" appear like it's behind a glassy reflection, you can lower the Opacity of that layer to around 65%. That's it!

Quick Tip:
Finding the right palette has actually become easier

This is going to sound so simple, and it is, but it will make your life a little easier when you're searching through the Window menu to open a palette you need. In Photoshop CS (after 11 long years) Adobe has put the Window menu's listing of palettes in alphabetical order. If this isn't proof positive that the apocalypse is near, really, what is?

Realistic Neon

This technique (created by Felix Nelson) was featured on the July/August 2003 cover of *Photoshop User* magazine. Unlike some simple neon text effects done with Photoshop, this actually looks like real neon tubes. You know, if he really works hard, and applies himself, this Felix joker just might have a future in this business.

STEP ONE: Create a new document at 72 ppi in RGB mode. Click on the Foreground Color Swatch, choose a light pink color in the Color Picker, and click OK. Choose the Type tool from the Toolbox and enter some text (we used 130-point Helvetica Black in our example).

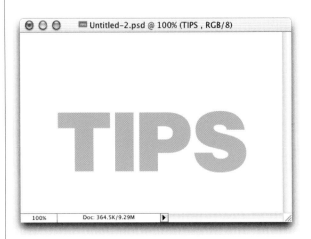

STEP TWO: Duplicate the Type layer by dragging it into the New Layer icon at the bottom of the Layers palette. With the Type tool, click anywhere in the text, and press Command-A (PC: Control-A) to select all the letters. Go to the Character palette, and change the font to VAG Rounded Thin, 112 pts, and the font color to red. Now, adjust the kerning (the space between two characters) so that the thinner red text fits inside the thicker pink text. To adjust the kerning, just click between two letters and change the kerning value in the Character palette.

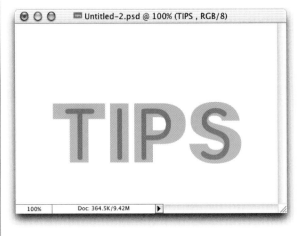

STEP THREE: Control-click (PC: Right-click) on the Type layer copy, and choose Rasterize Layer. Choose the Rectangular Marquee tool from the Toolbox and make a selection around the letter "i." Press Command-T (PC: Control-T) to bring up Free Transform. Rotate the "i" slightly counterclockwise, and press Enter to apply the transformation.

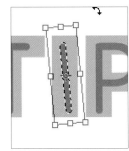

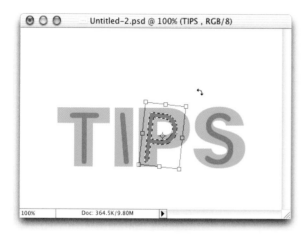

STEP FOUR: Now, make a selection around the letter "p" using the Rectangular Marquee tool. Press Command-T (PC: Control-T) to bring up Free Transform. Click-and-drag outside the bounding box to rotate the "p" slightly clockwise, and press Return (PC: Enter) to apply the transformation.

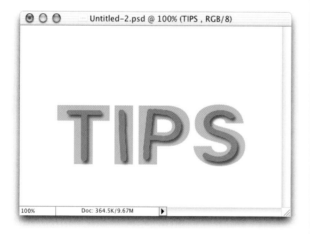

STEP FIVE: Click on the Add a Layer Style icon (the black circle with the "ƒ" in it) at the bottom of the Layers palette, and choose Drop Shadow. Click on the Blend Mode Color Swatch and choose a purple color in the Color Picker. Click OK in the Color Picker but not in the Layer Style dialog yet.

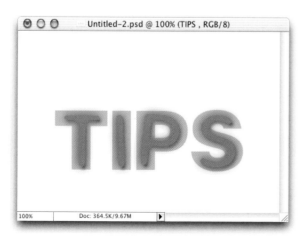

STEP SIX: Click directly on the name "Outer Glow" in the list of Styles on the left side of the Layer Style dialog box to reveal the Outer Glow options. Click on the Color Swatch and choose red for the color in the Color Picker. Choose Hard Light for Blend Mode, 65% for Opacity, and 15 for Size. Don't click OK yet.

continued

Quick Tip:
Trying out different levels of magnification

If you enter magnification values in the View field in the bottom-left corner of your image window, here's a tip that will save you some time: once you've entered the percentage of Zoom that you want, don't just press the Enter key—instead press Shift-Enter. That way, the photo zooms in, but the view percentage field stays highlighted so if you want to type in a different percentage, you don't have to re-highlight the field—it's ready to go—just type in a new percentage. Try it once, and you'll see what I mean.

STEP SEVEN: Click directly on the name Inner Glow in the list of Styles on the left side of the Layer Style dialog box. Click on the Color Swatch and choose pink for the color in the Color Picker. Don't click OK yet.

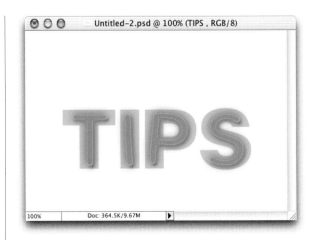

STEP EIGHT: Click directly on the name Bevel and Emboss in the list of Styles on the left side of the Layer Style dialog box. Enter 0 for Size. Uncheck the Use Global Light box, and then enter 22 for Angle and 30 for Altitude. Click on the down-facing arrow next to the Gloss Contour thumbnail, and choose the Ring contour (it's the one with one steep hill). Check the Anti-aliased box, and lower the Highlight Mode Opacity to 45%. Click on the Shadow Mode Color Swatch, choose a dark red color in the Color Picker and click OK. Lower the Shadow Mode Opacity to 60%.

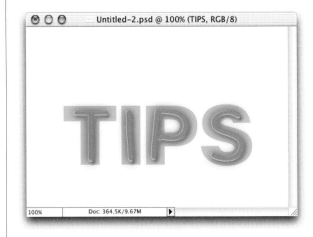

STEP NINE: Click directly on the name Contour in the list of Styles on the left side of the Layer Style dialog box to reveal the Contour options. Check the Anti-aliased box. Now you can click OK in the Layer Style dialog.

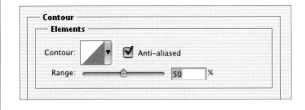

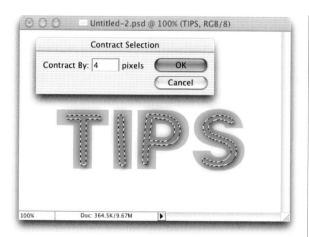

STEP TEN: Create a new layer by clicking on the New Layer icon at the bottom of the Layers palette. Command-click (PC: Control-click) on the red, rasterized type layer to put a selection around it. Go under Select, under Modify, and choose Contract. Enter 4 pixels and click OK.

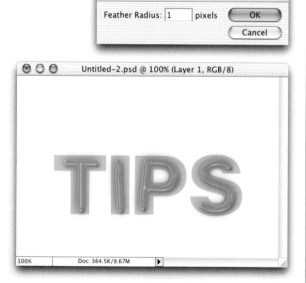

STEP ELEVEN: Go under Select, and choose Feather. Enter 1 pixel and click OK. Press the letter "d" then "x" to set your Foreground color to white. Press Option-Delete (PC: Alt-Backspace) to fill with white. Change the layer Blend Mode from Normal to Hard Light. Press Command-D (PC: Control-D) to deselect.

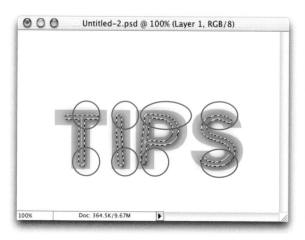

STEP TWELVE: Create a new layer (Layer 2). Command-click (PC: Control-click) on the red text layer. Change the Foreground color to a bright orange. Choose the Brush tool from the Toolbox. With a large soft-edged brush (about 17 pixels), paint in the areas shown in our example (the tops, bottoms, and some of the sides of each character). Change the layer Blend Mode to Darken, and lower the Opacity to 75%.

continued

STEP THIRTEEN: Create a new layer (Layer 3). Press the letter "d" then "x" to change the Foreground color to white. Go under Select, under Modify, and choose Contract. Enter 1 pixel and click OK. With a soft-edged brush (about 8 pixels), paint in the highlight areas shown in our example.

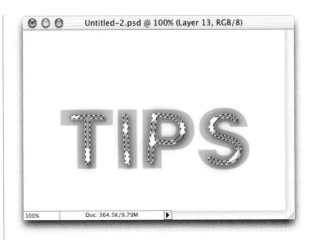

STEP FOURTEEN: Go under Filter, under Blur, and choose Gaussian Blur. Enter 2 pixels, and click OK. Change the layer Blend Mode from Normal to Overlay. Press Command-D (PC: Control-D) to deselect.

STEP FIFTEEN: Create a new layer (Layer 4). Drag this layer down in the Layers palette so it's above the original Type layer and below the red, rasterized text layer.

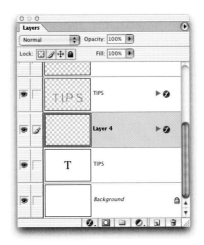

STEP SIXTEEN: Choose the Elliptical Marquee tool from the Toolbox. Hold the Shift key and make a circular selection on the left side of the neon text (the top-left of the "t" in our example). Keep the selection inside the pink type behind the neon type.

STEP SEVENTEEN: Hold the Shift key to add another circular selection on the right side of the neon text (the bottom portion of the "s" in our example). Again, keep the selection within the pink type.

STEP EIGHTEEN: Press the letter "d" to change the Foreground color to black. Press Option-Delete (PC: Alt-Backspace) to fill your circular selections with black.

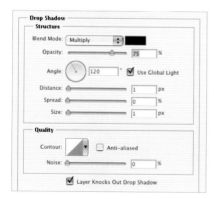

STEP NINETEEN: Click on the Add a Layer Style icon, and choose Drop Shadow. Enter 1 for Distance and 1 for Size. Don't click OK yet.

STEP TWENTY: Click on the words Bevel and Emboss in the list of Styles on the left of the Layer Style dialog box. Enter 570% for Depth, 3 for Size , and click OK. Press Command-D (PC: Control-D) to deselect.

continued

continued

Quick Tip:
Tired of the sRGB mismatch warning dialog? Have Photoshop ignore it.

There's a new preference in Photoshop CS that may be my favorite single preference of all. It's a checkbox (found under the Photoshop menu [PC: Edit menu], under Preferences, choose File Handling) named "Ignore EXIF sRGB tag." When you turn this on, it ignores the sRGB tag that is embedded into many digital camera images. This alone may be worth the price of the upgrade, in terms of sheer aggravation relief.

Quick Tip:
Spend less time in the File Browser's Navigation panel

If you find yourself accessing photos from the same folder again and again, you can save yourself a load of time (and the hassle of digging through your hard drive via the File Browser's Navigation panel) by saving that folder as a Favorite in Photoshop CS's File Browser. To do this, make your way to that folder, then in the File Browser's mini-menu, under File choose Add Folder to Favorites. From that point on, you can jump straight to this folder by choosing it from the pop-up menu at the top of the File Browser. Pretty darn sweet!

STEP TWENTY-ONE: Hold the Shift key and make a small circular selection on the left side of the "t" near the middle. Press Option-Delete PC: Alt-Backspace) to fill with black. Now, while holding down Option-Command (PC: Alt-Control), click-and-drag the selection to make a duplicate on the right side of the "t."

Duplicate enough of the "black dots" to have a pair for each of the neon letters (see example).

STEP TWENTY-TWO: Create a new layer (Layer 5). Use the Rectangular Marquee tool to join the first two neon letters at the top. Hold the Shift key to make additional selections that join the rest of the neon letters (see example). Press Option-Delete (PC: Alt-Backspace) to fill the selections with black.

STEP TWENTY-THREE: Click on the Add a Layer Style icon, and choose Bevel and Emboss. Change the Size to 1. Click on the down-facing arrow next to the Gloss Contour thumbnail, and choose the "Ring" contour again. Check the Anti-aliased box and click OK. Lower the layer Opacity to 65% and the Fill Opacity to 50% in the Layers palette. Press Command-D (PC: Control-D) to deselect.

STEP TWENTY-FOUR: Click on the Background layer, and fill with black to complete the effect.

OPTIONAL STEP: Open an image that you want to use the neon type in (a diner sign in our example). Choose the Move tool, then click-and-drag the image into the neon text document. We added the chrome circle and the words "100 Photoshop" (using Brush Script MT as the font).

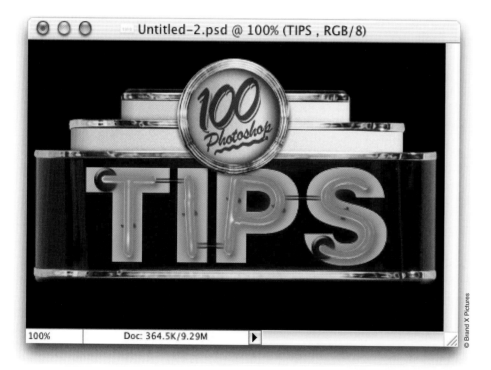

© Brand X Pictures

Quick Tip:
Ranking's out; flagging's in.

Okay, ranking still exists in the Photoshop CS File Browser, but its importance has been diminished because now there's something better—Flags. Now when you see a photo you want to keep, just press Command-' (PC: Control-') and that image is flagged. Then you can choose to see just your flagged photos, your unflagged photos, or both by making your choice from the "Show" pop-up menu at the top right of the File Browser. If you still insist on ranking (with the old A, B, C, method) you still can by Control-clicking (Right-clicking) on an image, and then choosing Rank from the pop-up menu.

Magnifying an Object

I saw this popular effect recently in a Xerox print ad that ran in *USA Today*. When I took a close look at the ad, not only was the magnification effect created from scratch, but the magnifying glass as well. It's actually very simple, thanks to Felix Nelson (the photo-realistic genius guy) who figured out the gradients you'll need to create a realistic magnifying glass. (Note: If nothing else, you'll want to keep Felix's great metal gradients for future use.)

STEP ONE: Open a new document in RGB mode. Create a new blank layer by clicking on the New Layer icon at the bottom of the Layers palette. Get the Rounded Rectangle tool (it's under the Shape tools in the Toolbox). Up in the Options Bar click on the third icon from the left (so it will create a pixel-based shape), then set the Radius (corner roundness) to 5. Click-and-drag out a horizontal bar like the one shown here.

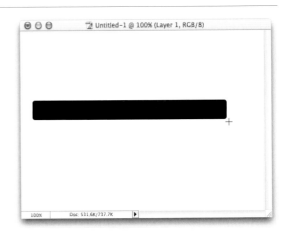

STEP TWO: Press "g" to get the Gradient tool, then click once on the Gradient thumbnail (up in the Options Bar) to bring up the Gradient Editor. Create a gradient like the one shown here (from light gray, to black, to white, then back to black). To change a color—double-click on the Color Stop below the gradient bar. To add a Color Stop, click right below the gradient bar. To make a hard edge between colors, click on the Stop and a little diamond will appear. Drag that diamond close to a Stop for a hard edge.

STEP THREE: Go to the Layers palette and Command-click (PC: Control-click) on your black bar layer to put a selection around it. Then, take the Gradient tool and drag from the bottom of the selection to the top, to fill the bar with your gradient (as shown).

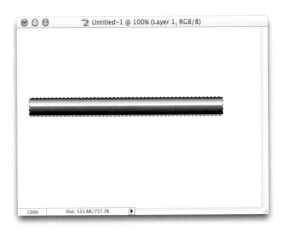

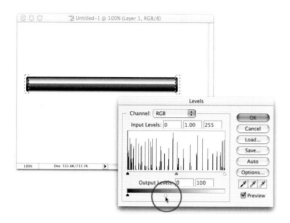

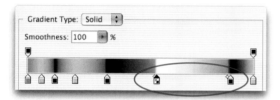

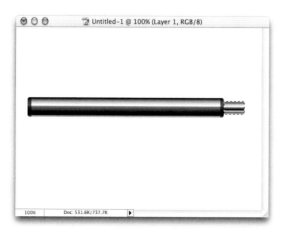

STEP FOUR: Press Command-D (PC: Control-D) to deselect. Press the letter "m" to get the Rectangular Marquee tool and drag out a thin vertical selection around the left end of your shape (like the one shown here). Hold the Shift key, then drag out another selection on the right end, so both ends are selected (as shown). Press Command-L (PC: Control-L) to bring up the Levels dialog. Drag the bottom right Output Levels slider to the left to darken the ends (as shown) and click OK. Press Command-D (PC: Control-D) to deselect.

STEP FIVE: Now for the second gradient. Bring up the Gradient Editor again. Create a gradient that goes from medium gray, to light gray, to a solid black line (the diamonds on both sides are moved right up against the Stop), to light gray, to black (with a close diamond on the left), then to white (you can see the close diamond in the example here), then to black (with another close diamond), and ending with medium gray. This is a great gradient for creating a metallic look.

STEP SIX: Get the Rectangular Marquee tool and draw a small horizontal rectangular selection that butts right up against the right side of your bar (as shown here). Take the gradient tool (using your newly created metal gradient) and drag from the bottom of your selection to its top (as shown). Don't deselect yet.

continued

Quick Tip:
When it comes to EXIF data, less may be more

If you've ever read the EXIF data compiled and embedded in your photos by today's digital cameras, chances are there's about 30 or so pieces of info you just don't care about. Stuff like the amount of "compressed bits per pixel," or whether the EXIF color space was calibrated or uncalibrated. Well, Photoshop CS can set you free by displaying only the EXIF data fields you care about. Just go to the File Browser, and from the Metadata tab's pop-down menu choose Metadata Display Options, and then uncheck every field you just don't care a flip about.

Quick Tip:
Nesting File Browser tabs

In Photoshop CS, you now have some control over the workspace in the File Browser, because it lets you reorder the individual panels. You do this just like you would when you're nesting palettes—just click on the tab you want to move, and drag it up with the other tab you want it to live with. A popular workspace is to move the Metadata and Keywords tabs up with the Folders tab. That way, you can make the Preview pane much, much deeper, providing dramatically larger previews of portrait oriented photos.

STEP SEVEN: Get the Line tool (from the Shape tool flyout), set the Width to 1 pixel in the Options Bar, hold the Shift key, and drag a vertical line right through the right side of your selection (from top to bottom), and then draw another line on the left side of your selection, to create the lines shown here. Now press Command-D (PC: Control-D) to deselect.

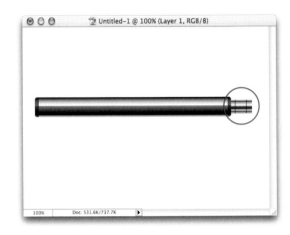

STEP EIGHT: We created this bar bigger than we need it, so press Command-T (PC: Control-T) to bring up Free Transform. Hold the Shift key (to keep things proportional), then grab a corner point and drag diagonally inward to scale the handle down in size (as shown here).

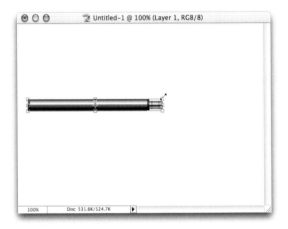

STEP NINE: Create a new blank layer by clicking on the New Layer icon at the bottom of the Layers palette. Then, get the Elliptical Marquee tool, hold the Shift key, and draw a large circular selection (like the one shown here) with the left side of the circle butting up against your handle.

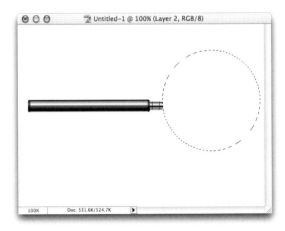

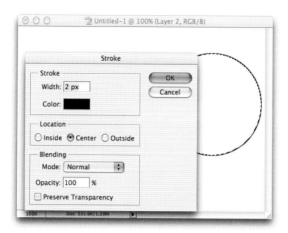

STEP TEN: Go under the Edit menu and choose Stroke. When the Stroke dialog appears, for Width choose 2 pixels, for Location choose Center, and click OK to apply a stroke around your circle (as shown).

STEP ELEVEN: The third (and final) gradient is a breeze: open the Gradient Editor and create a gradient that goes from a very light gray (like 10% black) to a dark gray (like 60% black) as shown here. Next, go up in the Options Bar and choose the Reflected Gradient, the fourth of the five gradient icons to the right of the Gradient thumbnail.

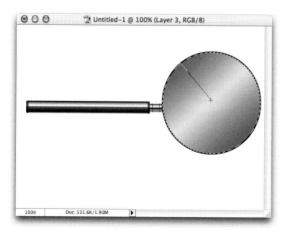

STEP TWELVE: Hold the Command key (PC: Control key) and click on the New Layer icon at the bottom of the Layers palette to create a new blank layer beneath your currently active layer. Next, click in the center of your circular selection, and drag outward to the top-left side of the circle (as shown here) to apply the reflected gradient. Don't deselect yet.

Quick Tip:
Can't remember how to get to Full Screen Mode?

If you don't remember the little keyboard shortcuts (or which icons to click) to get into Full Screen Mode now you don't have to. To get into either Full Screen Mode, Full Screen Mode with Menu Bar, or Standard Screen Mode, just go under the View menu, and under Screen Mode make your choice.

continued

Quick Tip:
Making all your tiled images zoom at once

If you have more than one photo open in Photoshop CS, you can view these side-by-side by going under the Window menu, under Arrange, and choosing Tile. I know, you could do that in Photoshop 7 too, but in CS you can make it so when you zoom in on one photo, they all zoom in the exact same amount, at the same time. Just hold the Shift key as you zoom, and the other documents will follow right along.

STEP THIRTEEN: Next, press "m" to switch back to the Elliptical Marquee tool. Press the Left Arrow key on your keyboard six times to nudge your circular selection over to the left. Then press the Down Arrow key six times to nudge the selection down. Press Delete (PC: Backspace) to knock a hole out of your gradient (as shown here). Don't deselect yet.

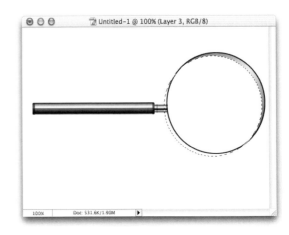

STEP FOURTEEN: Create another new blank layer beneath your current layer by Command-clicking (PC: Control-clicking) on the New Layer icon at the bottom of the Layers palette. Get the Gradient tool again, drag the Reflected Gradient tool from the center of the selected area to the top-left edge of your circle (as shown here).

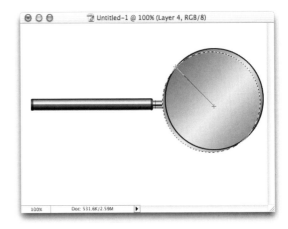

STEP FIFTEEN: Press the Up Arrow key on your keyboard six times then press the Right Arrow key six times to nudge the selection back to where it was before you moved it in Step Thirteen. Press Delete (PC: Backspace) to knock another hole out of your selection. This forms the frame of the magnifying glass. Deselect by pressing Command-D (PC: Control-D).

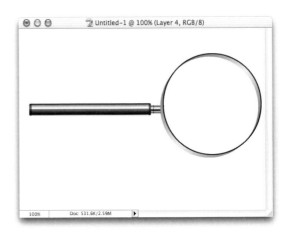

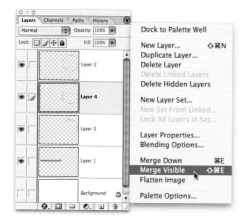

STEP SIXTEEN: Go to the Layers palette and hide the Background layer from view by clicking on the Eye icon in the first column next to it. Then, choose Merge Visible from the palette's pop-down menu to merge all the magnifying glass layers into just one layer. Click where the Eye icon used to be next to the Background layer to make the Background layer visible again.

Quick Tip:
Zooming in the Filter Gallery

The new Filter Gallery has a huge preview window, but you'll probably find yourself constantly enlarging your photo to at least a 100% view (if not closer), which is made a bit tedious by clicking on the plus button at the bottom-left corner, or using the pop-up menu of magnification views. However, if you move your cursor over the Preview area and hold the Command key (PC: Control key), your Hand cursor changes into the Zoom tool, enabling you to zoom right into the area you want. Just hold the Option key (PC: Alt key) and click to zoom back out.

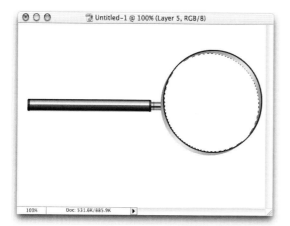

STEP SEVENTEEN: Get the Magic Wand tool from the Toolbox. Click it once within the magnifying glass area to select the circle (as shown). Hold the Command key (PC: Control key) and click to create a new blank layer under your current layer. Press "d" then "x" to make white your Foreground color, then press Option-Delete (PC: Alt-Backspace) to fill this circle with white. Lower the Opacity of this white layer to 20% in the Layers palette.

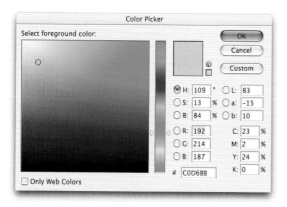

STEP EIGHTEEN: Click on the Foreground Color Swatch (in the Toolbox) and choose a light green (the build shown here is R=192, G=214, B=187). Create a new blank layer by clicking on the New Layer icon at the bottom of the Layers palette.

continued

Quick Tip:
Showing just one effect in the Filter Gallery

One of the advantages of the Filter Gallery is that you can apply multiple applications of any filter, and create numerous filters, all one on top of the other to create some pretty wild effects. However, after you've created a number of effects, you may want to view the effect of just one of the filters in the Filter Gallery. To do that, use the same trick you would to view just one layer in the Layers palette: Option-click (PC: Alt-click) on the Eye icon next to the effect you want to see, and all the other effects will be temporarily hidden from view.

STEP NINETEEN: Press "g" to get the Gradient tool, then press Return (PC: Enter) to make the Gradient Picker appear onscreen. Choose the second gradient (Foreground to Transparent) as shown.

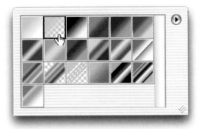

STEP TWENTY: Up in the Options Bar, click on the first gradient button (the Linear gradient), next to the Gradient thumbnail, then click in the center of your circular selection and drag down to the bottom right (as shown here). Press Command-D (PC: Control-D) to deselect.

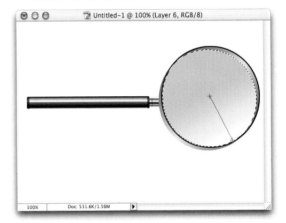

STEP TWENTY-ONE: Get the Elliptical Marquee tool again, and drag out a large oval-shaped selection like the one shown.

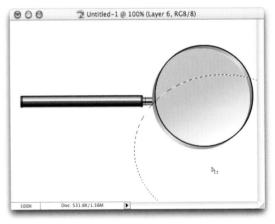

STEP TWENTY-TWO: Go under the Select menu and choose Inverse, to inverse your selection (as shown here), then press Delete (PC: Backspace) to knock a hole out of the top of the glass area, to help create the reflective effect in the glass. Press Command-D (PC: Control-D) to deselect. Lower the Opacity of this layer to 35%.

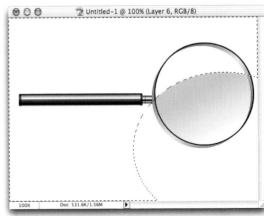

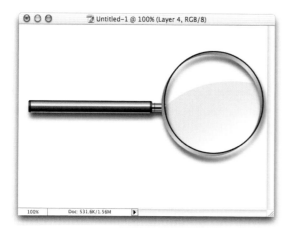

STEP TWENTY-THREE: Click on the magnifying glass layer in the Layers palette to make it active. Choose Drop Shadow from the Add a Layer Style pop-up menu at the bottom of the Layers palette. When the dialog appears, increase both the Size and Distance to 10, then click OK to apply a soft drop shadow to your magnifying glass (as shown here). Now, hide the Background layer, and choose Merge Visible from the palette's pop-down menu, to merge the magnifying glass and the reflections into just one layer.

STEP TWENTY-FOUR: Get the Move tool and drag your magnifying glass into a document that has some large type. (In the example shown here, I dragged it over an ad layout that's similar to the layout of the Xerox ad. The type at the top is in Optima Bold.) Press Command-T (PC: Control-T) to bring up Free Transform, then move your cursor outside the bounding box, and click-and-drag upward to rotate the magnifying glass into position over your type. Press Return (PC: Enter) to lock in your transformation.

STEP TWENTY-FIVE: Get the Elliptical Marquee tool and make a circular selection inside the glass area (as shown here). If you have trouble positioning the circular selection, hold the Spacebar after you start dragging out your selection—this enables you to readjust the position of your selection as you drag it out. Pretty handy.

Quick Tip:
Setting defaults in the Filter Gallery

If you want to have your own custom Defaults for the Filter Gallery, all you have to do is set up the Filters you want, with the settings you want, then hold the Command key (PC: Control key) and you'll notice that the Cancel button changes to the Default button. Click that button, and those settings will now become your defaults.

continued

Quick Tip:
Reordering filters in the Filter Gallery

The order in which you stack filters in the Filter Gallery greatly effects how they look, so changing their stacking order is a great tool for experimentation. To do so, you do it just like you would a layer—click on the effect, and drag it upward or downward in the list of filters on the bottom right side of the dialog.

STEP TWENTY-SIX: Go to the Layers palette and click on your Type layer. In the next step, you'll need to apply a filter to your type, so first you'll have to convert your Type layer into a regular image layer. To do that, Control-click (PC: Right-click) on the Type layer, and choose Rasterize Layer (as shown) from the pop-up menu.

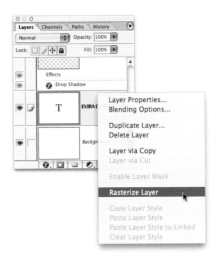

STEP TWENTY-SEVEN: To make the area under your magnifying glass look larger, go under the Filter menu, under Distort, and choose Spherize. This filter applies a spherical effect to your selected area (as shown in the filter's preview). When the Spherize dialog appears, lower the Amount to 75%.

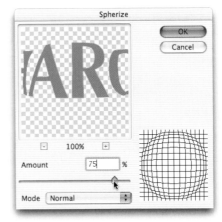

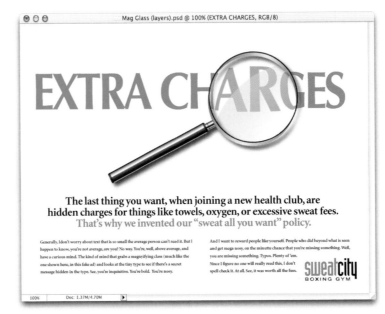

STEP TWENTY-EIGHT: Click OK and it's done! Better yet, you drew it yourself, and you've got two butt-kicking metallic gradients you can save for other projects.

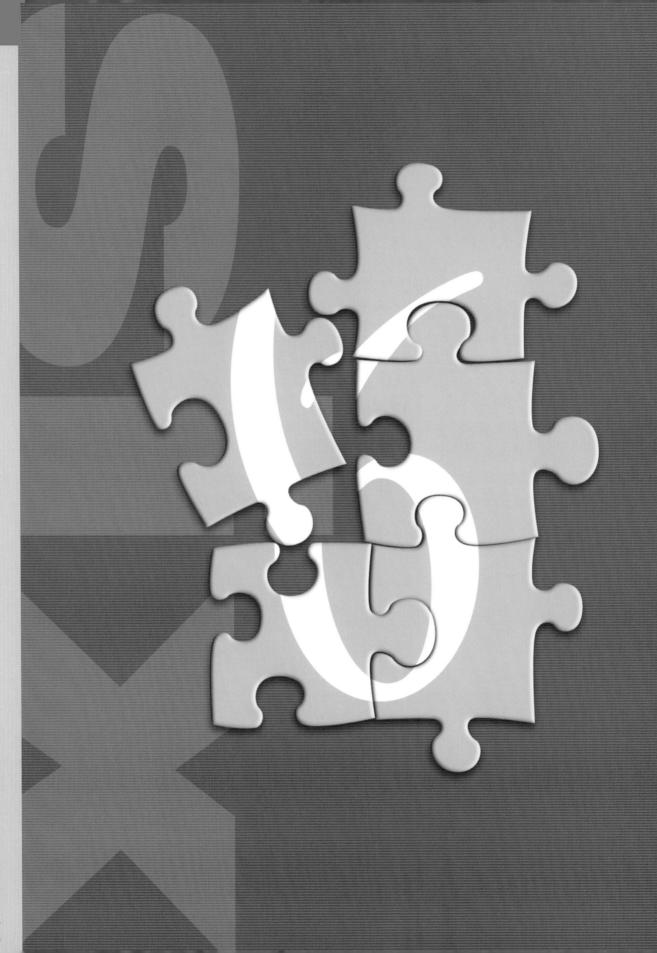

This is where it all pays off. These are the effects that you can use when it's time to present your work to the client.

Show Me the Money
Portfolio Effects

Whether it's in a Web portfolio, in a printed book, a brochure, or a flyer, this is where you go to add your finishing touches. This is where you learn how to add those little extras that make you and your work stand out from the crowd. This is where your "click-click" turns into "bling-bling!" Where your "tap-tap" turns into "cha-ching" Where your "pipp-pipp" turns into your "ace-duce." OK, I should've stopped with "bling-bling." These are the kinds of effects that can transform you from a scrappy kid in the streets, struggling along with some off-brand 3-megapixel point-and-shoot, and turn you into a real playa, poppin' Cristal corks at one of P-Diddy's parties, and cranking off shots with your Nikon D2H. That is, provided you actually are a scrappy kid in the streets. If you're not, and instead you're a middle-aged wedding photographer from Grand Rapids, I don't think you'll make it past the bouncers where P-Diddy hangs. But it's certainly worth a try. It's all gravy.

Quick Tip:
**Saving your own
custom new
document sizes**

When you choose to create
a new document, Photo-
shop provides you with
a pop-up list of common
document sizes in the
New dialog. Of course, the
size you really want, the
one you use all the time,
doesn't appear in that
list. Why? Because that's
the way life works. Adobe
knew that, and that's why
in Photoshop CS you can
now create and save your
own custom sizes (includ-
ing saving your favorite
color mode, resolution, and
Background color). Just
enter your desired new
document specs in the New
dialog box, then click the
Save Preset button right
under the Cancel button.
Do that, and from now on
your custom new docu-
ment size will appear at the
top of the list. (Note: You're
not limited to just one
custom new doc size—add
a bunch. Live a little.)

Filmstrip Templates

Photographers use this technique for a host of reasons: displaying client photos
(especially modeling shots), high school senior portraits, travel shots, and
shots used in online portfolios. One great thing about it is—once you've created
one, you can save it as a template and apply it to any photo in seconds.
Here's how it's done:

STEP ONE: Open a new document
in RGB mode at a resolution of
300 ppi. Click on the New Layer
icon at the bottom of the Layers
palette to create a new blank layer.
Press "d" to set your Foreground
color to black. Get the rectangular
Marquee tool and drag a large
rectangular selection. Fill it with
black by pressing Option-Delete
(PC: Alt-Backspace), then deselect
by pressing Command-D (PC:
Control-D). Next, inside your black
rectangle, draw a smaller selection
(like the one shown here).

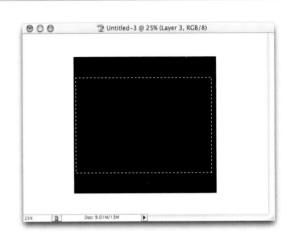

STEP TWO: You're going to
need this smaller rectangular
selection later in this project,
so save it by going under the
Select menu and choosing Save
Selection. When the dialog box
appears, just click OK. Now,
press Delete (PC: Backspace) to
knock the smaller rectangular
selection out of the larger black
rectangle (as shown here).

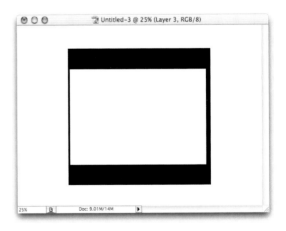

STEP THREE: Deselect by pressing Command-D (PC: Control-
D). Next, go to the Toolbox and
get the Rounded Rectangle
tool (shown here). Press the
letter "x" to set white as your
Foreground color. Next, go to
the Layers palette and create a
new blank layer.

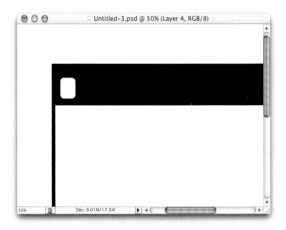

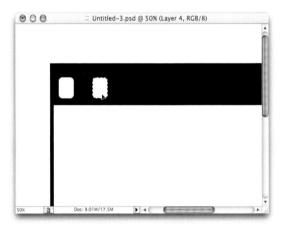

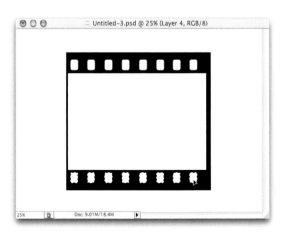

STEP FOUR: You'll need to zoom in close for this step, so press Option-Command-+ (PC: Alt-Control-+) to zoom in without changing your window size. Now, up in the Options Bar, click on the third icon from the left for creating pixel-based shapes, then for Radius Amount enter 15 (the higher the number, the rounder the corners). On this new layer, draw a small rounded corner shape in the top black border area (as shown here).

STEP FIVE: Once you've got your first shape drawn, press the letter "v" to switch to the Move tool, then go to the Layers palette and Command-click (PC: Control-click) on this layer to put a selection around your shape. Now, hold Shift-Option (PC: Shift-Alt) and drag to the right to create a duplicate of your shape (the Shift key keeps your dragged copy perfectly aligned). Continue dragging copies until you have a whole row across the top, then press Command-D (PC: Control-D) to deselect.

STEP SIX: Go back to the Layers palette and Command-click (PC: Control-click) on this "row of rounded rectangles" layer to select all of the rectangles. Hold Shift-Option (PC: Shift-Alt) but this time, drag straight down to the bottom border (as shown) to duplicate this row of rectangles at the bottom, and then deselect.

Quick Tip:
Zooming in without changing window size

In Step Four of the technique shown here, I give you the keyboard shortcut for zooming in your image without resizing your document window in the process. However, this is a workaround, because by default every time you zoom in, your window size increases, and when you zoom out, it shrinks. But believe it or not, you can change that default. That's right, you can set it so every time you zoom in or out, the windows stays the same size.

It's not really a preference setting, it's more of an option. To toggle this window zoom option on/off, click on the Zoom tool in the Toolbox, then up in the Options Bar, turn off "Resize Windows to Fit." Once you do that, your window will stay put, but your image will zoom in and out as you command it to ("Command it to." Ya like that? I thought you might.)

continued

Quick Tip:
How to hit those tiny checkboxes

If there's a program with more impossibly small checkboxes to click than Photoshop, I'd like to see it (actually, I don't care to see it, but…). Anyway, here's the good news: You don't have to be so precise, because in most cases you can toggle on/off checkboxes by just clicking on the word beside the checkbox, rather than on the checkbox itself. Give it a try—click on a tool like the Move tool (for example) and then head on up to the Options Bar, but instead of clicking on the checkbox for Auto Select Layer, just click on the words "Auto Select Layer" and you'll see the checkbox toggle on (unless of course, it was already turned on, in which case it will toggle off).

STEP SEVEN: After you de-select, go back to the Layers palette and Command-click (PC: Control-click) on the layer to put a selection around all the white rounded rectangles (as shown). Once the selection appears around all of them, you can drag this layer into the Trash to delete it (you don't need it anymore). In the Layers palette, click on the black rectangle layer (your selection should still be in place) and press Delete (PC: Backspace) to knock that selection out of your black rectangle.

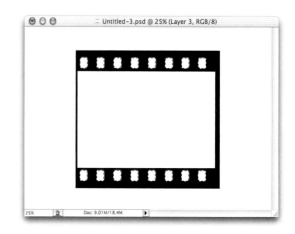

STEP EIGHT: Choose Drop Shadow from the Add a Layer Style pop-up menu at the bottom of the Layers palette. In the Structure selection (shown here) increase the Distance to 21 and the Size to 25, then click OK to apply a drop shadow to your black rectangle layer (we'll now refer to this as our filmstrip layer).

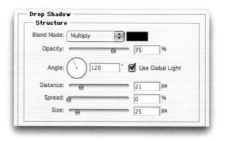

STEP NINE: Click the Foreground Color swatch in the Toolbox, and when the Color Picker appears, choose an olive color (I used R=141, G=162, and B=68, as shown here), and then click OK.

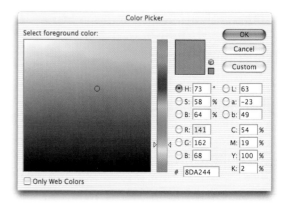

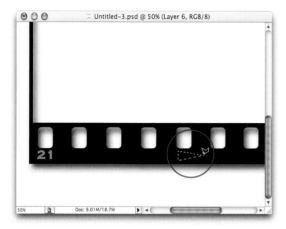

STEP TEN: Now zoom in to the lower left-hand corner, press the letter "t" to get the Type tool, and type the number "21" (as if this was the 21st frame on the roll). I used Adobe's font Copperplate Gothic Bold in the example shown here. Now, create a new blank layer, then get the Polygonal Lasso tool from the Toolbox, and use it to draw a long thin triangle like the one shown. To use the Polygonal Lasso tool, click once and drag out a straight line. Click again where you want to change directions. Then, either click back where you started or double-click to close the selection.

STEP ELEVEN: Go under the Edit menu and choose Stroke. When the Stroke dialog appears, for Width choose 3 pixels and click OK to stroke your triangular selection with the olive green color that you chose in Step Nine (as shown). Deselect by pressing Command-D (PC: Control-D).

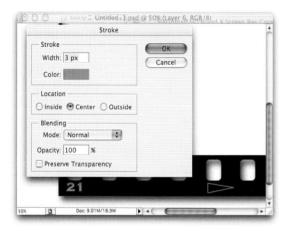

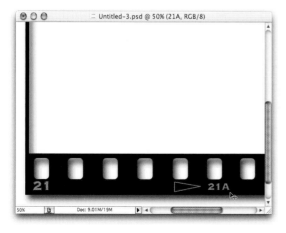

STEP TWELVE: Now switch back to the Type tool and type "21A" to the right of your triangle. We're adding this type, and the triangle to help the filmstrip look more realistic.

Quick Tip:
Getting a perfectly circular path to wrap type around

If you're trying to put type on a perfect circle, don't use the Pen tool (that takes way too much effort). Instead, choose the Ellipse tool (it's one of the Shape tools found directly below the Type tool in the Toolbox). Once you have the tool, go up to the Options Bar and click on the center icon of the three icons on the left. This creates a path, rather than a filled region. Then hold the Shift key, click, and drag yourself out a circular path.

continued

Quick Tip:
Better patching

If you ever wanted a reason to switch from the Healing Brush to the Patch tool as your favorite retouching tool, Photoshop CS gives you a pretty good reason—now you get live previews of your patchwork. Here's how it works: Let's say you want to patch over a mole on someone's face. Get the Patch tool, and draw a selection around the mole. Click inside the Lasso-like selection created by the Patch tool and drag that selection to a clean area of the person's face. As you do, the original area still has a selection around it and it gives you live feedback as to how the retouch will look as you drag across different areas of the person's face. It makes getting a perfect retouch dramatically easier. How cool is that? Seriously, that rocks!

STEP THIRTEEN: Open the photo that you want to appear within your filmstrip. Switch to the Move tool by pressing the letter "v."

STEP FOURTEEN: Drag this photo directly into your filmstrip document. In the Layers palette, drag it down in the stack until the photo appears directly below your filmstrip layer. If you need to resize the photo, press Command-T (PC: Control-T) to bring up Free Transform, hold the Shift key, grab any corner point, and resize the photo to fit within the opening (as shown).

STEP FIFTEEN: Remember that selection we saved back in step two? Well, Bunky, now you need it. Press Option-Command-4 (PC: Alt-Control-4) to reload that saved selection of the smaller rectangle (as shown here).

STEP SIXTEEN: Now you need to remove the excess areas of the photo that extend outside the center rectangle. To do that, press Shift-Command-I (PC: Shift-Control-I) to select everything on this layer *but* the photo in the center (in other words, all the excess is selected), and press Delete (PC: Backspace) to erase those areas. Now you can deselect. Save this file now (it's your template).

STEP SEVENTEEN: In the Layers palette, you'll need to link all your layers together, so click once in the second column of the filmstrip layer, each Type layer, the triangle layer, and your photo layer to link them together. Now press Command-T (PC: Control-T) to bring up Free Transform. Move your cursor outside the bounding box, and click-and-drag upward to rotate your film strip (as shown).

STEP EIGHTEEN: Press Return (PC: Enter) to lock in your rotation and complete the effect. Note: Remember how you saved the file back at Step Sixteen, before the rotation? You did that because it can now act as a template. To use this effect again on a different photo, just choose Revert from the File menu, trash the photo layer, open a different photo, drag it in, crop away the excess, link the layers, rotate, and you're done!

Creating Gallery Prints

This is a really slick technique for turning a regular photograph into what looks like a gallery print. In the project shown here, you'll start by transforming a color photograph into an Ansel Adams-like black-and-white photo but we're only doing that because the photo is a mountainous landscape. You can use a regular less "contrasty" conversion to grayscale for other photos you'll apply this effect to.

STEP ONE: Open the photo you want to turn into a gallery print.

STEP TWO: Duplicate the Background layer by pressing Command-J (PC: Control-J). It's this duplicate that we'll convert into a black-and-white image. Rather than just choosing Grayscale from the Image>Mode menu, choose Channel Mixer from the Adjustment Layer pop-up menu at the bottom of the Layers palette (as shown here).

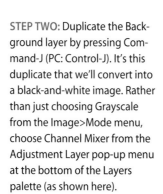
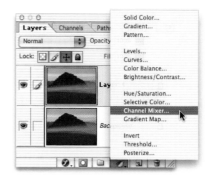

STEP THREE: When the Channel Mixer appears, click on the Monochrome checkbox at the bottom of the dialog, and you'll see your photo turn black-and-white. We're going for that Ansel Adams effect, so drag the Red slider over to +200. Lower the Green to -30, and increase the Blue to +20.

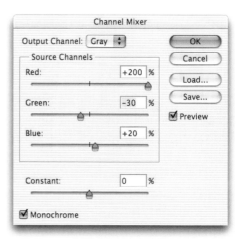

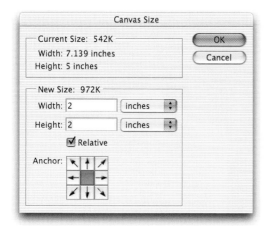

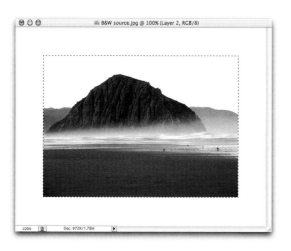

STEP FOUR: When you click OK you'll have a very "contrasty" black-and-white image. Now, merge the Channel Mixer Adjustment Layer permanently with your duplicate layer by pressing Command-E (PC: Control-E).

STEP FIVE: Now you'll need to add some white space around your photo, so go under the Image menu and choose Canvas Size. In the Canvas Size dialog box, check the Relative checkbox, then add 2 inches of Width and 2 inches of Height (as shown).

STEP SIX: When you click OK, the 2 inches of white space is added around your photo (as you can see in the capture shown here). Now you need to get a selection around your photo. Hold the Command key (PC: Control key), go to the Layers palette, and click on the black-and-white layer, which puts a selection around your photo (as shown). Next, create a new blank layer by clicking on the New Layer icon at the bottom of the Layers palette.

Quick Tip:
Setting your tracking back to 0 (its default)

The tracking control (in the Character palette) controls the amount of space between your letters. A negative setting moves your letters closer together; a positive number moves them farther apart. If you're like me, you're constantly tweaking this spacing, and if you're like me, you'll be as happy as I was when I learned that you can reset the tracking to zero for your selected type by simply pressing Shift-Command-0 [zero] (PC: Shift-Control-q) [the letter q]). The only catch is—your type has to be highlighted (which frankly is weird because you can increase or decrease the amount of tracking any time the Type layer is active in the Layers palette, but unless the type is highlighted, that keyboard shortcut doesn't work. See, it is weird isn't it?).

continued

Quick Tip:
Getting your last settings back

If you're working on a project in Photoshop and you apply Levels, Curves, etc., and click OK, when you open the dialog box again, you start back at square one. For example, if you apply a custom curve, click OK, and go back to the Curves dialog box, all you'll find is the default straight curve. However, there's a trick for bringing back the last settings you used in a dialog—just add the Option key (PC: Alt key) when you press the keyboard shortcut. For example, to bring up Curves with the last curve setting you applied, press Option-Command-M (PC: Alt-Control-M) instead of just pressing Command-M (PC: Control-M), the regular keyboard shortcut.

STEP SEVEN: Now you're going to put a very thin stroke around your photo to create a subtle border. Go under the Edit menu and choose Stroke. When the Stroke dialog appears, for Width enter 1, for Color click on the Swatch and choose a light gray in the Color Picker (as shown), and for Location choose Center.

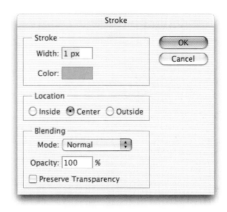

STEP EIGHT: Click OK and the thin gray stroke is applied around your photo (don't deselect yet). Since you applied this stroke on its own layer, if the stroke seems too bold, or calls too much attention to itself, you can simply lower the Opacity of the layer in the Layers palette until it looks right to you.

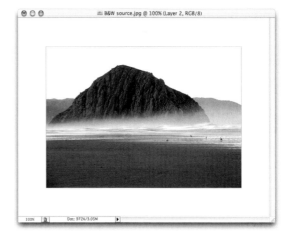

STEP NINE: Your selection should still be in place, so go under the Select menu and choose Transform Selection (as shown). We'll use Transform Selection to expand our selection outward without rounding its corners.

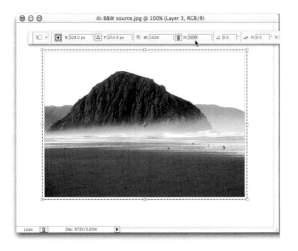

STEP TEN: To expand your selection, go up to the Options Bar and enter 102% for the W(idth), and 103% for the H(eight) as shown, then press Return (PC: Enter) to lock in your transformed selection. With your expanded selection in place, create a new layer, then go under the Edit menu and choose Stroke. Leave the Width at 1 pixel, but change your stroke Color to black by clicking on the gray Color Swatch and choosing black in the Color Picker.

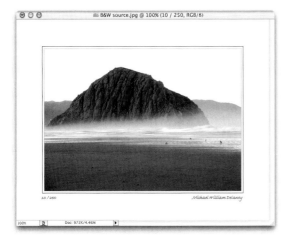

STEP ELEVEN: Click OK to stroke this outer border with a thin black stroke (as shown), and deselect. Now you'll use the Type tool to sign the print (if you indeed shot the shot, of course) using a font that looks like handwriting (I used ITC Bradley Hand), and position it under the right bottom border. Under the left corner, I used the same font to give that "numbered print" look.

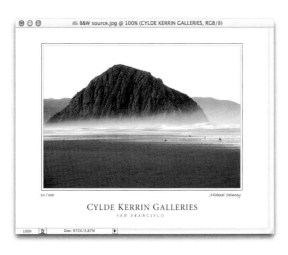

STEP TWELVE: Lastly, I added the name of a fictitious gallery, using the font Minion (from Adobe) in all caps at 24 point size. However, once I added the type, I left the first letter of each word of the gallery name at 24 points, but I highlighted the rest of the letters and lowered their size to 21 points in the Options Bar, to give a "small caps" feel. The words "San Francisco" are in Minion Italic, with the Tracking set at 400 in the Character palette.

Quick Tip:
High-powered chiseling

Photoshop allows you to create a hard-edged chisel effect via the Bevel and Emboss Layer Style by changing the Technique to Chisel Hard.

Another way to create a hard-edged chisel effect is to use Alien Skin's Bevel Boss plug-in from their Eye Candy 4000 collection of Photoshop plug-in filters. For more information on their way-crazy, cool plug-ins, visit them at www.alienskin.com.

Photo Mount Effect

Here's a handy technique for adding visual interest by adding photo mounts to your corners. This is popular with wedding and travel photographers and photo retouchers. What's nice about this is that once you've created one set of mounts, you can save the layered file and use them again and again. Plus, at the end of the effect, there's a pretty cool background texture you create from scratch.

STEP ONE: Open a new document in RGB mode. Create a new blank layer by clicking on the New Layer icon at the bottom of the Layers palette. Press the letter "m" to get the Rectangular Marquee tool, hold the Shift key, and draw a square selection in the middle of your image area (as shown). Press "d" to set your Foreground color to black then fill your square with black by pressing Option-Delete (PC: Alt-Backspace).

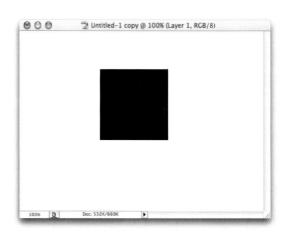

STEP TWO: Deselect by pressing Command-D (PC: Control-D). Get the Polygonal Lasso tool, and draw a straight line diagonally through the center of your square, then draw straight lines like the ones shown here until you get back where you started to select the top left half of the black square. Press Delete (PC: Backspace) to remove that area of the square. Press Command-D (PC: Control-D) to deselect.

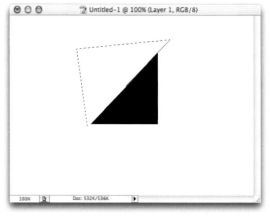

STEP THREE: Switch to the Rectangular Marquee tool, hold the Shift key, and drag out a small square selection (like the one shown here). With the Rectangular Marquee tool, click-and-drag inside the selection, and drag it to overlap a small section of the black triangle, as shown here.

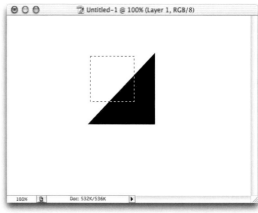

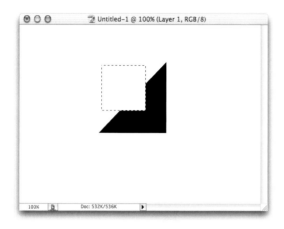

STEP FOUR: Press Delete (PC: Backspace) to knock a little triangular chunk out of your black triangle (as shown here). Deselect by pressing Command-D (PC: Control-D).

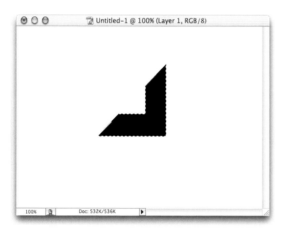

STEP FIVE: Next you'll need a selection around your entire shape, so hold the Command key (PC: Control key), go to the Layers palette, and click on your layer. This puts a selection around your entire shape (as shown here). In the next step you're going to shrink your selection.

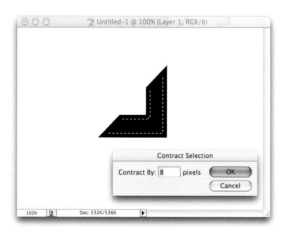

STEP SIX: Go under the Select menu, under Modify, and choose Contract. When the Contract Selection dialog appears, enter 8, then click OK to shrink your selection inward by 8 pixels (as shown). Create a new blank layer by clicking on the New Layer icon at the bottom of the Layers palette. Fill your selection with black by pressing Option-Delete (PC: Alt-Backspace). Now you can deselect by pressing Command-D (PC Control-D).

Quick Tip:
How to find the Chrome gradient

When you select the Gradient tool, the Options Bar immediately displays the Gradient tool options. If you click on the down-facing triangle immediately to the right of the Gradient thumbnail of your currently selected gradient, a flyout Gradient Picker will appear with all the gradient presets you have loaded. Now, how do you know which one is the Chrome gradient? Well, if you have the Tool Tips preference turned on (it's on by default), just hold your cursor over any gradient swatch and its name will appear. If you've turned off Tool Tips (frankly, they drive me crazy, except for finding gradients), then you can choose to view your gradients by name rather than by thumbnails. You do that by clicking on the right-facing triangle in the Gradient Picker to display a pop-up menu where you can choose Text Only to display the gradients by name. This makes finding the Chrome gradient a snap.

continued

Quick Tip :

Creating
another
document
with the same
exact specs as
your current
document

If you do much collaging
of images, this tip will save
you boatloads of time
(meaning a cargo bay of
cheap watches). To create
a new document with the
same size, resolution, and
color mode as your current
document, go under the
File menu and choose New.
While the New dialog box
is onscreen, go under the
Window menu, and there
you'll see a list of all your
currently open documents
at the bottom. Choose the
one you want, and Pho-
toshop will automatically
load its size, resolution, and
color mode into your New
dialog box. All you have to
do is click OK.

STEP SEVEN: Choose Bevel and
Emboss from the Add a Layer
Style pop-up menu at the bottom of the Layers palette. When
the dialog appears, for Style
choose Pillow Emboss. Decrease
the Size to 3, and increase the
Soften amount to 5.

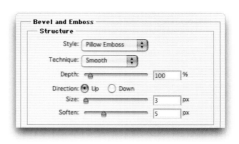

STEP EIGHT: When you click OK,
it adds some soft highlights
and shadows inside your
contracted shape, which helps
make the smaller shape appear
embedded into the larger shape
(as shown here).

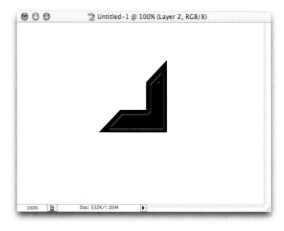

STEP NINE: In the Layers
palette, click on the larger black
shape layer (Layer 1), then
choose Bevel and Emboss from
the Add a Layer Style pop-up
menu at the bottom of the Layers palette. Decrease the Size
setting to 3, but increase the
Soften amount to 7.

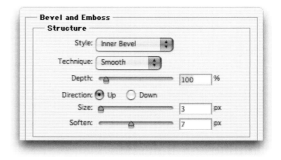

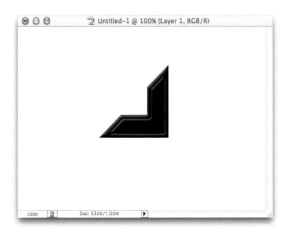

STEP TEN: When you click OK, it applies a soft bevel to the larger of your shapes (as shown here).

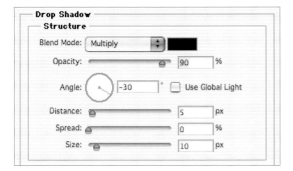

STEP ELEVEN: Choose Drop Shadow from the Add a Layer Style pop-up menu at the bottom of the Layers palette. When the Drop Shadow dialog appears (shown in the inset) increase the Opacity to 90%, turn off Use Global Light, set your Angle to -30°, and increase your Size to 10.

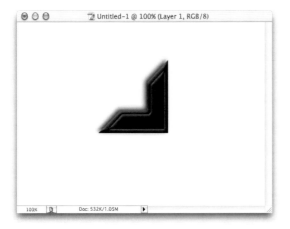

STEP TWELVE: Click OK to apply this drop shadow to your photo frame corner. In the following steps, we'll add this mount to the four corners of a photograph.

Quick Tip:
The advantage of Adjustment Layers

In many projects shown in this book, we use Adjustment Layers and I have to tell you that Adjustment Layers freak people out. They shouldn't, but they do. However, if you know a little history about them, they're not only easier to understand but it may also encourage you to use them as well.

Adjustment Layers were introduced back in Photoshop 4.0 (which was 14 years before Ben Franklin discovered electricity), and back then Photoshop didn't have multiple undos like we do today. So, Adobe came up with Adjustment Layers as a way to give users an "undo" for tonal adjustments such as Curves, Levels, Color Balance, etc. When you applied one of these, they appeared in your Layers palette as an Adjustment Layer. This was great because, if after working on a file for several hours you suddenly decided that you wanted to undo that tonal adjustment you made hours earlier, you could just drag that layer into the Trash and it would undo. Better yet, you could save Adjustment Layers with your file for undos at a later date.

continued

Quick Tip:
Using big effects at small sizes

In a number of places in this book I mention that you need to create the effect at a large size. For example, if it's a Type effect, I might tell you to create the effect at 200- or 300-point size so the effect looks right. But don't let that tie your hands if you need to use that big effect at a small size—just create it at the larger size, then use either the Image Size command or Free Transform to scale it down to the size you really need later. The effect will usually hold when scaled down but if you start at that smaller size, oftentimes the effect won't look right, so you're better off to start off big, and shrink it down later. This is a very common technique with pro Web designers.

STEP THIRTEEN: Open the photo you want to apply the effect to. Then, open a new larger blank document (in RGB mode) and use the Move tool to drag your photo onto this new document. Your photo will show up on its own separate layer. Use the Move tool to center your photo within the image area (as shown here).

STEP FOURTEEN: Now you're going to add a border around your photo. Choose Stroke from the Add a Layer Style pop-up menu at the bottom of the Layers palette. In the Stroke dialog, increase the Size to 11, choose Inside for Position, and then click on the Color Swatch and choose a very light gray color in the Color Picker. When you click OK, it puts a Polaroid-like border around your photo (which can be seen in the capture in the following step).

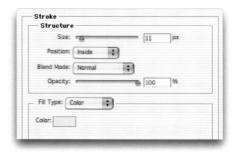

STEP FIFTEEN: Now go back to your photo frame document. Merge your two layers together by clicking on the top layer in the Layers palette and pressing Command-E (PC: Control-E). Get the Move tool, click on the photo frame corner, and drag-and-drop it onto your photo document (as shown here). It'll probably be too big, so in the next step you'll scale it down to size.

STEP SIXTEEN: Press Command-T (PC: Control-T) to bring up Free Transform. Hold the Shift key, grab a corner point, and drag inward to scale the photo corner down to size. When the size looks right, move your cursor within the bounding box, and click-and-drag it into position at the bottom-right corner (as shown here). Press Return (PC: Enter) to lock in your transformation.

STEP SEVENTEEN: Duplicate your photo frame corner by pressing Command-J (PC: Control-J). Press Command-T (PC: Control-T) to bring up Free Transform. Control-click (PC: Right-click) within the bounding box and choose Flip Horizontal from the pop-up menu to flip your duplicate layer (this will become your left side corner).

STEP EIGHTEEN: Click-and-drag in the bounding box to position the left corner piece (as shown), and press Return (PC: Enter). Then, repeat the process for the top two corners: duplicate the layer, bring up Free Transform (but this time choose Rotate 90° CW), and position it in the upper left-hand corner. Then duplicate that corner, bring up Free Transform, and this time choose Flip Horizontal, and position in the top right-hand corner as shown.

continued

Quick Tip:
How to see feathering before you apply it

One downside of the feathering feature is that you can't see how much you're really feathering: it's pretty much a guess because there's no preview. Here's a cool trick that many people use to see a feathered edge effect before they apply it: First, make a selection (inside the edges of your image) and then press the letter "q" to enter Quick Mask Mode (your selection will be surrounded by red by default). Go under the Filter menu, under Blur, and choose Gaussian Blur. When you apply the blur, you'll see the edges become very soft. When the softness of the edges looks right, click OK and press the letter "q" again to return to Standard Mode to make your selection active. The selection is now feathered the amount that you visually selected using Gaussian Blur. To see the feather in action, go under the Select menu and choose Inverse to choose the background edges, rather than the inside of your selection, and press Delete (PC: Backspace). The area that remains should be feathered at the exact amount you saw in the Quick Mask preview.

Quick Tip:
**Opening
multiple images
at once**

If you're going to open
more than one image from
the same folder, Photoshop
will allow you to open them
all at the same time (rather
than choosing one, open-
ing it, and then choosing
another, etc.). While in the
Open dialog box, click on
the first image you want
to open, then hold the
Command key (PC: Control
key), and click on any
other images you want to
open. When you click OK,
Photoshop will open all the
selected images.

STEP NINETEEN: Now you're
going to add a background
texture. In the Layers palette,
click on the Background layer
and then press Command-J
(PC: Control-J) to duplicate it.
Choose Pattern Overlay from
the Add a Layer Style pop-up
menu at the bottom of the
Layers palette. When the dialog
appears, click on the down-facing arrow next to the Pattern
thumbnail to bring up the Pattern Picker. In the Picker's pop-
down menu, choose Texture
Fill to load that set of texture
patterns.

STEP TWENTY: From the pop-
up menu in the Picker, choose
Small List so you can see the
patterns by name. Choose
the pattern named Noise (as
shown), then lower the Opacity
amount to 29% and click OK to
apply this texture to the Background copy layer. Now press
Command-L (PC: Control-L) to
bring up Levels. In the Levels
dialog box, grab the bottom-
right Output Levels slider
and drag it to the left at bit to
darken the pattern and make it
look a bit like marble.

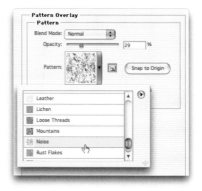

STEP TWENTY-ONE: Click OK in
the Levels dialog and the effect
is complete (as shown here).

Quick Slide Mounts

About three years ago, I did a tutorial here in the *Down & Dirty Tricks* book on how to make your own digital slide mounts. The end result looked authentic, but getting there was pretty brutal, because creating rounded corners for your slide took a series of channels, blurs, Levels adjustments, and a host of other "pain-in-the-butt" steps. The tutorial took four full pages, and 10 to 15 minutes. Now it's down to three pages and 60 seconds—thanks to new features in Photoshop—and that's good because displaying your photos in slide mounts (for online portfolios, wedding shots, ads, etc.) is becoming popular once again.

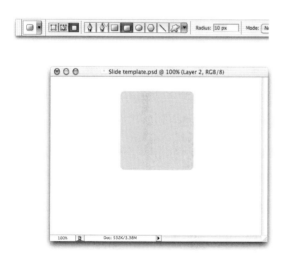

STEP ONE: Create a New document in RGB mode at whatever size and resolution you'd like. Click on the New Layer icon at the bottom of the Layers palette to create a new blank layer. Click on your Foreground Color Swatch and choose a gray (I used R=212, G=212, B=212), then choose the Rounded Rectangle tool from the Toolbox (as shown). Up in the Options Bar, click on the third icon from the left (as shown below right). This lets you draw round-cornered objects that are made up of pixels (rather than paths or Shape Layers).

STEP TWO: While you're up in the Options Bar, change the Radius setting to 10 for low-res 72 ppi images (or 40 for 300-ppi, high-res images). The Radius determines how round your corners will be. A setting of 10 is fairly low (so is 40 for high-res images), so there will only be a slight rounding of the corners, and that's what we want. Now that your Radius is set, click-and-drag out a tall rounded rectangle (as shown).

Quick Tip:
Find the right histogram by its color

In Photoshop CS's new Histogram palette, you can either view one histogram or you can view the histograms for all the channels at the same time, but they're all black. When it comes to making quick adjustments, nothing beats seeing your channels in color. To view the individual channels in their colors (red, green, and blue respectively) go to the Histogram palette's pop-down menu and choose All Channels View (to view the histograms for all the channels), then choose Show Channels in Color.

continued

Quick Tip:
Swapping sizes in measurement fields

Adobe added a very handy new button in many of the fields where you can enter a Height and Width setting (like the Crop tool options, or Marquee tool options) which lets you swap the Width and Height figures in just one click (for example, you could switch from cropping as a 5"x7" to a 7"x5" in one click). Once your measurements are entered in the appropriate fields, just click the "Swap" button which appears between the two fields, and the figures are swapped.

STEP THREE: Switch to the regular Rectangular Marquee tool and create a horizontal selection within the gray round-cornered rectangle (as shown here). Once your selection is in place, just press Delete (PC: Backspace) to knock a hole out of your slide, which creates the basic shape (as shown). Now deselect by pressing Command-D (PC: Control-D).

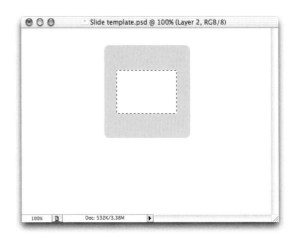

STEP FOUR: Choose Drop Shadow from the Add a Layer Style pop-up menu at the bottom of the Layers palette. When the Drop Shadow dialog appears, lower the Distance amount to 1 (for high-res, 300-ppi images, leave the Distance setting at the default setting of 5, but increase the Size setting to 20). Click OK to apply the shadow. You'll notice that the shadow not only appears on the outside edges, but also on the inside edges where the knocked out area is. This shadow will cast onto the photo you place on the layer beneath the slide, and will help make the photo look like it's inside the mount itself (even though the shadow effect is a bit exaggerated).

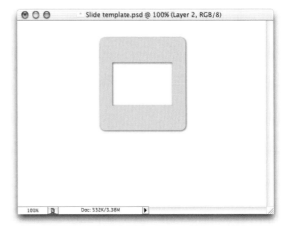

STEP FIVE: To finish off your slide template we'll add some text for added realism (I call it a template, because once you've built this one slide, you can use it as a template to create as many as you'd like). Add

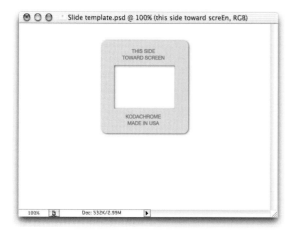

the type (as shown here) in black using the font Helvetica (or Arial) in all caps. Once the type has been added, lower the Opacity setting for your type layer to 50% to help it blend in. Then, click on the Eye icon next to the Background layer to hide it and choose Merge Visible from the Layers palette's pop-down menu. This leaves you with one single layer with the completed slide on it. Now you can make the Background layer visible again.

STEP SIX: The last step is the fun part: pick a photo you want to appear within your slide, and use the Move tool to drag it into your slide template. In the Layers palette, position the photo layer just below your slide layer (as shown here). To get your photo small enough to fit inside the slide window, press Command-T (PC: Control-T) to bring up Free Transform. Hold the Shift key, grab a corner point, and drag inward to shrink it until it's just slightly larger than the opening. Press Return (PC: Enter) to lock in your resize. Merge the two together by clicking on the slide mount layer, then pressing Command-E (PC: Control-E). Now you can drag your completed slide into a new document, then go back to your template, undo the merged layers, trash the photo layer, and repeat this step using different photos. In the final piece (shown here) I made four slides, and rotated each in a different direction.

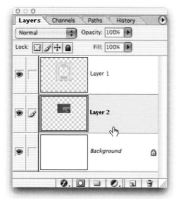

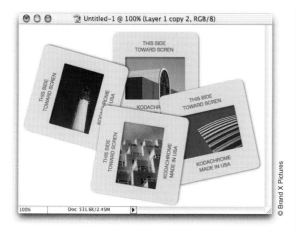

© Brand X Pictures

DVD Packaging

In Chapter 4 of this book, I showed you how to create a DVD disc and then showed how to make
it look as if the disc was protruding from a 3D DVD package because right now, that's what everybody
seems to be doing to make it clear that the package contains a DVD, not a VHS tape. In the effect here,
I show you how to take a flat photo and create the 3D DVD package that we used in the earlier project.

STEP ONE: Open a new document in RGB mode, and make it
fairly wide (like the one shown
here) because you're going
to need some working space.
Open the photo you want to
use as the cover of your DVD,
press the letter "v" to get the
Move tool, and drag it into your
blank working document. Use
the Move tool to position it on
the right side of your window
(as shown).

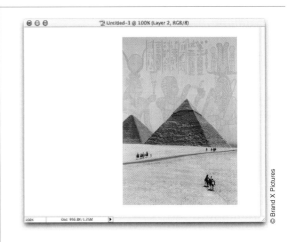

© Brand X Pictures

STEP TWO: Create a new blank
layer by clicking on the New
Layer icon at the bottom of the
Layers palette. Get the Rectangular Marquee tool and drag out
a rectangular selection around
the bottom quarter of your
photo (as shown here). Click on
the Foreground Color Swatch
and choose a dark gray, then fill
this selection with that dark
gray by pressing Option-Delete
(PC: Alt-Backspace).

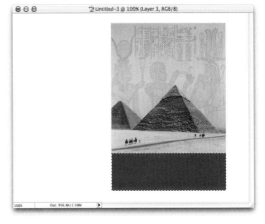

STEP THREE: Now create a thin
rectangular selection at the top
(like the one shown here). This
time set your Foreground color
to light gray then fill this selection with light gray by pressing
Option-Delete (PC: Alt-Backspace). Deselect by pressing
Command-D (PC: Control-D).

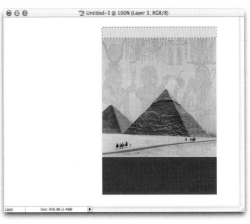

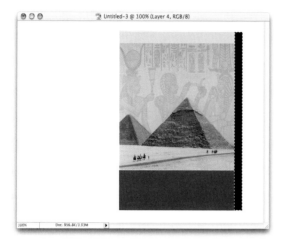

STEP FOUR: Create another new blank layer. With the Rectangular Marquee tool, drag out a tall, thin rectangular selection on the right side of your photo (like the one shown here). Press "d" to set your Foreground color to black then fill this selection with black by pressing Option-Delete (PC: Alt-Backspace).

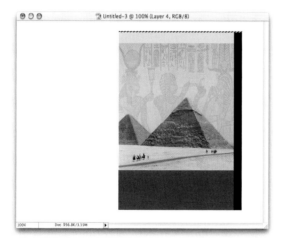

STEP FIVE: While on the same layer, drag out a very thin rectangular selection across the top of the photo (as shown here). Fill it with black by pressing Option-Delete (PC: Alt-Backspace).

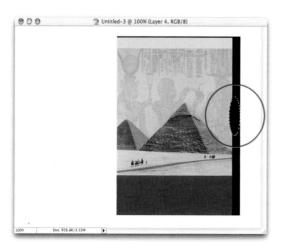

STEP SIX: Switch to the Elliptical Marquee tool and drag out a vertical oval-shaped selection (like the one shown here) that is mostly in the vertical black bar, but extends into the photo a little bit. Fill it with black by pressing Option-Delete (PC: Alt-Backspace). This will be the tab that is used to open the DVD box. Deselect by pressing Command-D (PC: Control-D).

continued

Quick Tip:
Resizing multiple layers at one time

Here's a real timesaving tip that enables you to resize objects or text on multiple layers—all at the same time. Just link together the layers that you want to resize, then press Command-T (PC: Control-T) to bring up the Free Transform bounding box. Hold the Shift key (to constrain proportions), then grab any of the bounding box handles and drag. As you drag, all of the linked layers will resize at the same time.

Quick Tip:
How to switch to the Precise Cursor any time

When using Photoshop's paint tools, your cursor displays the size of the brush you're using. But if you ever need a more-precise cursor for really detailed work, you can temporarily switch to the "Precise Cursor," which looks like a crosshair. To do this, just press the Caps Lock key on your keyboard and your cursor (not just your paint cursor, but any cursor) will switch to the crosshair cursor. To switch back, press the Caps Lock key again.

If you don't know about this Caps Lock trick, it can be quite confusing because you could be using the Type tool with the Caps Lock turned on to type some text in all caps, and when you switched to another tool, it would be the crosshair cursor, and you wouldn't know why. Freaky!

STEP SEVEN: In the Layers palette, you'll need to merge these black box parts and the gray bars with the photo itself. To do that, just press Command-E (PC: Control-E) twice to merge all the parts into one single layer. Now press Shift-M to switch back to the Rectangular Marquee tool, and drag out another tall rectangular selection, but this time position it on the left side of the box, from the top to the bottom of the box (as shown here). This selected area will become the spine of your DVD box.

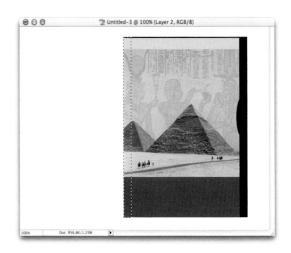

STEP EIGHT: Once your selection is in place, you're going to need to cut it from this layer and copy this spine area onto its own separate layer. To do that, simply press Shift-Command-J (PC: Shift-Control-J). Then, press "v" to switch to the Move tool, and move your spine over to the left a little to create a visual separation (as shown here).

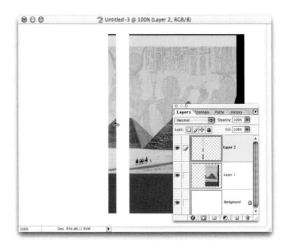

STEP NINE: Click on the front of the box layer and add your type to the DVD box with the Type tool. (In the example shown here, the word "Egyptian" is set in Papyrus. The words "Secrets of the Pharaohs" are set in Herculanum. The words "National Geothermal DVD" at the top are set in Gill Sans Regular with 90% Horizontal Scaling in the Character palette.) Duplicate the "Secrets of the Pharaohs" Type layer by pressing Command-J (PC: Control-J).

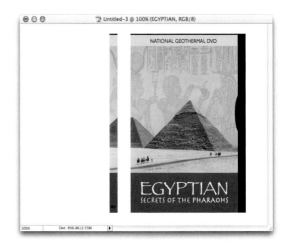

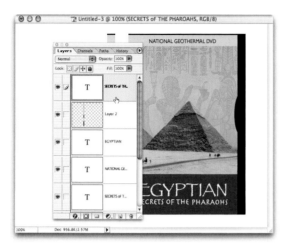

STEP TEN: In the Layers palette, drag this duplicate Type layer so it appears directly above the spine layer (as shown here). Press Command-T (PC: Control-T) to bring up Free Transform. Under the Edit menu, under Transform, choose Rotate 90° CW, then press Return (PC: Enter) to lock in your transformation. Position this type over the spine, highlight it with the Type tool, click on the Color Swatch in the Options Bar, and change the color to black. Press Command-E (PC: Control-E) to merge it with the spine layer, making it just one layer.

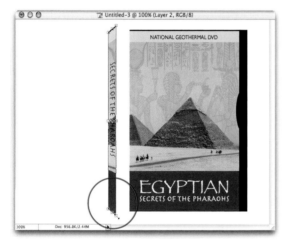

STEP ELEVEN: In the Layers palette, click on the spine layer. Press Command-T (PC: Control-T) to bring up Free Transform. Go under the Edit menu, under Transform, and choose Perspective. Click on the bottom right-hand corner point and drag downward to add a perspective effect to your spine (as shown here). Then, grab the bottom left-hand corner point and drag upward to exaggerate the effect.

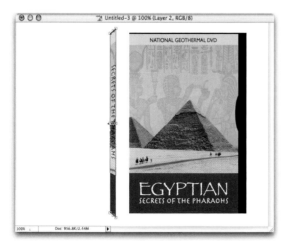

STEP TWELVE: That stretches out the spine a bit too much, making it look visibly stretched, so go under the Edit menu, under Transform, and choose Scale. Then grab the left center point and drag inward a bit to remove the stretching that the Perspective effect created. Then press Return (PC: Enter) to lock in your changes.

Quick Tip:
You can still apply most transformations to editable Type layers

Many people don't realize that while you have an editable Type layer, you can still apply a number of transformations (such as Scale, Rotate, Skew, Flip Horizontal, and Flip Vertical), and your type will remain fully editable (meaning you can change the letters, tracking, leading, etc.). However, to apply Distort or Perspective transformations, you'll first have to Rasterize the Type layer by going under the Layer menu, under Rasterize, and choosing Type.

continued

STEP THIRTEEN: In the Layers palette, click on the front of the DVD box layer, and then link all of your Type layers to it by clicking in the second column of each layer. Press Command-E (PC: Control-E) to merge these linked layers. Press Command-T (PC: Control-T) to bring up Free Transform. Go under the Edit menu, under Transform, and choose Perspective. Grab the bottom left-hand corner point and drag downward (as shown). Try to visually match the amount of perspective that you applied to the spine.

STEP FOURTEEN: Now grab the bottom right-hand corner point and drag upward to exaggerate the perspective effect (as shown here).

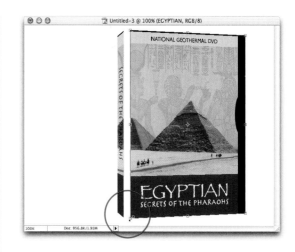

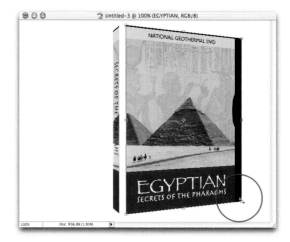

STEP FIFTEEN: Again, adding this perspective effect tends to give your box a stretched look, so go under the Edit menu, under Transform, and choose Scale. Then grab the right center point and drag to the left a bit to remove the stretching that the Perspective effect created. Then press Return (PC: Enter) to lock in your changes.

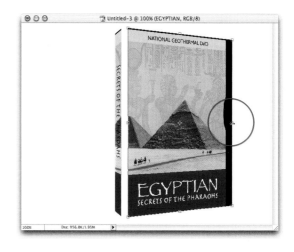

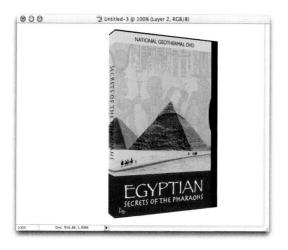

STEP SIXTEEN: Switch to the Move tool and move your front layer until it touches the spine layer and then line them up. Note: if they don't line up perfectly, use Free Transform and Scale the spine up (or down) to match the front of the box.

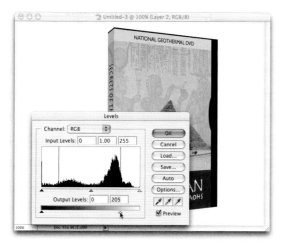

STEP SEVENTEEN: In the Layers palette, click on the spine layer. You're going to darken the spine layer a bit to help it look like it has natural shadows. Press Command-L (PC: Control-L) to bring up the Levels dialog. Then drag the bottom right Output Levels slider to the left (as shown) and click OK to darken the spine a bit.

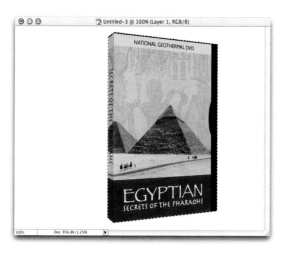

STEP EIGHTEEN: Now, press Command-E (PC: Control-E) to merge the spine layer and the box front layer together into one layer. Hold the Command key (PC: Control key) and in the Layers palette click on the merged box layer to put a selection around the entire box (as shown here). Now create a new blank layer by clicking on the New Layer icon at the bottom of the Layers palette.

Quick Tip:
Where has the "Blur" gone?

By now you've probably noticed that starting back in Photoshop 6.0, Blur and Intensity have disappeared from some of the Layer Style dialog boxes (Inner Glow, Outer Glow, and Drop Shadow). But never fear; Adobe didn't remove these effects, they simply renamed them.

What used to control the amount of Blur is now controlled by Size, and what used to affect the Intensity is now called Spread.

These effects have also been enhanced. By changing the Spread (formerly Intensity), you can get a completely solid edge with just a small amount of Blur (I'm sorry Size). This is something that previously couldn't be accomplished in these dialog boxes.

The name change is a little weird, but hey, they could have changed the name to "Softening the edges of a predetermined selection in which the amount of said selection can be affected by the front-end user."

continued

STEP NINETEEN: Press "d" then "x" to set white as your Foreground color. Press "b" to get the Brush tool, and choose a very small, soft-edged brush (I used a 5-pixel brush here). Click once at the top of your box at the spot where the spine meets the front, hold the Shift key, and click once at the bottom (as shown), and a perfectly straight white line will be drawn right along the spine.

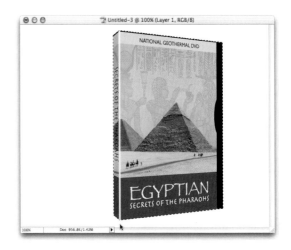

STEP TWENTY: Go to the Layers palette and lower the Opacity setting for this white brush stroke to 50%. This makes it look like there's a natural bend in the cover (as shown here). Deselect by pressing Command-D (PC: Control-D) to complete the box. However, if you want to create the DVD disc that I mentioned in the intro of this technique and then add it to this image, keep this image open and flip back to Chapter 4.

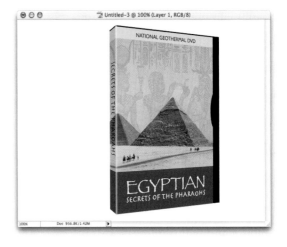

Framing Your Work

It's amazing how just putting a frame around a photo can transform it from a snapshot into a piece of art, and this technique shows you an easy way to create a photo-realistic frame, all from right within Photoshop, without using any third-party filters or images. The frame you'll create here is in red; however, you can use a medium gray instead, and then use Hue/Saturation after it's done to make the frame any color you'd like.

Quick Tip:
The limits of Bevel and Emboss

Photoshop's Bevel and Emboss Layer Style works really well on low-res, 72-ppi images, but unfortunately when you're using high-res, 300-ppi images, the effect of the Bevel and Emboss filter is much less. For example, a Depth of 20 gives a very thick, sharp inner bevel on a 72-ppi image, but the same setting of 20 on a 300-ppi image gives a softer, smaller bevel that seems to have about 30% to 40% of the intensity of the low-res version.

There's really no practical way around this in Photoshop, but if you want this type of bevel effect for high-res images, Alien Skin's Eye Candy 4000 collection of Photoshop plug-ins has a Bevel Boss filter that's first-rate, and it works well on high-res images. Find out more at their Web site at www.alienskin.com.

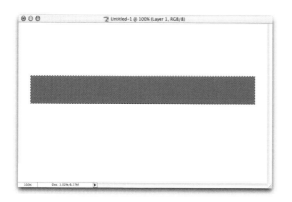

STEP ONE: Open a new document in RGB mode. Create a new layer by clicking on the New Layer icon at the bottom of the Layers palette. Get the Rectangular Marquee tool and drag out a horizontal rectangular selection like the one shown here. Click on your Foreground Color Swatch and choose a medium red, and fill your selection with this red by pressing Option-Delete (PC: Alt-Backspace).

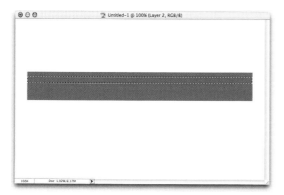

STEP TWO: Deselect by pressing Command-D (PC: Control-D). Take the Rectangular Marquee tool and drag out a thin horizontal rectangular selection inside the red rectangle that goes from side to side and is near the top (like the one shown here). Then press Command-J (PC: Control-J) to copy this selected area up on its own layer.

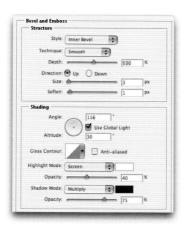

STEP THREE: Choose Bevel and Emboss from the Add a Layer Style pop-up menu at the bottom of the Layers palette. When the dialog appears, increase the Depth to around 500%, lower the Size to 3, increase the Soften setting to 1, and in the Shading section, lower the Highlight Opacity to 40% (as shown here).

continued

Quick Tip:
Moving selections from one document to another

If you have an active selection in a document, and you want the exact same selection in another open document, you can drag-and-drop just the selection (and not its contents) from one open document to another. To make this work, all you have to do is make sure you have a selection tool active (e.g., Lasso, Rectangular Marquee, Magic Wand, etc.), and with that tool, click in the center of your selection and drag it over to the other open document.

STEP FOUR: Click OK and a bevel (the white highlight and black shadow) will be added to your thin red bar (as shown here). To add more shadows beneath your bar, choose Drop Shadow from the Add a Layer Style pop-up menu. Decrease the Distance to 2, then click OK to apply a small drop shadow to your beveled thin red bar (as shown).

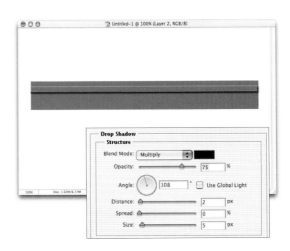

STEP FIVE: Use the Rectangular Marquee tool to create another rectangular selection (like the one shown here, which is below the beveled bar and goes almost all the way to the bottom of the red rectangle). In the Layers palette, click on your original red rectangle layer, then press Command-J (PC: Control-J) to copy this selected area up on its own layer. Next, go to the Layers palette, and click directly on the word "Effects" (from the layer you just beveled) and drag-and-drop this word directly on the new layer you just created. This copies the same bevel and shadow to your new layer.

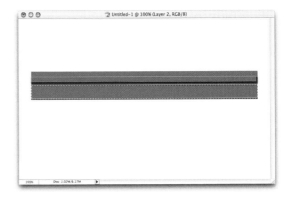

STEP SIX: On your new layer, double-click on the words Bevel and Emboss. When the Bevel and Emboss dialog appears, for Direction click the Down button to reverse your bevel (on just this layer) so the shadow is on top and the highlight is on bottom. Don't change anything else, just the Direction, then click OK.

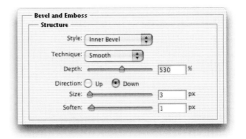

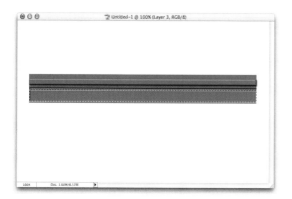

STEP SEVEN: Use the Rectangular Marquee tool to create another rectangular selection that's a little shorter than your last selection but still goes almost to the bottom of the red rectangle (like the one shown here). Press Command-J (PC: Control-J) to copy this selected area up on its own layer. Since you're copying this selected area from an area that is already beveled, the beveled effect will come right along with it. However, you'll need to double-click on the words Bevel and Emboss attached to this layer, and change the Direction back to Up, then click OK.

Quick Tip:
Rotating through open documents

If you have more than one document open at the same time in Photoshop, you can rotate through your open documents by pressing Control-Tab.

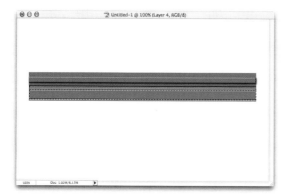

STEP EIGHT: Drag out another rectangular selection (like the one shown here, that's even shorter than your last selection). Press Command-J (PC: Control-J) to copy this selected area up on its own layer (as shown).

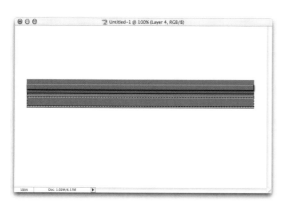

STEP NINE: Do the same thing again: make a shorter rectangular selection, and press Command-J (PC: Control-J) to put your selected area up on its own layer. Each of these selections should be just a little thinner than the one before, giving your layers a "stacking effect."

continued

When it's time for me to show a client the final image (or an onscreen proof along the way), I don't like them to see the application running, just the image.

One reason is that I've had clients say, "Hey, is that Photoshop? My next-door neighbor Earl has Photoshop on his home computer and he does some really neat stuff." At this point I start to cringe because you can tell he's thinking "Hey, my neighbor could do this for me, and I'd save a bundle."

Secondly, it puts the client's focus on the image, and not the software surrounding it (which can be distracting), and third, it just looks more professional.

To get into what I call "Presentation mode" press "f," "f," Tab (press the letter "f" twice, then the Tab key once). This centers your image on screen, puts a black background behind your image, and hides Photoshop's menus and palettes. It looks great.

When you're done and your client steps away, just press "f," Tab to get all your goodies back.

STEP TEN: Go to the Layers palette and hide the Background layer by clicking on the Eye icon in the first column beside it. Then go to the palette's pop-down menu and choose Merge Visible (as shown here). This merges all your beveled layers into just one layer. Click where the Eye icon used to be for the Background layer to make it visible again.

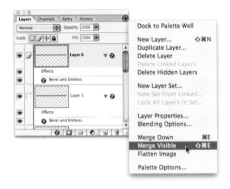

STEP ELEVEN: Now it's time to miter cut the ends. Get the Polygonal Lasso tool, hold the Shift key to get a perfect 45° angle, and create a triangular selection (like the one shown here) and align the diagonal side of your triangular selection with the top-left corner of the bar (as shown). Press Delete (PC: Backspace) to knock this selection out of your bar (as shown here).

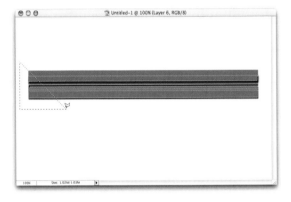

STEP TWELVE: Don't deselect yet. Instead, go under the Select menu and choose Transform Selection. Then Control-click (PC: Right-click) within your selected area and choose Flip Horizontal from the pop-up menu (as shown).

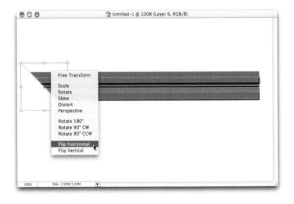

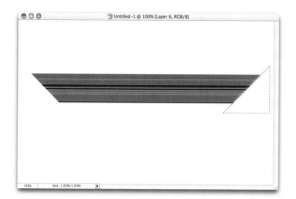

STEP THIRTEEN: Press Return (PC: Enter) to lock in your horizontal flip. Click the Polygonal Lasso tool inside your flipped selection and drag it over to the right side of the bar, and align the angled side of your triangular selection with the top-right corner of your bar. Then, press Delete (PC: Backspace) to knock out the selected area (as shown here).

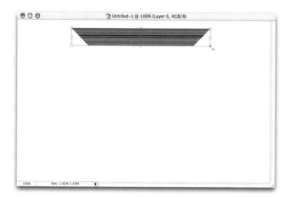

STEP FOURTEEN: Deselect by pressing Command-D (PC: Control-D). Press Command-T (PC: Control-T) to bring up Free Transform. Hold the Shift key, grab a corner point, and drag inward to scale this top portion of your frame down to the size you want for the final frame (as shown here). Press Return (PC: Enter) to lock in your transformation.

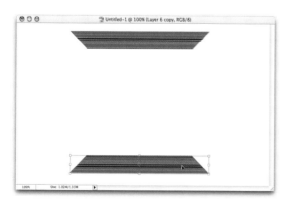

STEP FIFTEEN: Press Option-Command-T (PC: Alt-Control-T) to bring up Free Transform. This particular shortcut makes a duplicate of your layer. Control-click (PC: Right-click) in the bounding box and choose Flip Vertical. Hold the Shift key, and-click-and-drag the flipped copy to the bottom of the image (as shown). Press Return (PC: Enter) to lock in your transformation.

Quick Tip:
Healing on a blank layer

Back in Photoshop 7, if you used the Healing Brush, it "bruised the pixels" (meaning your changes where made directly on your image, changing the pixels forever). Although the Clone Stamp tool let you clone onto a blank layer above your photo (protecting your original pixels) the Healing Brush did not. But now, in Photoshop CS, you can indeed save your pixels from extinction by Healing to a blank layer. Start by creating a new layer (in the Layers palette), then get the Healing Brush, and up in the Options Bar turn on the checkbox for "Use all Layers." Now you can heal safely on a layer above your original photo layer.

continued

This isn't really a Photoshop tip as much as it's a
tip about this book. If you
see a project in the book
that uses type, you can
find out which typeface
(font) I used to achieve
the final effect. In the
last version of this book,
we had an appendix that
listed all the fonts that
were used in the tech-
niques, but many readers
didn't realize it was there.
Thanks go out to read-
ers of the previous book
who came up with the
great idea to include the
fonts right along with this
technique.

STEP SIXTEEN: Press Option-
Command-T (PC: Alt-Control-T)
to bring up Free Transform.
Control-click (PC: Right-click)
within the bounding box and
choose Rotate 90° CCW. Drag
this rotated duplicate into place
on the right side. Press Return
(PC: Enter). Transform this right
side, and drag the duplicate
over to the left and choose Flip
Horizontal. You may need to
move the bottom section up/
down to align all the pieces.

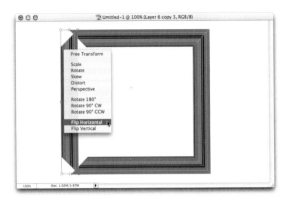

STEP SEVENTEEN: In the Layers
palette create a new layer, then
Command-click (PC: Control-
click) on the top frame layer to
put a selection around it. Get the
Brush tool, choose the 3-pixel,
hard-edged brush, hold the Shift
key, and paint a white stroke
along the top bevel highlight (as
shown here) on this new layer.

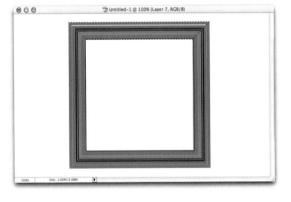

STEP EIGHTEEN: Click on the
down-facing arrow next to the
Brush thumbnail up in the
Options Bar to bring up the
Brush Picker, and use the
Master Diameter slider to lower
your brush size to 2 pixels.
Paint three thin lines, from left
to right, along the three highlights created by the bevels
(as shown here).

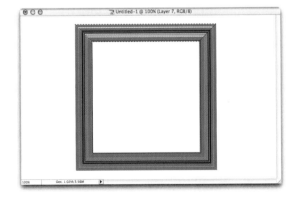

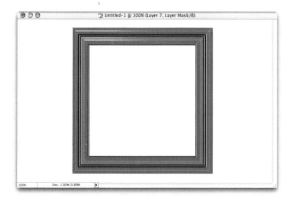

STEP NINETEEN: Click on the Layer Mask icon at the bottom of the Layers palette. Get the Gradient tool. Click on the Gradient thumbnail up in the Options Bar and from the Gradient Picker choose the third gradient (the Black to White gradient). Click-and-drag the Gradient tool from the center of your top frame over to the left (as shown) to fade out the right side of your white paint strokes.

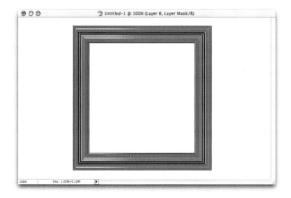

STEP TWENTY: Repeat this process for the bottom frame: create a new layer; select it; paint the white, hard-edged brush strokes on it; then create a Layer Mask; and fade the right side by dragging a Black to White gradient from the center to the left (as shown here).

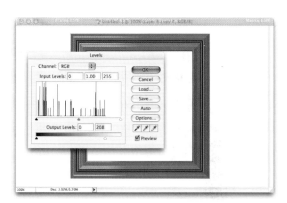

STEP TWENTY-ONE: In the Layers palette, click on the right frame layer. Press Command-L (PC: Control-L) to bring up the Levels dialog. Drag the bottom-right Output Levels slider to the left to darken this side of the frame (as shown here) and click OK. Do the same thing to the left frame layer. Next, hide the Background layer (click on its Eye icon) then choose Merge Visible from the palette's pop-down menu to combine all your frame layers into just one layer.

continued

Quick Tip:
File Browser tips

When you're working in Photoshop's File Browser you can use the Arrow keys to move from image to image in the preview window. But if you hold the Shift key while you use the Arrow keys, it will keep your original image selected, then select the image in the direction you moved with the Arrow key. For example, if you click an image, hold the Shift key, and click the Right Arrow, it adds the image to the right of your current image to your selection of images. Every time you Shift-Right Arrow over, it adds another image. If you then Shift-Up Arrow, that image is added, and so on.

Ever since the introduction of layers (back in Photoshop 3.0) you've been able to drag-and-drop layers between documents. When you do this, the image you're dropping lands wherever you release your mouse (by default). So if you drag it over and let go of the mouse button right away, chances are your image will be off to the left or right a bit.

To get your image to be perfectly centered when you drag from one document to another, all you have to do is hold the Shift key as you drag. Your dragged layer will then appear centered within your target document.

STEP TWENTY-TWO: Choose Pattern Overlay from the Add a Layer Style pop-up menu. Click on the Pattern thumbnail to bring up the Pattern Picker. From the palette's pop-down menu choose Nature Patterns (then click Append) to add this new set of patterns. Click on the pattern named Yellow Mums (as shown). Change the Blend Mode to Overlay, then lower the Opacity to 30%.

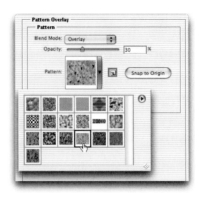

STEP TWENTY-THREE: In the Layer Style dialog, click on the word Drop Shadow to bring up its options. Lower the Opacity to 50%, increase the Distance to 14, and increase the Size to 9, then click OK to apply both the pattern and a drop shadow (as shown here). Lastly, open the photo you want in your frame, drag it into your frame document, and in the Layers palette drag it beneath your frame layer (as shown below).

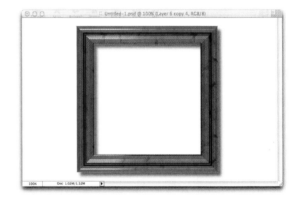

© Brand X Pictures

OK, if you're not into pro or college football, you might not make a connection with the term "Special

Special Teams
Photoshop Special Effects

Teams." In football, the term "Special Teams" is actually a misnomer, because it really only refers to one "special" team. My team. The Tampa Bay Buccaneers. That's right, baby, we're the World Champions. (We're #1. We're #1. Come on, chant with me: We're #1 [you're not chanting]. We're #1.) So what does all this have to do with Photoshop Special Effects? Not a dang thing—I just had to find a way to work some kind of football phraseology into at least one chapter intro which would then enable me to put into print for all the world to see "We're the world champions, baby!" Sad, isn't it? Now, you'll be happy to know that I did refrain from using any Bucs photos, logos, or other Buccaneer references in this entire chapter, which I think shows amazing restraint on my part. Oh yeah, did I mention: We're #1? (You're not chanting!)

Quick Tip:
The express lane to backscreening

If you're not too fussy about the exact percentage of backscreening, there's a faster way to backscreen an image. Make your selection and then press Command-L (PC: Control-L) to bring up the Levels dialog box. Drag the left bottom Output Levels slider to the right to instantly backscreen your selected area.

3D Photo Cubes

I've seen people create these photo cubes before, but it's always been such a long and laborious process that I usually went a different direction. However, using the 3D Transform filter, it suddenly becomes really simple. Don't let the number of steps fool you—this is a very easy project. You may have already learned in another technique in this book that 3D Transform no longer installs along with Photoshop. You'll have to find it on the install disc and drag it into your Photoshop Plug-Ins folder.

STEP ONE: Open a new document in RGB mode. Start by creating a new blank layer by clicking on the New Layer icon at the bottom of the Layers palette. We'll use this layer to create a 3D cube, which we'll use as our guide.

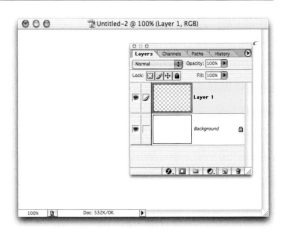

STEP TWO: Go under the Filter menu, under Render, and choose 3D Transform. When 3D Transform appears, click on the Cube tool (highlighted in the Toolbar shown here), then hold the Shift key, and drag out a cube shape (as shown).

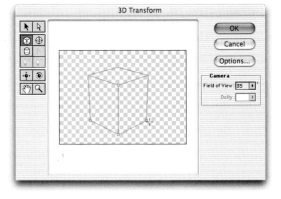

STEP THREE: Switch to the Trackball tool (shown highlighted here), click within your preview area and drag to the right. As you drag, the cube will rotate, exposing its back side (shown here), which includes shading on all three sides. Note: You'll have to click-and-drag quite a ways to the right—in fact, your cursor will actually extend outside the 3D Transform dialog as you drag to the right.

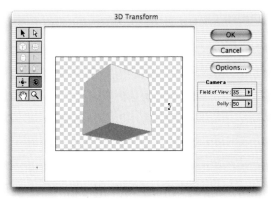

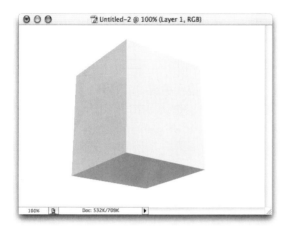

STEP FOUR: When you click OK in the 3D Transform dialog, your shaded cube will appear on your blank layer (as shown).

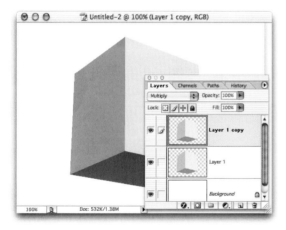

STEP FIVE: The shading is somewhat subtle, so to intensify it, duplicate the cube layer by pressing Command-J (PC: Control-J). Then, change the Layer Blend Mode in the Layers palette for this duplicate layer to Multiply. This has a multiplying effect and makes the shading on the cube more pronounced. Now press Command-E (PC: Control-E) to merge the Multiply cube layer permanently together with the original cube layer (creating just one layer).

STEP SIX: Open the first photo you want to use on your photo cube (here I've opened the photo that I want to appear on the right face of my cube).

© Brand X Pictures

Quick Tip:
Backscreens aren't just white

Depending on the image, sometimes when you attempt a backscreen effect, a light backscreen won't work. If the image is already of a lighter nature, a light backscreen can get lost, so instead, try a dark backscreen. You can do this in the Levels dialog. Press Command-L (PC: Control-L) to bring up the Levels dialog box, and drag the right Output Levels slider to the left. This will darken your selected area. If you prefer to use Curves, you can add a light backscreen by dragging the bottom point of the curve straight upward. To add a dark backscreen, drag the top-right point straight downward.

continued

Quick Tip:
Quick Tip:
Formatting ®, ™, and other symbols in Photoshop

To visually adjust the baseline shift (great for adjusting trademark and registration mark symbols), highlight the character you want to affect and press Shift-Option-Up Arrow (PC: Shift-Alt-Up Arrow) to move the character above the baseline, and of course, use the same shortcut with the Down Arrow to move text below the baseline (for things such as H_2O, etc.).

STEP SEVEN: Press "v" to switch to the Move tool, and click-and-drag this photo over to your cube document. It will appear on its own layer above your cube layer (as shown).

STEP EIGHT: The cube has perfectly square sides, so to keep from distorting your photos as you place them into the cube shape, you'll need to make a perfectly square photo. To do that, switch to the Rectangular Marquee tool, hold the Shift key, and drag out a square selection (as shown here). If you need to reposition your square once it's in place, just click the Rectangular Marquee tool within your selection, and you can move just the selection itself.

STEP NINE: When it's positioned correctly, go under the Select menu and choose Inverse. This inverses the selection, which selects everything *but* the square photo you want to keep (as shown here).

STEP TEN: Press Delete (PC: Backspace) and everything outside your perfectly square selection is erased, leaving you with a perfectly square photo (as shown here). Press Command-D (PC: Control-D) to deselect.

Quick Tip:
Accessing Free Transform functions

Although we're constantly accessing Free Transform functions, such as Skew, Scale, Flip Horizontal, etc., from either the contextual pop-up menu or by use of a keyboard shortcut, you can access these functions by going under the Edit menu, under Transform.

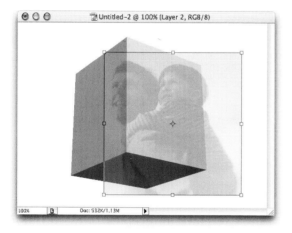

STEP ELEVEN: In the Layers palette, lower the Opacity of this layer to 20% so you can see the cube below (the cube is there to be your guide, so being able to see it is critical). Now, press Command-T (PC: Control-T) to bring up Free Transform (this puts the Free Transform bounding box around your square photo, as shown).

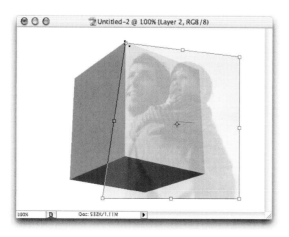

STEP TWELVE: Hold the Command key (PC: Control key), grab the top-left corner of the bounding box, and drag it until it aligns with the top-left corner of the right face of the cube (as shown here). Because you lowered the opacity of your photo layer, this is very easy. By the way, holding the Command/Control key as you drag, invokes Free Transform's Distort feature.

continued

Quick Tip:
Zoom shortcut

To jump instantly to a 100% view of your image, double-click on the Zoom tool. To have your image instantly "Fit on Screen," double-click on the Hand tool.

STEP THIRTEEN: Next, while still holding the Command/Control key, grab the top-right Free Transform point and drag it until it aligns with the top-right corner of the cube (as shown).

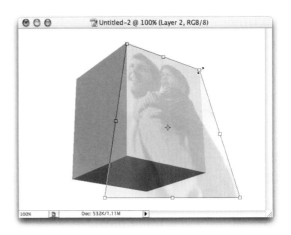

STEP FOURTEEN: Now, while still holding the Command/Control key, grab the bottom-right corner of your photo, and align it with the bottom-right corner of your cube (as shown).

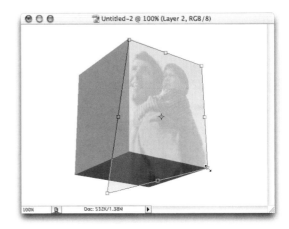

STEP FIFTEEN: Now, while *still* holding the Command/Control key, grab the left corner point, and drag it up to where it aligns with the left corner point of the cube's right face. Now press Return (PC: Enter) to lock in your transformation (as shown).

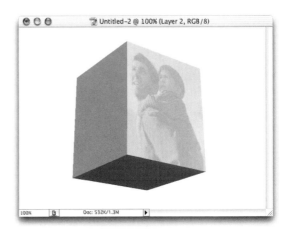

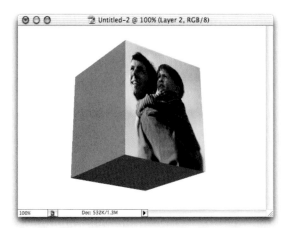

STEP SIXTEEN: Remember how you lowered the opacity of this layer earlier? Well, now that the photo's been aligned to the cube, you can go to the Layers palette and raise the Opacity of your photo layer back up to 100% to bring the photo back to full strength (as shown here).

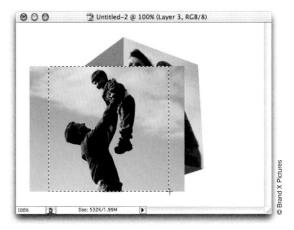

STEP SEVENTEEN: Now you're going to repeat the process for the left face of the cube: open another photo, drag it over into your cube document, put a square selection around the most important part of the photo, inverse your selection and press Delete (PC: Backspace), lower the Opacity of this layer to 20%, bring up Free Transform, hold the Command key (PC: Control key), align the corner points to the cube, press Return (PC: Enter) to lock in your transformation, and raise the Opacity back to 100%.

STEP EIGHTEEN: Open your third photo, drag it over to the cube, and follow the same steps for aligning it to the bottom of the cube, just like you did the other two photos.

continued

Quick Tip:
Putting a selection around your type

In this book, when I want you to put a selection around your type, I generally have you Command-click (PC: Control-click) on the Type layer in the Layers palette. There's another way to do this but because it's not just a keyboard shortcut, it takes longer to get to. I still thought you'd want to know it (especially if you're charging by the hour).

Just go under the Select menu and choose Load Selection. When the dialog pops up, click OK, and it'll put a selection around your type.

Quick Tip:
Sharpen that gel

Gel effects are an example of those effects that seem to really jump off the page if you apply the Unsharp Mask filter (under Sharpen in the Filter menu). In fact, try these settings and run the filter twice in a row: Amount: 150%, Radius: 1, and Threshold: 7.

STEP NINETEEN: Once you align all three photos, and raise their Opacity settings back to 100%, you'll see the photo cube take shape. The only problem is, we've covered up all the shading from the cube (the photo on the bottom isn't darker, the right side isn't lighter, etc.).

STEP TWENTY: Go to the Layers palette, and as you can see (from the Layers palette shown here), each photo is on its own separate layer, and the cube is still positioned behind them on Layer 1.

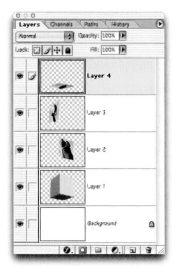

STEP TWENTY-ONE: Press Command-E (PC: Control-E) twice, to merge the three photo layers into just one layer, right above the cube layer (as shown here).

STEP TWENTY-TWO: Now you're going to use the shaded cube itself to add the shading to your photo cube. In the Layers palette, drag the cube layer above your photo layer (as shown), then change the Blend Mode of this layer to Soft Light. When you do this, your photo cube will now appear subtly shaded, with the bottom photo becoming darker, the right photo lighter, and the left side not as light.

© Brand X Pictures

STEP TWENTY-THREE: The effect is essentially complete, but I thought I'd put it on a background just to show you the final effect. I opened a photo of some clouds (shown here).

STEP TWENTY-FOUR: Now return to your photo cube layer, and press Command-E (PC: Control-E) to merge your shaded cube and photo cube permanently together. Switch to the Move tool and drag this cube over onto the clouds background to complete the effect. (Notice how the bottom of the cube is now darker?) This is just one way to use this effect; try creating multiple cubes, with other photos, and rotate each slightly for a different effect.

Quick Tip:
Avoiding pixelation

When you're resizing images, there's a simple rule of thumb: making your image smaller is good, making it larger is bad. That's a huge over-simplification of the wild and woolly subject of resolution, but in general, scaling an image down in size increases the resolution of the image, and generally doesn't do the image much harm. (The resampling sometimes makes it lose a little clarity, but the amount varies from image to image.) However, increasing the size of an image, especially a low-res image (72-ppi) is generally a recipe for disaster, creating images that are blurry and pixelated. Therefore, starting with a large image and scaling down is by far preferable to starting with a small image and scaling up. If you must start with a small image, if you're scanning it, try to scan it at a high enough resolution to keep the image from falling apart (e.g., 600 dpi). If you're shooting digitally, try a minimum, 3-megapixel camera so you start with a large image that you'll likely want to scale down.

Faking Hand-Drawn Illustrations

The inspiration for this one came from a zoo T-shirt I saw someone wearing. You start with photographs and convert them into silhouettes, and the final effect looks as if you drew the figures in Adobe Illustrator. At the end of the technique, I give you a couple of different examples of how this handy technique can be utilized.

STEP ONE: In this project, we're going to build a T-shirt design for a zoo by converting three typical animal photos into drawings. Start by opening the first of these three photos.

STEP TWO: Use any selection tool you'd like to put a selection around the elephant (I used the Magnetic Lasso tool). As usual, the Magnetic Lasso tool didn't do a perfect job all by itself, so after it was done, I had to add some areas of the elephant to the selection by holding the Shift key and using the Regular Lasso tool.

STEP THREE: Once the elephant is fully selected, press Command-J (PC: Control-J) to put the elephant up on its own separate layer above the Background layer (as shown here in the Layers palette).

© Brand X Pictures

STEP FOUR: Slide the elephant photo over to one side of your screen and open the second photo—in this case a giraffe. Put a selection around the giraffe (again, I used the Magnetic Lasso, and then the Regular Lasso tool to add any areas that the Magnetic Lasso tool missed). When your giraffe is selected, press Command-J (PC: Control-J) to put a copy of the giraffe up on its own layer.

© Brand X Pictures

STEP FIVE: Slide the giraffe photo out of the way and open the third photo—in this case a rhino. Put a selection around him, then press Command-J (PC: Control-J) to put a copy of the rhino up on its own layer. You should now have three open documents, each with an animal on the top layer.

© Brand X Pictures

STEP SIX: Now open the photo that will serve as a background for the animals (in this case, it's a photo of a sunset).

Quick Tip:
Precise-sized selections— method #2

Another way to make a selection in the exact size that you need is to click on the Rectangular Marquee tool and change the style in the Options Bar Style pop-up menu. By default it's set to Normal, but if you choose Fixed Size, you can type in your desired size in the Width and Height fields just to the right of the pop-up menu in the Options Bar.

Now, when you click the Rectangular Marquee tool anywhere within your image, a selection in that fixed size (and only that size) will appear.

continued

Quick Tip:
Hide that path!

If you've been tromping over to the Paths palette every time you want to hide a path from view, there's actually a quicker way—just press Shift-Command-H (PC: Shift-Control-H) and your path will be temporarily hidden. To make it visible again, just press the same shortcut.

STEP SEVEN: Go to the Layers palette, and click on the New Layer icon to create a new blank layer. Then get the Rectangular Marquee tool and draw a rectangular selection across the bottom quarter of your photo. Press "d" to set your Foreground color to black, then press Option-Delete (PC: Alt-Backspace) to fill this rectangle with black (as shown here). Press Command-D (PC: Control-D) to deselect.

STEP EIGHT: Now switch back to one of the animal photos. Press the letter "v" to get the Move tool, then drag the animal over onto your sunset background. Once it's in your sunset document, you'll need to scale it down in size. Press Command-T (PC: Control-T) to bring up Free Transform. Hold the Shift key, grab a corner point (as shown), and drag inward to shrink the rhino.

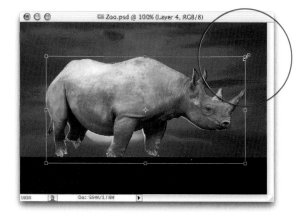

STEP NINE: Scale the rhino to the size shown here, and place him as though he's walking on the black rectangle. Now, repeat this process for the other two animals: drag them over into your sunset document using the Move tool, then use Free Transform to scale them down to size, to make a row of animals (as shown here).

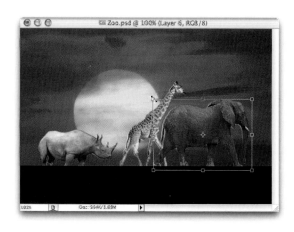

STEP TEN: These animals will be on three separate layers, and we need all three on just one layer, so in the Layers palette, click on the top animal layer, then press Command-E (PC: Control-E) two times. This will merge the three animal layers down into one layer (as shown here in the Layers palette).

The only time you really need to check (turn on) the Colorize box in the Hue/Saturation dialog is when the image or selected area you're working on doesn't already contain color. Turning this checkbox on adds color to the image. If your image is already in color, and you want to change the color, you don't need to click Colorize, just move the Hue slider to pick a new color.

STEP ELEVEN: Black should still be your Foreground color, so all you have to do is press Shift-Option-Delete (PC: Shift-Alt-Backspace) to fill the animals with black, creating a hand-drawn silhouette look (as shown here).

STEP TWELVE: The final step is simply to add some type. I used the font Herculanum, in all caps with the tracking set to 345 in the Character palette (tracking is the amount of space between letters). On the following page, I included two more examples of how to use this technique.

continued

Quick Tip:
Getting
realistic colors

When colorizing grayscale images, one trick you can use to get more realistic colors for critical areas, like flesh tones, grass, hair, sky, etc., is to open a full-color image at the same time that you're trying to colorize your grayscale image. That way, when you're in the Color Picker, you can move your cursor outside the dialog to sample real colors right from the color image, and then return to your image and paint with those colors.

EXAMPLE TWO: Here I used a photo of a bicycle, dragged it onto a cloud background, filled the bike with black, and added some type (in the font American Typewriter Bold, from Adobe).

EXAMPLE THREE: Here's a golf photo, where I selected the golfer, moved him onto a different sunset photo, and turned him into a silhouette for a golfing event. The technique is actually easy—what will take the most time is finding a photo that translates well into a black silhouette.

Info Pop-Down with Cutaway Styles

There are about a dozen ways to use this technique, which lets you take a beveled object and cut away parts of it to reveal a different beveled object inside of it (it's actually just the same object, scaled down a bit, with a different colored bevel). The example you'll create here might be used on a Web site or in video production, but I think once you try it yourself, you'll find ten more ways to incorporate this cool technique.

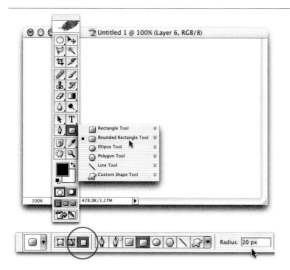

STEP ONE: Open a new document in RGB mode. Create a new layer by clicking on the New Layer icon at the bottom of the Layers palette. Press the letter "d" to set your Foreground color to black, and then get the Rounded Rectangle tool from the Toolbox (as shown here).

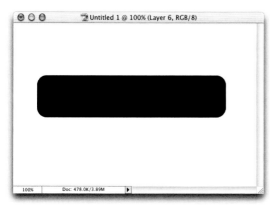

STEP TWO: Up in the Options Bar, click on the third icon from the left (as shown above at left) to create pixel-based shapes with this tool. Then, set the Radius (the roundness of your corners) to 20. Drag out a round-cornered shape (like the one shown here).

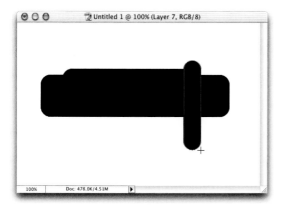

STEP THREE: Now you're going to build on that shape by adding more rounded rectangles to this same layer. Add a thin rectangle across the top of the original shape so that half of it extends into the white background, then add a thin vertical one on the right, as shown here. In the following steps we'll keep building upon this shape until we have our finished console.

continued

Quick Tip:
Design tip

When colorizing line art, filling your selections with a flat color can make your colorization look, well…flat. Instead, try filling your line art with a gradient that goes from a lighter color to a much darker shade of that same color. For example, set your Foreground color to light pink and your Background color to a very dark pink. Make your selection on the line art layer, create your new layer below it, switch to the Gradient tool by pressing the letter "g" (make sure your chosen gradient is Foreground to Background), then drag this gradient from left to right through your selection. This gives the illusion of a light source and adds interest to your image. Note: Remember to drag your gradient in the same direction consistently so that your "shadows" will fall on the same side throughout your image (i.e., always drag from left to right, top to bottom, etc.).

STEP FOUR: Use the Rounded Rectangle tool to add another shape to the bottom of your console (as shown here).

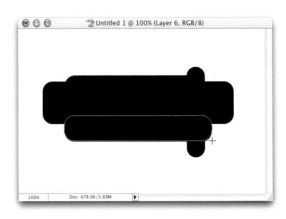

STEP FIVE: Now switch to the Polygon tool (it's two tools below the Rounded Rectangle tool in the flyout list of Shape tools). Up in the Options Bar, set the number of Sides to 5, then draw a polygonal shape like the one shown here. If you hold the Spacebar after you start dragging out your shape you can reposition it, as long as you keep the mouse button held down. You can also rotate it a bit (as we have here) by simply dragging the mouse up or down.

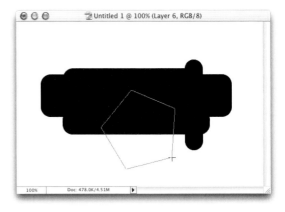

STEP SIX: Finish your console by adding a couple of other polygons, one to the left of your large one, and a smaller one to the right (as shown here). Once you've done this, you have the basic shape of your console. (By the way, you can create any style of console you like—you don't have to stick to the one shown here—it's just an example.)

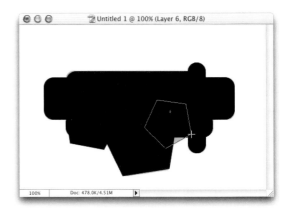

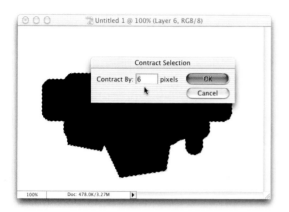

STEP SEVEN: Hold the Command key (PC: Control key), go to the Layers palette, and click on your shape layer to put a selection around it. Now you're going to shrink that selection, so go under the Select menu, under Modify, and choose Contract. When the Contract Selection dialog appears, enter 6.

Quick Tip:
What about the Art History Brush?

The Art History brush, (which is what we used in previous versions of Photoshop to replicate traditional art effects) is still there, but with the Brush engine that was introduced in Photoshop 7, I haven't yet found an occasion to use it. But in case you feel the need to use it, press Shift-Y until you see it appear in the Toolbox (where the History Brush usually lives). My tip: Use a very small brush and paint over your existing image. It's pretty limiting, and maybe that's why Adobe introduced a whole new Brush engine.

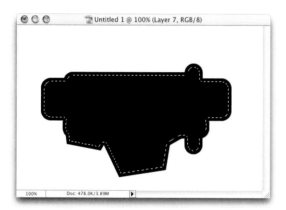

STEP EIGHT: When you click OK, your selection will shrink by 6 pixels. Don't deselect yet. Create a new layer by clicking on the New Layer icon at the bottom of the Layers palette. Fill this selected area with black by pressing Option-Delete (PC: Alt-Backspace). Next, you'll apply a series of Layer Styles.

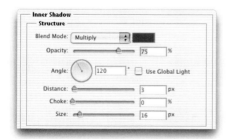

STEP NINE: Choose Inner Shadow from the Add a Layer Style pop-up menu at the bottom of the Layers palette. Click on the Color Swatch next to the Blend Mode pop-up and choose a reddish brown in the Color Picker for the shadow color. Then, turn off Use Global Light, and set the Distance to 3 and the Size to 16. Don't click OK yet.

continued

Quick Tip:

Getting around your image, one button at a time

There are a dozen or so keyboard shortcuts for zooming in and out of your image: switching to the Zoom tool, zooming to Fit on Screen, and a bunch more. But there are some lesser-known navigation shortcuts that can be helpful when you're working on large, high-res images. These are mostly one-button wonders that are available to anyone with an extended keyboard (which is just about everybody not using a laptop). Here goes: To jump up one full screen in your image, press the Page Up key. To jump down one full screen, press the Page Down key. To move to the left one full screen, press Command-Page Up (PC: Control-Page Up). To move right one full screen, press Command-Page Down (PC: Control-Page Down). To jump to the upper-left corner of your image, press the Home key. To jump to the lower-right corner of your image, press the End key.

STEP TEN: In the list of Styles on the left side of the dialog, click directly on the words Bevel and Emboss. Increase the Size to 9 and Soften to 2. Then in the Shading section, turn off Use Global Light, and set the Angle at 120° and the Altitude at 70°. Click on the Highlight Mode Color Swatch and choose a light gray in the Color Picker. Do the same for the Shadow Mode color but choose a medium brown. Raise the Highlight Opacity to 100% and lower the Shadow Opacity to 66%. Don't click OK yet.

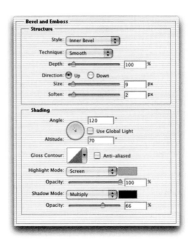

STEP ELEVEN: In the list of Styles, click directly on the word Satin. Change the Blend Mode to Overlay and the color to a light blue. Increase the Opacity to 100%. Change the Angle to 90° and increase the Distance to 30 and the Size to 43. Click on the down-facing arrow next to the Contour thumbnail to bring up the Contour Picker. In the Contour Picker, choose the "Half Round" contour shown here, and then click on the Anti-aliased checkbox. Don't click OK yet.

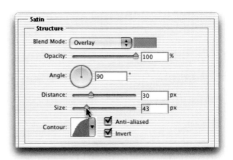

STEP TWELVE: Last, in the list of Styles, click on the words Color Overlay. Choose an orange color (like the one shown here) and click OK to apply all four effects at once. Press Command-D (PC: Control-D) to deselect.

STEP THIRTEEN: Go to the Layers palette and click on your original shape layer (the larger of the two shapes—the one with no effects applied). Drag this layer to the top of the layers stack (as shown). You're now going to apply a bit of a metallic look to this larger shape.

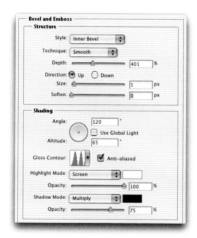

STEP FOURTEEN: Choose Bevel and Emboss from the Add a Layer Style pop-up menu at the bottom of the Layers palette. Increase the Depth to around 400%. Then in the Shading section, turn off Use Global Light. Set the Angle at 120° and the Altitude at 65°. Bring up the Gloss Contour Picker and choose the default contour with two hills called "Ring-Double" (as shown), then click on the Anti-aliased checkbox. Increase the Highlight Opacity to 100%. Don't click OK yet.

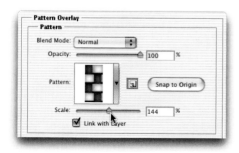

STEP FIFTEEN: Choose Pattern Overlay from the list of Styles on the left side of the dialog. Click on the Pattern thumbnail to bring up the Pattern Picker, and from the Picker's pop-up menu choose Patterns to load the Patterns set into the Picker. Choose the pattern called Woven Wide shown here, then increase the Scale to 144% and click OK.

Quick Tip:
If you don't like your Layer Mask, start over

If you applied a Layer Mask to your image and you can't get it to look quite right, sometimes the best thing to do is just start over. There are a couple of ways to do this. You can click directly on the Layer Mask thumbnail and drag it into the Trash icon at the bottom of the Layers palette, but there's another way that may be quicker because you don't have to create a new mask in the Layers palette. Hold the Option key (PC: Alt key) and click on the Layer Mask icon (this displays the mask). Then, with your Foreground color set to white, press Option-Delete (PC: Control-Backspace), which fills your Layer Mask with white; you're "reset" and ready to start over. Option-click (PC: Alt-click) on your Layer Mask thumbnail again, then drag a gradient through your image, or start painting directly on your image (of course, you're really painting on the mask).

continued

STEP SIXTEEN: Get the Rectangular Marquee tool and drag a rectangular selection like the one shown here. Press Delete (PC: Backspace) to knock a chunk out of the top layer, revealing the orange gel-like layer beneath it (as shown).

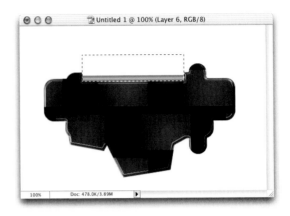

STEP SEVENTEEN: Now you can knock out some other chunks: Just drag out a selection, hold the Shift key, and you can keep adding selections. When you have them in place, press the Delete key (PC: Backspace) to knock out those areas, revealing the gel layer beneath again (as shown here). Deselect by pressing Command-D (PC: Control-D).

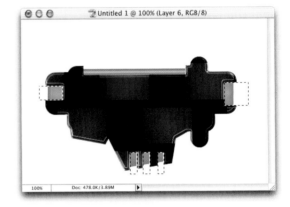

STEP EIGHTEEN: In the Layers palette, create a new layer, then get the Rounded Rectangle tool again. Drag out a rounded shape on this new layer, like the one shown here.

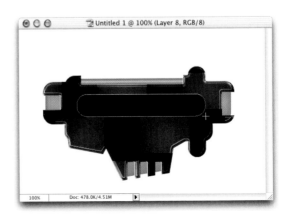

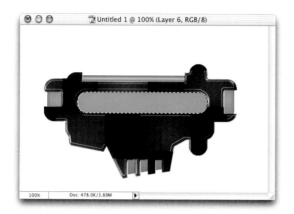

STEP NINETEEN: Hold the Command key (PC: Control key), go to the Layers palette, and click on this black rounded rectangle to put a selection around it. Delete this layer by dragging it into the Trash icon, then press Delete (PC: Backspace) to knock another chunk out of your top layer to reveal the layer beneath (as shown here).

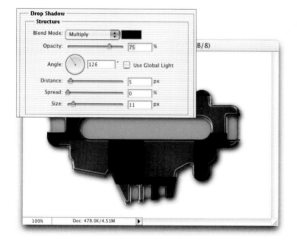

STEP TWENTY: Deselect, then choose Drop Shadow from the Add a Layer Style pop-up menu at the bottom of the Layers palette. Increase the Size to 11 and then click OK to apply a drop shadow to your top layer. In the Layers palette, click on the words Drop Shadow under the top layer and drag it to the gel shape layer to apply the same drop shadow. Create a new layer, and in the Layers palette drag this new layer beneath your orange gel shape layer.

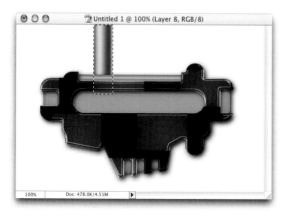

STEP TWENTY-ONE: Get the Rectangular Marquee tool and drag out a vertical selection like the one shown here. Press the letter "g" to get the Gradient tool, and press Return (PC: Enter) to bring up the Gradient Picker. Choose the Copper gradient, then drag the Gradient tool from left to right through your selection (as shown here).

continued

Quick Tip:
What to check if you can't save your file in the format you want

If you try to save your Photoshop document and you see a warning symbol at the bottom of the dialog saying that the "File must be saved as a copy with this selection," here's what to check for:

(1) Layers: If you have layers in your document, you can only save in Photoshop or TIFF format without losing data. You'll see a warning symbol next to the Layers checkbox near the bottom of the Save dialog.

(2) Check for extra channels: If you have an extra channel (perhaps a saved selection), you cannot save in the EPS format without losing data. You'll see a warning symbol next to the Alpha Channels checkbox near the bottom of the Save dialog. Go to the Channels palette, drag the channel to the Trash, and then you can save as an EPS.

(3) You need a Background layer: If your only layer is named Layer 1 or Layer 0, Photoshop treats it as a layered document. You first have to go under the Layers palette's pop-down menu and choose Flatten Image.

(4) Check your color mode: Some file formats aren't available for certain color modes; for example, BMP doesn't show up as a choice when you're in CMYK mode.

Quick Tip:
Too much
Liquid? Undo it!

If you're used to the
Photoshop 6 version of
Liquify, you're used to the
"one undo" limitation that
makes you really stay on
your toes when working
in Liquify. Well, you'll be
happy to know that since
Photoshop 7 you can now
"mess up" all you want,
because Adobe added
multiple undos.

STEP TWENTY-TWO: Remove
the color from this gradient by
pressing Shift-Command-U (PC:
Shift-Control-U) which is the
shortcut for Desaturate. Now
you can Deselect by pressing
Command-D (PC: Control-D).

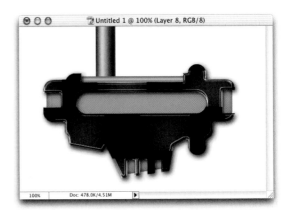

STEP TWENTY-THREE: Press
Command-J (PC: Control-J) to duplicate your gradient layer. Press
"v" to switch to the Move tool
and drag this duplicate gradient
to the right to form a second
tube, then merge these two tube
layers into one layer by pressing
Command-E (PC: Control-E). Hold
the Command key (PC: Control
key), go to the Layers palette,
and click on the tube layer to put
a selection around the tubes
(as shown).

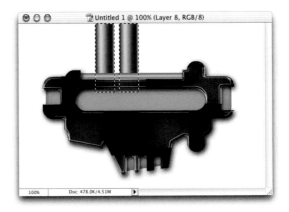

STEP TWENTY-FOUR: Create
a new blank layer. Press "d" to
make sure your Foreground
color is still black, then press
Command-Delete (PC: Control-
Backspace) to fill these two
rectangular selections with
your Background color (which
is white).

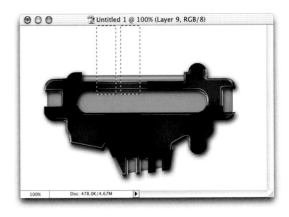

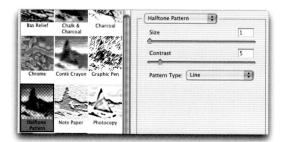

STEP TWENTY-FIVE: Go under the Filter menu, under Sketch, and choose Halftone Pattern to bring up the Filter Gallery. In the options on the right side of the dialog set the Size to 1, the Contrast to 5, and for Pattern Type choose Line.

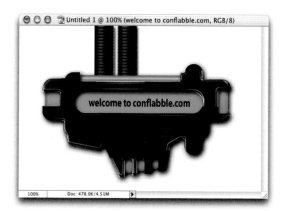

STEP TWENTY-SIX: Click OK to apply these gray lines over your white fill. Deselect by pressing Command-D (PC: Control-D), then go to the Layers palette and change the Blend Mode of this layer to Multiply to have it blend in with the gradient tubes (as shown). Last, add some type to the center (I used the font Myriad from Adobe) .

Quick Tip:
If the blend isn't right, drag again

In a tutorial elsewhere in the book, I ask you to drag a gradient on a Layer Mask to reveal the photo on the layer below it. The nice thing about this technique is that if it's not right the first time you try it, just keep dragging until it does look right. Every time you drag again, it creates an entirely new mask. Also, try painting on the mask (actually, it looks like you're painting on the layer, but it's really painting on the mask, so don't let that throw you) using solid black to reveal the layer below, or solid white to cover it back up.

Reverse Restoration

It seems that everyone has a new technique for repairing or restoring images. You can find a gazillion tutorials on the subject just about anywhere. But what about aging an image? It takes a special kind of twisted individual to destroy a perfectly good image. Try it out; it's very therapeutic.

STEP ONE: Open the image you wish to age (a classic Chevy in our example). Press the letter "d" to set your Foreground color to black and your Background color to white. Go under Image, and choose Canvas Size. When the Canvas Size dialog box appears, add at least 2 inches to both the Width and Height, and click OK.

© Brand X Pictures

STEP TWO: Choose the Rectangular Marquee tool from the Toolbox and make a selection slightly larger than the original image (see example). Press Command-J (PC: Control-J) to copy the selection onto its own layer (Layer 1).

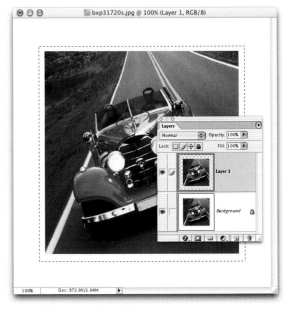

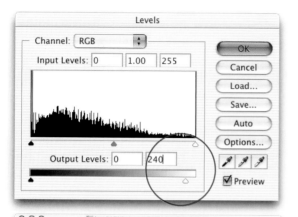

STEP THREE: Press Command-L (PC: Control-L) to bring up the Levels dialog box. Move the highlight Output Levels slider (the white slider in the lower right) toward the left until the Output Levels field on the right reads 240, and click OK.

STEP FOUR: Choose the Lasso tool from the Toolbox. Make a selection of the upper-left corner of the image like the one shown here. Press Command-J (PC: Control-J) to copy the selected area up onto its own layer (Layer 2).

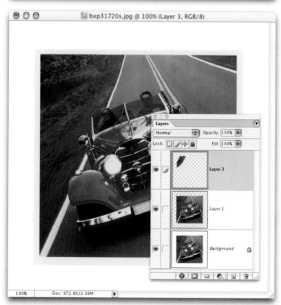

STEP FIVE: Create a new layer (Layer 3) by clicking on the New Layer icon at the bottom of the Layers palette. Drag this new layer beneath the layer with the small photo chunk on it. With the new layer still highlighted, Command-click (PC: Control-click) on the photo chunk layer to make a selection. Press Command-Delete (PC: Control-Backspace) to fill the selection with the Background color (white). Click on the photo chunk layer, and press Command-E (PC: Control-E) to merge down. Press Command-D (PC: Control-D) to deselect.

continued

Quick Tip:
Saving your brushes

After you've created a cus-tom brush and saved it as a Brush Preset by choosing New Brush Preset from the Brushes palette's pop-up menu, the next time you launch Photoshop, that brush will appear in the same position in your Brushes palette. However, if you reset your brushes to their factory defaults (by choosing Reset Brushes from the Brushes palette's drop-down menu), all of your custom brushes will be gone forever. If that's a concern to you, make sure you save your new set of brushes by going under the Brushes drop-down menu and choosing Save Brushes. What I do is de-lete all the other brushes by holding the Option key (PC: Alt key) and clicking once on each of them. Then, when I'm down to just the new brushes I've created, I choose Save Brushes from the Brushes palette's pop-up menu, name that brush set with a name I'll remember (such as Acme Co. logos), and save it in the Brushes folder, inside the Preset folder, inside my Photo-shop folder. Whew!

STEP SIX: Click on the Add a Layer Style icon (the black circle with the "f" in it) at the bottom of the Layers palette, and choose Bevel and Emboss. When the Layer Style dialog box appears, enter 115 for Size, set the Angle to 120˚, and lower the Highlight Mode to 40%, and then click OK.

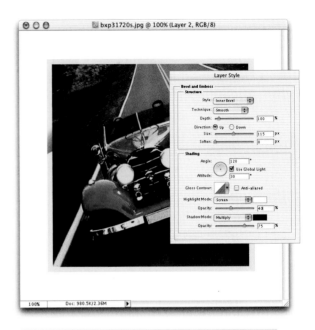

STEP SEVEN: Go under the Filter menu and choose Liquify. To slightly bend the top portion of the image, use the Forward Warp tool (the top tool in the Toolbar) and adjust your Brush Size so that it's approximately the same width as the top of the photo chunk (see example). Click-and-drag from the top of the image toward the bottom (not too much). Now, use a smaller brush to bend in the left side of the image (see below right), and click OK.

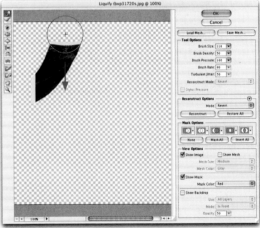

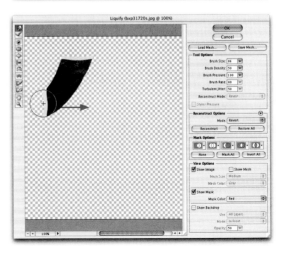

STEP EIGHT: Click on Layer 1 (the duplicate photo layer) in the Layers palette to make it active. Choose the Eraser tool from the Toolbox, and remove the areas that extend out past the bends on the photo chunk layer (see example).

STEP NINE: Press Shift-O until you get the Burn tool. Choose a medium-sized, soft edged brush from the Brush Picker in the Options Bar and darken some of the corners and sides of the image (as shown).

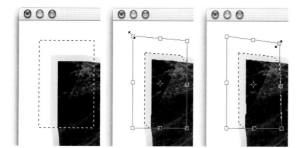

STEP TEN: With the duplicate photo layer still active, use the Rectangular Marquee tool to make a selection over the top-left corner of the image (as shown far left). Press Command-T (PC: Control-T) to bring up Free Transform. Command-click (PC: Control-click) on the top left adjustment point, and move it slightly upward and to the right. Now, Command-click (PC: Control-click) on the top-right adjustment point, and move it down just a bit (see example).

continued

Quick Tip:
See your documents side by side

Since the beginning of Photoshop history (back when dinosaurs roamed the earth) when you had one image open onscreen and you opened a second image, the way the images were displayed within your monitor was called cascading. What that meant was, when you opened an image, it would open in front of the existing image (as you've already experienced countless times). However, back in Photoshop 7, Adobe added a new document view that has been in page layout programs for years, and my guess is you're going to love it. It's called Tile and what it does is tile all your open documents one beside the other filling your monitor. Photographers should love this, because they can open up to 10 or 12 proofs and display them side-by-side on their monitor. Tile is found under the Window menu under Arrange. Open up three or four images then choose Tile and you'll see what all the fuss is about.

Quick Tip:
Brush size changes since Photoshop 7

Here's a tip about a feature that was added in Photoshop 7 that didn't make big headlines, but when you realize what it means, it's absolutely mondo-crazy big! The feature is the Master Diameter slider in the Brushes palette (found under the Window menu, choose Brushes). This enables you to change the size of a selected brush. I know that sounds like no big deal because you could always change the size of a brush, right? Well, not always. You see, previous versions of Photoshop let you change the size of round soft-edged and hard-edged brushes, but NOT the custom brushes. This meant that if Adobe created a cool custom brush at 25 pixels, that's the size it was stuck at. So, for high-res images, many of those smaller custom brushes were totally unusable because they were too small. Now, just pick *any* custom brush and make it the size you want it. Even if you create your own custom brush, it's totally scalable with the Master Diameter slider. Way, mondo-crazy cool!

STEP ELEVEN: Press Return (PC: Enter) to lock in the transformation, then press Command-D (PC: Control-D) to deselect. Click on the photo chunk layer (Layer 3) and press Command-E (PC: Control-E) to merge down. Now, press Command-T (PC: Control-T) to bring up the Free Transform bounding box. Rotate the image by moving your cursor outside of the bounding box (your cursor will turn into a double-sided arrow), and rotate as desired. Press Return (PC: Enter) to apply the transformation. Click on the Background layer and press Command-Delete (PC: Control-Backspace) to fill it with the Background color (white).

STEP TWELVE: Click on the photo layer (Layer 1) to make it active. Now, click on the Add a Layer Style icon and choose Drop Shadow. Change the Size to 10, and click OK. Go under the Layer menu, under Layer Style, and choose Create Layer. When the warning dialog box appears, click OK. This will place the drop shadow on its own layer.

STEP THIRTEEN: Click on Layer 1's Drop Shadow in the Layers palette. Go under the Filter menu, under Distort, and choose Shear. When the dialog box appears, click on the center of the vertical line in the grid to add a new adjustment point. Then, click-and-drag the top and bottom adjustment points toward the right (see example), and click OK. Lower the layer Opacity to 50%, and use the Move tool to drag the shadow to the right.

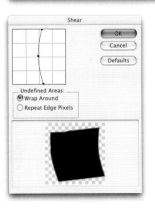

STEP FOURTEEN: Open a background image for your car photo (a map in our example). Use the Move tool to click-and-drag the new background into your original document. Drag this new background image to the bottom of the layer stack, just above the Background layer, in the Layers palette.

STEP FIFTEEN: Press Command-Shift-U (PC: Control-Shift-U) to desaturate Layer 2. Click on Layer 1 and Desaturate this layer as well. Create a new layer (Layer 3), and move it to the top of the layer stack in the Layers palette. Click on the Foreground Color Swatch and choose a light cream color. Press Option-Delete (PC: Alt-Backspace) to fill the new layer with the Foreground color. Change the Layer Blend Mode to Color to complete the effect.

Before

After

Quick Tip:
Load those sets, baby!

Back in Photoshop 6, Adobe introduced loadable Presets (collections) of Brushes, Patterns, Shapes, etc. What was nice, rather than digging through dialog boxes to dig up sets buried in folders on your computer, you could load these presets right from the palette's drop-down menus. What was bad was the quality of those presets. They were, (and I'm being as kind as possible here) incredibly lame. Adobe fixed that in Photoshop 7 and included lots of usable shapes, patterns, brushes, and other presets, and Photoshop CS added even more.

Not only that, there are many more sets than in Photoshop 7. So if you haven't loaded some sets in a while, it's time to take another look.

Quick Tip:
**Getting rid of
blemishes and
scratches on
your image**

If you have an image
with blemishes, spots, or
scratches (generally called
"artifacts"), here's a little
trick that will help. Click
on the Blur tool, and in
the Options Bar, lower the
tool's Opacity setting to
20%, change the blend
Mode to Lighten, and
start painting over
your scratches. In just a
few strokes you'll see your
scratches start to disappear.

From Human to Cyborg

This technique of "revealing the inner robot" has become incredibly popular lately, and it's showing up in print, on the Web—just about everywhere. At first you might think, "I don't have any
robot innards photos" but you'll be amazed at how a photo of mechanical parts (from car engines
to industrial plants to a photo of the inside of your computer) will do the trick. This one looks complicated, but it's surprisingly simple.

STEP ONE: Open the photo
of a person that you want to
"robotize." The photo in this
example captures the exact
moment at which the man
in the photo has passed out
and is totally unconscious,
due to smelling his own
underarm odor.

STEP TWO: Press "p" to get
the Pen tool and draw a path
like the one shown here, going
down his arm. If you're not
familiar with the Pen tool, here's
what to do: Click once (just below the wrist, on the left side of
his arm), then move to the right,
and click-and-drag slightly upward for the next point (and to
put a slight downward curve in
your path). Move down the arm,
and click-and-drag to the left
to curve the path outward and
create the next point. Then click
over on the left (as shown).

STEP THREE: Click back on the
point where you started, to
complete your path (as shown).
If you're uncomfortable with
the Pen tool, you could use the
Polygonal Lasso tool, but your
lines will be straight instead of
slightly curved, so it won't follow the contours of his arm, and
thus it will look a little "fakey."
Hey, it's a tradeoff.

STEP FOUR: Press Command-Return (PC: Control-Enter) to turn your path into a selection (as shown here).

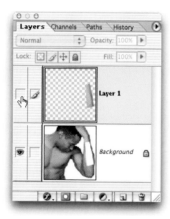

STEP FIVE: Now, press Shift-Command-J (PC: Shift-Control-J) to cut this selected area out of your Background layer and copy it on its own separate layer above the background. Go to the Layers palette, and hide this new layer from view by clicking on the Eye icon in the first column next to your layer (as shown here).

STEP SIX: In the Layers palette, click on the Background layer to make it active. Press "w" to get the Magic Wand tool, and click once within the white area you cut out of his arm. This will select this entire white area (as shown).

continued

Quick Tip:
Save that mesh!

If you're a Liquify user (and I know that you are), Photoshop lets you save the mesh that you create and apply it to another image. So what's the big deal about that? Well, you could apply your Liquify adjustments on a low-res version of your image, save the mesh, then apply that same mesh to a high-res version of the same image. This has some very interesting implications (none of which I can think of at this time, but I've always wanted to use that sentence).

Quick Tip:
Color-correction shortcut

If you're new to color-correcting images, you've probably already learned that Auto Levels and Auto Contrast are pretty limited. However, back in Photoshop 7, Adobe introduced its best "color-correction one-trick pony" yet. It's called Auto Color and it can help your color images look better by analyzing the image's highlights, midtones, and shadows. It then tries to neutralize any color casts in those areas. Give it a try next time you're stuck with a yucky photo (that's a technical term).

STEP SEVEN: Open the photo that you'll use for your "robot guts." The photo shown here is taken inside an industrial plant but a lot of photos work well for this, including auto parts, the insides of watches, factory and plant photos, and basically any photo with lots of visible cables and wires. Press Command-A (PC: Control-A) to put a selection around the photo, then press Command-C (PC: Control-C) to copy the photo into memory.

STEP EIGHT: Go back to the photo of the man. Your selection should still be in place, so go under the Edit menu and choose Paste Into. This will paste the photo that's in memory into your selected area (as shown here). Chances are, it will be too big, so in the next step, you'll scale it down to size.

STEP NINE: Press Command-T (PC: Control-T) to bring up Free Transform. You probably won't be able to reach the Free Transform handles, so press Command-0 (zero) (PC: Control-0) and Photoshop will automatically resize your window, making the handles all within reach (as shown). Hold the Shift key, grab one of the corner points and drag inward to scale the robot guts down in size (as shown here). You can position them by clicking-and-dragging within the bounding box.

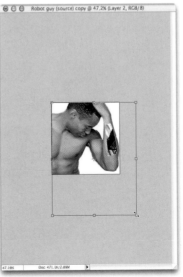

STEP TEN: When the size and position look right to you, press Return (PC: Enter) to lock in your transformation (as shown here).

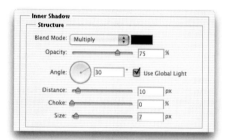

STEP ELEVEN: To make it look like the robot guts are really inside his arm, we're going to add a shadow inside, which will help add depth. Choose Inner Shadow from the Add a Layer Style pop-up menu at the bottom of the Layers palette. When the dialog appears, increase the Distance to 10 and the Size to 7.

STEP TWELVE: When you click OK, the shadow is applied to the top and right side of your robot guts, making it look like the guts are inside the arm. In the next step, we'll help make it look even more like it's really inside.

continued

Quick Tip:
How to copy a flattened version in a multilayered document

When you make a selection on a layer and press Command-C (PC: Control-C), Photoshop copies the selected area from that layer into memory. But did you know that you can copy from all your visible layers (as if from a flattened image), by adding Shift to that keyboard shortcut? That's right. To do that press Shift-Command-C (PC: Shift-Control-C), and it captures everything inside your selected area as if it was a flattened background image.

We've been using the Command-click (PC: Control-click) on the layer's name trick to put a selection around your type throughout this book. But that puts a selection around all your text. What if you want to select just one or two letters? You can do it, but first you have to rasterize your Type layer by going under the Layer menu, under Rasterize, and choosing Type. You might be tempted to try selecting the letter with the Magic Wand tool, but don't—it'll leave behind little edge pixels if you move the type. Instead, try this: Draw a very loose selection around the letter or letters that you want to select (don't touch the edges of the letters, just make a loose selection). Hold the Command key (PC: Control key) and press one of the Arrow keys on your keyboard. Your letter will be immediately selected with no messy edge pixels, so now you can colorize it, move it, or do whatever.

STEP THIRTEEN: In the Layers palette, hold the Command key (PC: Control key) and click once on the black and white Layer Mask thumbnail that appears to the right of your robot guts layer. This put a selection around your guts. Press "L" to switch to the Lasso tool, then press the Right Arrow key (on your keyboard) twice, and then the Down Arrow key twice to nudge the selection down and to the right.

STEP FOURTEEN: In the Layers palette, click on the Background layer (your selection should still be in place). Press Command-L (PC: Control-L) to bring up the Levels dialog. Click on the bottom-left Output Levels slider and drag it to the right (as shown) to add a highlight just outside the hole in his arm. This adds some depth to the wall of the arm. Click OK.

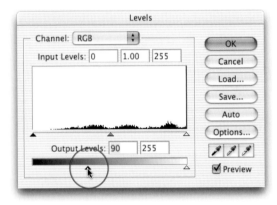

STEP FIFTEEN: Deselect by pressing Command-D (PC: Control-D) and you can see (in the example shown here) that the edges of the arm, where the hole is, now look as if they have some depth, thanks to the highlight you added in the last step. Note: You might be thinking, "Hey, aren't the highlight and shadow on the same side?" They are. I did that because the left side of the arm will be covered up in a minute, and it will need some more depth, so…we're going to cheat.

STEP SIXTEEN: Go to the Layers palette and click on the top layer (the cutout chunk of arm). Press the letter "v" to get the Move tool, then drag this layer down and to the left (as shown here) so it overlaps the arm.

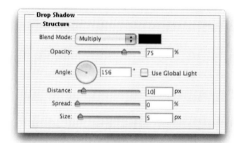

STEP SEVENTEEN: Choose Drop Shadow from the Add a Layer Style pop-up menu at the bottom of the Layers palette. When the dialog appears, turn off the Use Global Light checkbox (so we can position the shadow without disturbing shadows on other layers). Increase the Distance to 10, then set the Angle to 156°.

STEP EIGHTEEN: Because you changed the Angle setting, the shadow will now cast back onto the robot guts (as shown here). If it helps you mentally, just assume we're using multiple light sources. Now press OK to apply your shadow (as shown). Now, you'll need to make the chunk of arm look thicker, as if it has some depth.

Quick Tip:
Setting shades of gray

Photoshop is such an incredibly powerful program that surely there would be a little slider or pop-up menu for creating shades of gray, right? Well, there is one, it's just a bit hidden. Go under the Window menu and choose Show Color to bring up the Color palette. In the drop-down menu, choose Grayscale Slider. A slider will appear that goes from 0% to 100% and you can slide it to the percentage of gray that you want.

Another popular way, though a bit more cumbersome, is to click on the Foreground Color Swatch and in the CMYK fields of the Color Picker, enter 0 for Cyan, Magenta, and Yellow. Under Black, enter any number for the percentage of gray that you want, and click OK. This gives you a shade of gray without any CMY in it, whereas the Color palette gives you a gray color build, with percentages of Cyan, Magenta, and Yellow.

Quick Tip:
Adding spot colors

For years, Photoshop only wanted you to do one of three things: create a black-and-white image, a grayscale image, or a full-color image. However, back in Photoshop 5.0, Adobe introduced the ability to create spot color separations. To add a spot color to your grayscale image, make a selection of the area where you want to have a spot color, then go to the Channels palette, and from the drop-down menu choose New Spot Channel. When the dialog box appears, you can click on the Color Swatch and then click on the Custom button in the Color Picker to choose a PANTONE color to be your spot channel.

You can also add an extra spot color (or bump plate) to a four-color CMYK image in a similar fashion (giving you four color plates and a fifth spot color plate when you run your separations). There's even a special format for saving your image with spot colors: it's an EPS format called DCS 2.0 (which stands for Desktop Color Separation). There's a lot more to creating spot color seps, but at this point I just wanted to mention that they were there.

STEP NINETEEN: Hold the Command key (PC: Control key), go to the Layers palette, and click once on the arm chunk layer. This puts a selection around your arm chunk. Press "L" to switch to the Lasso tool, then press the Right Arrow key (on your keyboard) twice, and then the Down Arrow key twice to nudge the selection down and to the right (as shown here).

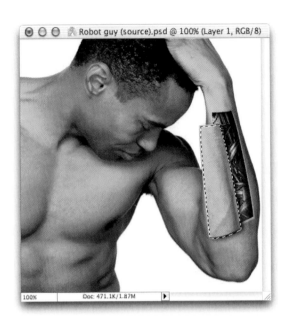

STEP TWENTY: You only want to effect the edge of your arm chunk, so go under the Select menu and choose Inverse to select everything except the area you selected in the previous step.

STEP TWENTY-ONE: Press Command-L (PC: Control-L) to bring up the Levels dialog. Click on the bottom-left Output Levels slider and drag it to the right (as shown) to add a highlight to that thin selected area. This helps to add depth to the arm chunk. Click OK.

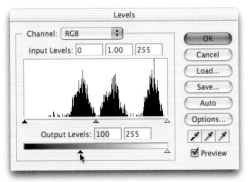

STEP TWENTY-TWO: Press Command-D (PC: Control-D) to deselect and the effect is complete (as shown here). You can see how adding the shadows (using Layer Styles) and highlighting just the edges (by nudging over that selection and using levels to brighten) makes all the difference.

OPTIONAL STEP: Now that you know the technique, it's simple to add other areas (in fact, the robot guts photo is still left in your memory) so pick a new spot, make your selection (remember to follow the contours of the body), then cut it out of the Background layer and copy it on its own layer. Go back to the Background layer, select the white hole, and choose Paste Into from the Edit menu. In the example shown here, you can see how leaving the chunk off the chest still looks good. (Most of the times I've seen this effect used, it doesn't have the arm chunk or chest chunk at all—just the exposed guts—so you can skip that whole part if you want, just showing the inside, and skipping the "door" effect.)

THIS SIDE
TOWARD SCREEN

CHAPTER 8
DOWN & DIRTY TRICKS

THIS SIDE
TOWARD SCREEN

CHAPTER 8
DOWN & DIRTY TRICKS

THIS SIDE
TOWARD SCREEN

CHAPTER 8
DOWN & DIRTY TRICKS

This chapter is where you learn the  effects that will subconsciously force people to purchase products and

Ad Libbing
Advertising Effects

services they neither want nor need, at prices they can't afford—increasing their personal debt, thereby putting them, and perhaps the entire country, on the verge of a financial collapse that can only be compared to "Black Saturday," when the market didn't drop because it was closed for trading, but had it been open surely something would've happened which I would then feel compelled to chronicle here; and that would have made this perhaps the longest run-on sentence in the history of modern literature, rather than the concise, straight-to-the-point introduction that you've come to expect from writers like me, who value your time, yet don't mind using a comma or two (but only when absolutely, positively necessary), like now. OK, keep breathing, keep breathing. In through the nose, out through the mouth. Or why not try Nasatrin, which provides 12-hour nondrowsy relief from common allergy symptoms, such as....

Quick Tip:
**Moving shapes
as you draw**

While you're using one of
Photoshop's Shape tools,
you can reposition the
shape as you're dragging
it out by holding down
the Spacebar.

Quick Elegant Product Background

This is a nice way to showcase an elegant product, such as jewelry, watches, etc.; and it really
gives that "shot-in-the-studio" look because it appears as though the red area is created by
a soft flood light. Best of all, this is one of those "create it from scratch in 60 seconds" type of
effects that appear to have taken hours.

STEP ONE: Open a new document in the size you'd like for
your background (the one
shown here is a 5"x7" document
in RGB mode). Press "d" to set
your Foreground color to black,
then press Option-Delete (PC:
Alt-Backspace) to fill the Background layer with black. Then
add a new blank layer by clicking on the New Layer icon at the
bottom of the Layers palette (as
shown here).

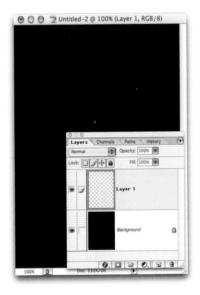

STEP TWO: Press Shift-M until
you get the Elliptical Marquee
tool, and draw a horizontal
oval-shaped selection (like
the one shown here) with each
end extending outside the
document's edges. Once you've
done that, if you have to center
your selection, just click the
Elliptical Marquee tool within
the oval selection area and
drag to reposition it.

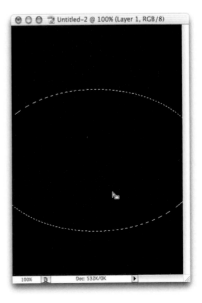

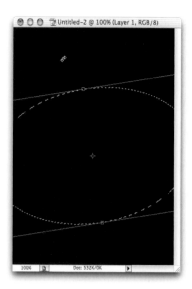

STEP THREE: Now you need to rotate your selection. Go under the Select menu and choose Transform Selection. When the Transform Selection bounding box appears, move your cursor outside the bounding box, above the oval. Your cursor will change into a two-headed curved arrow. Click-and-drag to the left and as you do your oval will rotate to the left (as shown here). When it looks like the one here, press Return (PC: Enter) to lock in your rotation. Don't deselect yet.

Quick Tip:
Unlinking layers the fast way

If you have a number of layers linked together and you want to quickly unlink them, you'll love this tip—just hold the Option key (PC: Alt key) and click directly on the tiny Brush icon in the second column beside your current layer. This will immediately unlink all layers linked to your current layer.

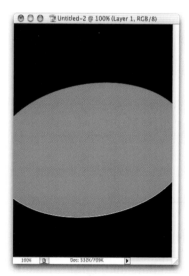

STEP FOUR: In the Toolbox, click on the Foreground Color Swatch to bring up the Color Picker, and then choose red for your Foreground color. Now, press Option-Delete (PC: Alt-Backspace) to fill your oval selection with red. Now you can deselect by pressing Command-D (PC: Control-D).

STEP FIVE: To soften the edges of our red oval (and make it look more like a soft red spotlight), go under the Filter menu, under Blur, and choose Gaussian Blur. When the Gaussian Blur dialog box appears, enter 48 pixels (for high-res, 300-ppi images, enter 230 pixels).

continued

Quick Tip:
Name it the
slow way?

Now that Photoshop has fixed the process of naming layers, do you miss the old Layer Properties dialog box? I know you don't, but just humor me. Hey, there actually is a reason you might want to access that annoying box—to color code your layer (ahhh, you forgot about that, didn't you?). Anyway, if you miss that annoying dialog, just Control-click (PC: Right-click) on the layer's thumbnail in the Layers palette and in the resulting pop-up menu, choose Layer Properties.

STEP SIX: When you click OK, this softens the edges of your red circle, creating the effect of a spotlight (this will look more realistic once you add a product to your image, as you'll soon see).

STEP SEVEN: Open an image of the product you want to place on your red spotlight background. In this case, it's a gold necklace with diamonds and a ruby (I'm guessing that's a ruby, which gives you an idea of how few rubies I've bought over the years). Use any selection tools you're comfortable with to put a selection around your product (it's on a white background, so the Magic Wand will probably do the trick).

© Brand X Pictures

STEP EIGHT: Once the object is selected, press the letter "v" to switch to the Move tool, click on the object, and drag it over into your red spotlight document (as shown here).

STEP NINE: Press Command-T (PC: Control-T) to bring up Free Transform. Move your cursor outside the bounding box (as shown), and click-and-drag to rotate the necklace to the left. Once the rotation looks right, move your cursor inside the bounding box, and click-and-drag to move the necklace up into the left corner (as shown). Then press Return (PC: Enter) to lock in your transformation.

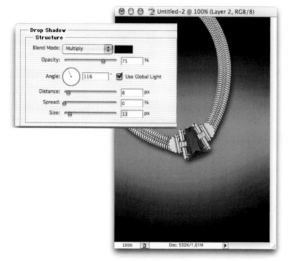

STEP TEN: To add some depth and to make it look as if the necklace is sitting over the background, choose Drop Shadow from the Add a Layer Style pop-up menu at the bottom of the Layers palette. When the Drop Shadow dialog appears, increase the Distance to 8 and the Size to 13 (as shown in the inset). Note: For high-res, 300-ppi photos, set your Distance to 33 and Size to 54. When the shadow looks like the one shown here, click OK.

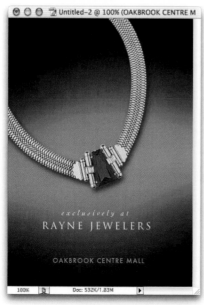

STEP ELEVEN: The effect is now complete. To finish things off you can add some type. In the example shown here, the words "exclusively at" are set in the font Cochin Italic (from Adobe) with 340 tracking (the spacing between letters). The words "RAYNE JEWELERS" is set in Trajan (also from Adobe) with 300 tracking, and at the bottom, "OAKBROOK CENTRE MALL" is set in Futura Medium (also from Adobe) with 105 tracking.

Quick Tip:
Change contours
for a new effect

If you like to experiment
with Layer Styles, chang-
ing the current contour of
your Bevel and Emboss,
or Satin effect, is a great
way to tweak an existing
effect and give it a totally
different look. Just click
the down-facing triangle
next to the current Contour
thumbnail. A library of
contours will appear, and
you can just start clicking
on each contour until you
see an effect you really like.
It sounds simple, and it is.

Quick Product Shot Background

Here's a very useful photographic background technique that not only looks great, but takes
only seconds to create. Perfect for catalog shots, magazine ads, and product shots of all kinds.
You can even use it as a background for portraits, but you might want to use a less warm
combination than yellow and brown. For portraits, start with a bright blue background in Step
One, and then add a dark blue in Step Two.

STEP ONE: Open a new document in RGB mode. Click on
the Foreground Color Swatch
in the Toolbox and choose a
bright yellow in the Color Picker
(the build shown here is R=252,
G=252, B=2). Fill your Background layer with this yellow
color by pressing Option-Delete
(PC: Alt-Backspace).

STEP TWO: Create a new
layer by clicking on the New
Layer icon at the bottom of the
Layers palette. Change your
Foreground color to a very
dark brown and fill your new
layer with this color by pressing
Option-Delete (PC: Alt-Backspace). Press the letter "m" to
get the Rectangular Marquee
tool and draw a thin rectangular
selection in the center of your
image area (as shown here).
Then, go under the Select menu
and choose Feather. When the
Feather dialog appears, enter
50 pixels (to soften the edges of
your selection).

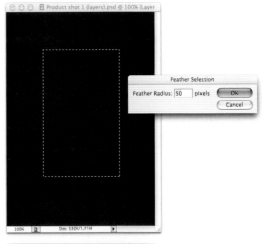

STEP THREE: When you click OK
in the Feather dialog, you'll see
the edges of your rectangular
selection become rounded (as
shown here).

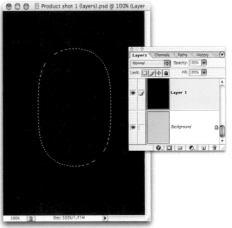

STEP FOUR: Now press Delete (PC: Backspace) to knock a large, soft-edged hole out of your brown-filled layer, revealing part of your yellow Background layer (as shown here). Deselect by pressing Command-D (PC: Control-D).

© Brand X Pictures

STEP FIVE: Open an image of the product you want to appear on this background. Use the selection tool of your choice to put a selection around the product, then get the Move tool and drag the product over to your brown/yellow background document (as shown here). To add some depth, in the next step you'll add a drop shadow.

STEP SIX: Choose Drop Shadow from the Add a Layer Style pop-up menu at the bottom of the Layers palette. When the Drop Shadow dialog appears, increase the Opacity to 85%, the Distance to 9, and the Size to 11, and click OK to apply your shadow. In the example shown here, I finished off by using the Type tool to add some type. The word "beautyscape" is set in the font Cochin (from Adobe) with the tracking set at 1000. The store name is Futura Light, and the cities are set in Cochin too.

Quick Tip:
Crop and straighten at the same time

When you're using the Crop tool, you can rotate your selected area before you crop by moving your cursor outside the bounding box that appears around your image where you dragged the Crop tool. You'll see that your cursor temporarily changes into a double-headed arrow, which enables you to freely rotate your object. When it's rotated just the way you like it, you have two choices: Double-click inside the bounding box or press Return (PC: Enter) to make the rotation permanent. If you're using the Crop tool and you decide that you don't want to crop the image after all, click once on the Crop tool icon in the Toolbox. A dialog box will appear giving you the option to Crop or Don't Crop.

Electronics Photo Background

You'll see this particular photo background used a lot in photos of electronic items like digital cameras, DV camcorders, cell phones, and things along those lines. The blue spotlight effect (created with a built-in preset in the Lighting Effects filter) works well for displaying high-tech gadgets, and the reflections and shadows you'll add really make it look like a studio job.

STEP ONE: Open a new document in RGB mode. Press "d" to set your Foreground to black, then click on the Background Color Swatch (in the Toolbox) and when the Color Picker appears, choose a light gray (as shown here). Now switch to the Gradient tool by pressing the letter "g."

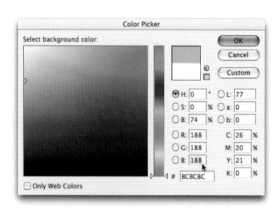

STEP TWO: Once you have the Gradient tool, press Return (PC: Enter) and the Gradient Picker will appear onscreen. Make sure the first gradient (Foreground to Background) is selected. Then click the Gradient tool about 1/3 of the way from the bottom of your image area, and drag downward (as shown) to create a gradient on your Background layer like the one shown here.

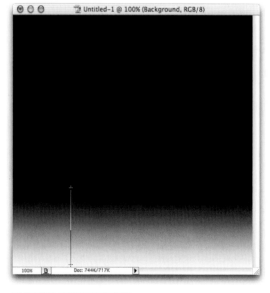

STEP THREE: Create a new blank layer by clicking on the New Layer Icon at the bottom of the Layers palette. Press "d" then "x" to set your Foreground color to white, then fill your layer with white by pressing Option-Delete (PC: Alt-Backspace).

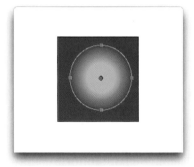

STEP FOUR: Go under the Filter menu, under Render, and choose Lighting Effects. When the Lighting Effects dialog appears, from the Style pop-up menu at the top, choose Blue Omni (as shown here). A preview of your lighting effect will be shown on the left side of the Lighting Effects dialog (the preview is shown here).

STEP FIVE: Within the Preview window, you'll see a circle with a center point and four outer points. Click directly on the center point (right within the Preview window) and drag it up and to the right just a little bit (as shown here). Compare this with the default position (shown in Step Four) and you'll see how this is now moved up and to the right just a little bit.

STEP SIX: Click OK in the Lighting Effects dialog box and your Blue Omni effect is applied to your white layer (as shown here).

Quick Tip:
If it's metal, sharpen the living heck out of it

First off, I had to say "heck," because there could be kids reading this book—and some of them might be really smart toddlers, so you can never be too careful. One thing I've found, and that *you* might find helpful is that when you have a chrome or metallic image, you can apply the Unsharp Mask filter with very high settings for Amount (such as 300 to 500) and it looks just fine. In fact, sometimes I'll apply Unsharp Mask to chrome type three or four times in a row (with Amount settings around 100 to 150). Those hard edges just soak up the sharpening.

The main things you need to look out for are halos or weird unwanted colors that can start to creep into your edges. Otherwise, sharpen till the cows come home (if you don't have cows, just keep sharpening until someone yells, "Stop!").

continued

Quick Tip:
Getting better results from the Eyedropper tool

There's one setting you should change immediately that will give you better results from your Eyedropper tool. Click on the Eyedropper, and in the Options Bar change the Sample Size from Point Sample to 3 by 3 Average. This helps keep you from getting erroneous readings when using the Eyedropper because when it's set to Point Sample, you get the reading from one single pixel, which may not be representative of the colors in the area where you're clicking. Set to 3 by 3 Average, it averages the color of the pixels surrounding the area that you clicked, which is considered by many to provide a much more usable reading when doing color correction.

STEP SEVEN: Click once on the Layer Mask icon at the bottom of the Layers palette (it's the second icon from the left). Make sure your Foreground color is set to black, and then get the Gradient tool, but this time, click in the bottom third of your image area and drag upward (as shown). This Layer Mask gradient blend reveals the bottom of your Background layer (as shown here).

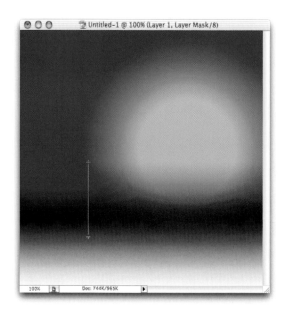

STEP EIGHT: Now you're done with the Layer Mask, so in the Layers palette, click directly on the Layer Mask itself (that's the extra thumbnail to the right of your layer, with a visible gradient) and drag it to the Trash icon at the bottom of the Layers palette. When the dialog appears asking "Apply mask to layer before removing?" choose Apply.

STEP NINE: Get the Elliptical Marquee tool, hold the Shift key, and draw a huge circular selection (like the one shown here). Click your cursor within the circle and drag the selection into position up and to the right (like the one shown here), with the top right of the circular selection extending outside your image area.

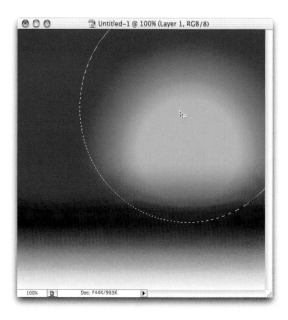

STEP TEN: To soften the edges of your circular selection, go under the Select Menu and choose Feather. When the Feather dialog appears, enter 50 and click OK (as shown here).

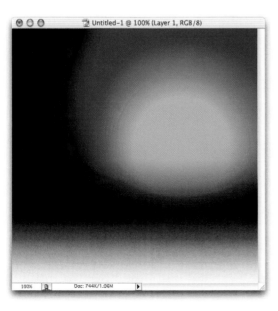

STEP ELEVEN: Go under the Select menu and choose Inverse, to inverse the selection, leaving the round bright omni spot unselected, and selecting the surrounding areas (as shown here).

STEP TWELVE: Press Delete (PC: Backspace) and those extra areas are deleted. Press Command-D (PC: Control-D) to deselect, leaving the image shown here.

Quick Tip:
Fill shortcuts

Here are some quick short-cuts that can be real time savers for filling selections or layers. For example:

- To fill an entire layer with your Foreground color, press Option-Delete (PC: Alt-Backspace).

- To fill just an object on a layer (not the entire layer), press Shift-Option-Delete (PC: Shift-Alt-Backspace).

- To fill with your Back-ground color, press Command-Delete (PC: Control-Backspace).

- To fill your layer with black, press the letter "d," then Option-Delete (PC: Alt-Backspace).

- To fill your layer with white, press the letter "d," then the letter "x," then press Option-Delete (PC: Alt-Backspace).

continued

Quick Tip:
Horizontal scaling without the palette

Throughout this book we often increase the amount of Horizontal Scaling of our type (the thickness of the letters) by typing in a percentage value in the Character palette. But there's another way to edit the Horizontal Scaling of your image without typing numbers in the Character palette. In Photoshop CS, after you enter your type, but before you press Enter to commit your type (in other words, your cursor is still blinking somewhere in your type), simply press and hold the Command key (PC: Control key). This will reveal a bounding box around your type. Then click-and-drag the right center adjustment point (on the bounding box) to the right. As you do, it will stretch the type (scaling it horizontally) and will give you the same effect as if you had typed a percentage in the Character palette in the first place. This is a much more visual way to scale your type horizontally.

STEP THIRTEEN: Open the photo you want to use as a product shot. If the product is not already on its own separate layer (with a transparent background) use the selection tool of your choice to put a selection around the product. (In the example shown here, I clicked the Magic Wand tool on the white background to select it all, then I chose Inverse to select just the computer.)

STEP FOURTEEN: Press the letter "v" to switch to the Move tool and drag the product onto your blue omni document. If the product appears too large (or too small), press Command-T (PC: Control-T) to bring up Free Transform. Hold the Shift key, click on one of the corner points of the bounding box, and drag inward to scale it down to size. Press Return (PC: Enter) to lock in your transformation.

STEP FIFTEEN: Once the product is at the right size, press Option-Command-T (PC: Alt-Control-T) to bring up Free Transform again. Adding the Option/Alt keys will create a duplicate of the computer on its own layer and any transformations will affect only the duplicate. Move your cursor inside the bounding box, then Control-click (PC: Right-click) to bring up a pop-up menu of transformations (shown here). Choose Flip Vertical (as shown).

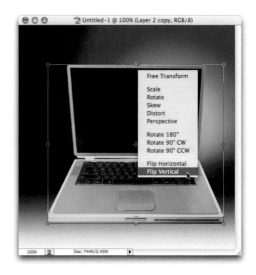

STEP SIXTEEN: When you choose Flip Vertical, it flips your product vertically (well, duh) as shown here. Press Return (PC: Enter) to lock in your transformation.

STEP SEVENTEEN: Hold the Shift key, and with the Move tool, click-and-drag the vertically flipped product straight downward (holding the Shift key will keep it perfectly aligned as you drag) until the bottom of your flipped version meets the bottom of your original version (as shown here).

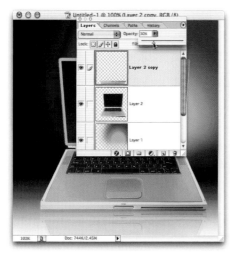

STEP EIGHTEEN: To make this flipped copy look like a reflection, go to the Layers palette and lower the Opacity to around 30% (as shown).

Quick Tip:
Saving time when creating custom gradients

If you're creating custom gradients and the colors you need for your gradient appear in the image you currently have open, you can really save yourself some time when changing the color of existing Color Stops. (Does that make any sense? Well, read on, and hopefully it will.) Here's how: Click on the Gradient thumbnail (in the Options Bar) to open the Gradient Editor. Then, click on the Color Stop you want to edit (don't double-click, just click once), then move your cursor out over your image. Your cursor immediately changes into an Eyedropper tool and you can sample a color directly from that image. Your Color Stop will change to that color—all without opening the Color Picker. Pretty neat! (Do people still say "neat"?)

continued

Quick Tip:
The "make anything chrome" trick

If there's anything that you want to turn into chrome, there's just one trick you have to know (besides the Curve mentioned in the Quick Tip on the opposite page): You've got to bevel the object first. To create a beveled effect we use the Lighting Effects filter on a blurred Alpha channel. The rest is simple enough—just add a Curves Adjustment Layer and draw a hill in the curves window.

So, any time you want to turn something into chrome, think first about how to bevel or emboss it, then think chrome.

Option #2: The Bevel and Emboss Inner Bevel Layer Effect will usually do the trick, but right after you apply it, you have to create a new blank layer, drag it below your beveled and embossed layer, click on your beveled layer, and choose Merge Down from the Layers palette's drop-down menu. Otherwise, the chrome curve interacts with the live bevel effect and it looks...well, bad.

Option #3: Alien Skin's Inner Bevel Boss plug-in from their Eye Candy 4000 collection also works like a charm.

STEP NINETEEN: To add more depth (and make it look more realistic) you can add a drop shadow. Do this by creating a new blank layer and then drag it beneath your original product layer in the Layers palette. Then, get the Brush tool, and choose a medium sized, soft-edged brush. Up in the Options Bar, lower the Opacity to 40%, hold the Shift key, and paint a straight line under the bottom of the keyboard (as shown).

STEP TWENTY: You've come this far, you're not going to just leave the monitor black are you? Nah! Go ahead and open a photo that you'd like to appear within the laptop's monitor (as if the photo were actually being displayed on the computer, full screen). Press Command-A (PC: Control-A) to select the entire photo. Then Press Command-C (PC: Control-C) to copy the photo into memory.

STEP TWENTY-ONE: Go back to your product shot, click on the computer layer in the Layers palette to make it active, then get the Magic Wand tool, and click it within the black monitor window (as shown). If it doesn't select the entire monitor at first, hold the Shift key then click on any areas it missed, until the entire screen area is selected (as shown here).

STEP TWENTY-TWO: Go under the Edit menu and choose Paste Into. This pastes the car photo (from memory) into your selected area (as shown). Chances are the photo you pasted is too big, and will need to be scaled down to size.

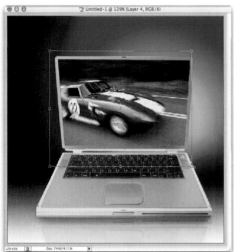

STEP TWENTY-THREE: To scale your photo down to size, press Command-T (PC: Control-T) to bring up Free Transform. Press Command-0 (zero) (PC: Control-0) to reach the Free Transform handles, then hold the Shift key and scale the photo down until it's pretty close to the size of the monitor (as shown here). Don't press Return (PC: Enter) yet.

STEP TWENTY-FOUR: The next problem to deal with is the fact that the photo looks flat, and doesn't match the angle of the monitor shown here. No sweat. Just hold the Command key (PC: Control key) grab the bottom-left corner point of the bounding box and drag it upward to the left corner of the monitor window (as shown). This begins the process of aligning your photo to the angle of the monitor.

Quick Tip:
Try different curve settings for different metallic effects

We often use Curves (Image>Adjustments>Curves) in conjunction with Lighting Effects (Filter>Render>Lighting Effects) that have been applied on a blurred Alpha channel to help produce metallic effects (see tip opposite page), and Curves is one area where you can experiment and have some fun. A curve with just one hill, then heads back up is usually enough to create the effect we're after, but for a more dynamic effect, try a curve with two or three hills. The more hills, the wilder it gets. If your curve starts introducing all sorts of weird colors, don't sweat it. When you're done with your curve, press Shift-Command-U (PC: Shift-Control-U) to take all the color out of your image, leaving just the shiny metal. The point is that there are no "right" curves; just move the points until something looks good to you.

continued

Quick Tip:
Finding out which gradient is which

Photoshop's gradients all have names, and even if you create your own, you're prompted to create a name for it. The problem is that the Gradient Picker shows thumbnails, so how do you know which gradient is which? There are two quick ways to make sure you're choosing the gradient you're looking for:

(1) Go under the Edit menu, under Preferences, and choose General. In the General Preference dialog box, turn on the checkbox for Show Tool Tips. With this preference turned on, if you rest your cursor over a gradient in the Gradient Picker, its name will "pop up"; and

(2) You can change the Gradient Picker to display the gradient names by choosing Text Only from the Picker's drop-down menu. However, the ideal solution may be to choose Small List from the drop-down menu, which gives you a small thumbnail followed by the gradient's name.

STEP TWENTY-FIVE: Continue to hold the Command key (PC: Control key) and grab the top-left corner point and do the same (align it to the top-left corner of the monitor). Repeat for the top right (as shown here), and finally the bottom right.

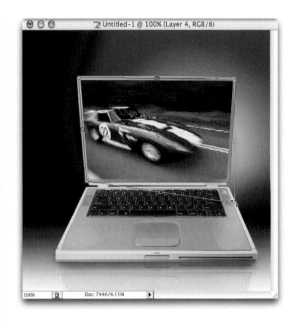

STEP TWENTY-SIX: When you press Return (PC: Enter) to lock in your transformation, the photo will now be angled as though it's really in the monitor's window, and the effect of building the studio background and putting the photo in the computer is complete (as shown here).

Adding a Window to Another Place

I saw this popular technique put to good use recently in a print ad for the Grand Dunes development. It makes use of one of the least-used Layer Styles (Inner Glow), and it's surprising what impact the final effect has, despite how easy it is to pull off. Here's a step-by-step.

© Brand X Pictures

STEP ONE: Open the photo you want to use as your background image. Get the Elliptical Marquee tool from the Toolbox, and drag a large circular selection just above the center of your photo (as shown here).

STEP TWO: Press Shift-M to switch to the Rectangular Marquee tool (pressing Shift-M toggles you between the Elliptical and Rectangular Marquee tools). Hold the Shift key (so you can add to the circular selection) and draw a rectangular selection that starts at the left of the circular selection at the center and extends downward to create the selection shown at right. Note: Be careful to make sure your rectangular selection is the exact same width as the circular selection, by dragging from the left center of the circle, to the right center.

continued

Quick Tip:
**Fast access to
Custom Shapes**

If you're using the Custom
Shape tool and want to
choose a new shape, don't
head all the way up to the
Options Bar. Instead just
press the Return key (PC:
Enter key) and the Shapes
Library will appear at the
location of your cursor. Just
double-click on the shape
you want, and the library
will automatically close.

STEP THREE: Now open
the photo that will appear
within your selection. Press
Command-A (PC: Control-A)
to put a selection around
the entire photo. Press Command-C (PC: Control-C) to
copy the selected image
into memory.

STEP FOUR: Switch back to the
document with your back-
ground photo (your selection
will still be in place) then go
under the Edit menu and
choose Paste Into. This will
paste the photo into your selection and doing so automatically
deselects your selection. If you
need to resize your photo, press
Command-T (PC: Control-T) to
bring up Free Transform, hold
the Shift Key, grab a corner
point, and drag inward to size it
down to fit.

STEP FIVE: Choose Inner Glow
from the Add a Layer Style pop-
up menu at the bottom of the
Layers palette (it's the first icon
from the left). When the Inner
Glow dialog appears (shown
here) near the top, change the
Blend Mode from Screen to
Normal. Then click on the beige
Color Swatch to bring up the
Color Picker and choose black
as your Inner Glow color. Last,
increase the Size (amount of
glow) to around 30 (try 80 for
high-res, 300-ppi photos).

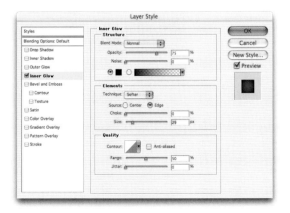

STEP SIX: When you click OK, it puts a shadow on all sides of the inner photo, making it look like it has depth, and you're looking into a window. Now all that's left is to add some type to turn this simple technique into a full page ad.

STEP SEVEN: Press "d" then "x" to set your Foreground color to white, then get the Type tool to create your headline type at the top of the ad. The headline shown here uses the font ITC Bradley Hand. The type directly below the photo is set in Minion (from Adobe). The "Mariner's Beach Club" logo is set in Trajan (also from Adobe) with more Minion below it for the price and phone number. The sun graphic above the Mariner's Beach Club type is one of Photoshop's built-in Custom Shapes. To add it, first get the Custom Shape tool from the Toolbox (it's right below the Type tool).

STEP EIGHT: Then, go up to the Options Bar, and click on the third icon from the right. Next, open the Shape Picker (shown here); then from the Picker's pop-down menu, add the Nature set by choosing Nature from the list. When the dialog appears, choose Append. Then, find the Sun graphic and simply click-and-drag out a sun right above your type to complete the effect.

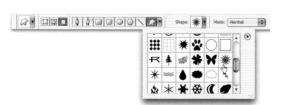

Quick Tip:
® and ™. They're there for you!

In Photoshop 6 and 7, Adobe included the © (copyright symbol) as a default Custom Shape (accessed from the Shape Library when using the Custom Shape tool). Well, in Photoshop CS, the copyright symbol is joined by ® (the registered mark) and ™ (the trademark symbol) in the default set of Custom Shapes. Ahh, it's the little things, isn't it?

Focus with an Inner Glow

I've seen all sorts of tricks for focusing the attention of a person viewing an image, but this glow effect (which I saw in a series of Bell South print ads) stopped me dead in my tracks for its ingenious use of an Inner Glow and backscreening. Although I'm showing the effect in the same context that Bell South did, you can use the same technique with different shapes to focus the reader as well.

STEP ONE: Open the photo you want to apply the effect to (in this case, I'm using a portrait-oriented photo because we'll be using it as the background for a print ad).

STEP TWO: Press Command-A (PC: Control-A) to put a selection around the entire photo, then press Shift-Command-J (PC: Shift-Control-J) to cut the photo off the Background layer and copy it on its own separate layer (as shown here in the Layers palette).

STEP THREE: Get the Polygonal Lasso tool (the lasso tool that draws straight selections) and create a triangular selection like the one shown here. (Note that the lines don't meet at a point on the right side—it's squared off). Now press Command-J (PC: Control-J) to copy the selected area and put it up on its own separate layer.

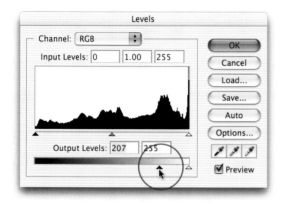

STEP FOUR: In the Layers palette, click back on your photo layer (Layer 1). Press Command-L (PC: Control-L) to bring up the Levels dialog. You're going to backscreen (greatly lighten) this photo by dragging the bottom left Output Levels slider over to the right quite a bit (as shown).

STEP FIVE: When you click OK, the layer is lightened, leaving the area you selected and copied on its own layer still visible (since it's above the backscreened layer in the Layers palette). Next, you'll add an Inner Glow to help define the edges of your triangle area. In the Layers palette, click on your triangle layer (Layer 2).

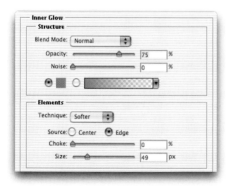

STEP SIX: Choose Inner Glow from the Add a Layer Style pop-up menu at the bottom of the Layers palette. Change the Blend Mode from Screen to Normal, then click on the beige Color Swatch to bring up the Color Picker. Choose a bright blue (like the one shown here). Then increase the Size to around 50 pixels.

continued

Quick Tip:
Getting back to a tool's default settings

Each tool in Photoshop has its own set of options, and chances are that you're going to be constantly changing them. You never have to worry about messing these tool options up, because you're always just one click away from resetting the tool to its defaults. Up in the Options Bar, on the far-left side of the Bar, Control-click (PC: Right-click) once on the icon for the tool you're using. Choose Reset Tool from the pop-up menu and that resets the tool to its default settings so you can play to your heart's content.

Quick Tip:
The advantage of loading the layer's transparency

Throughout this book, I have you hold down the Command key (PC: Control key) and click on a layer. This puts a selection around everything on the layer (for example, if it's a Type layer, it puts a selection around your type). What you're doing (in technical terms) is loading the layer's transparency (which you can do manually by going under the Select menu, choosing Load Selection, and then choosing to load the channel named "transparency"). What most people do who need to put a selection around their type, but don't know this trick, is use the Magic Wand tool to select each letter individually. It works—it does put a selection around the type—but if you move that type, it leaves little specks (well, pixels) behind that the Magic Wand misses. The advantage of loading the transparency instead is that it doesn't leave any little stray pixels behind. That's why we always choose to load transparency.

STEP SEVEN: Click OK and a blue Inner Glow is applied to your layer (as shown here). This is pretty much the basis of the effect, but since headlines and body copy will be added to this image, you can fade the photo away in most of that area.

STEP EIGHT: In the Layers palette, click back on Layer 1 (the backscreened layer). Get the Polygonal Lasso tool and create a selection like the one shown here that is larger than your Inner Glow area.

STEP NINE: To soften the edges of your selection (and make it appear to fade away into the white background), go under the Select menu and choose Feather. When the Feather Selection dialog appears, enter 30 pixels and click OK.

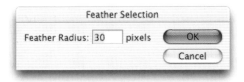

STEP TEN: Go under the Select menu and choose Inverse. This inverses your selection, selecting the top and bottom of your backscreened layer (which is the area that we want to fade away).

STEP ELEVEN: Press Delete (PC: Backspace) to erase those selected areas. Because we feathered that area so heavily, it makes it look like the photo gradually fades away (which it does).

STEP TWELVE: The effect is now complete, and all you have left to do is add the text for the ad. For the headlines, I used the font Trebuchet MS Bold. The body copy is set in Helvetica Light, 10 point with 24 leading. The type in the blue box is Trebuchet again. The logo of the fictitious Northern Phone is Helvetica Light Italic, and Helvetica Bold Italic. The slogan is set in Helvetica Regular Italic.

Quick Tip:
Change your view anytime

When you open a filter dialog, or any dialog such as Levels or Curves, most of your menus are grayed out while you're in that dialog. However, one menu that's almost always available is your View menu. Your keyboard shortcuts for accessing View menu items also still work, even though you're in a dialog box.

Try it for yourself: Open an image, bring up the Gaussian Blur filter dialog, then look at the Menu Bar up top. View is still available, you can just reach out and choose a new view or use the keyboard shortcut of your choice.

The Page Curl Finally Made Easy

Granted, this effect has been around for a while, but: (1) it's still widely used, (2) most people use a special plug-in filter to create it, and (3) if you don't use the plug-in, it's very complicated. Well, not anymore, Bunky, and that's why I included this new super-fast, super-easy version here in the book. See, I care.

STEP ONE: Open the photo you want to apply the effect to. Press "p" to get the Pen tool, and zoom in on the bottom right. Start by clicking once on the bottom of the photo, then move to right side of the photo, and click-and-drag upward to curve your path outward. Next, Option-click (PC: Alt-click) on the point you just created, then move down and to the left and click-and-drag to bend your path inward.

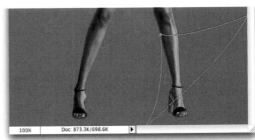

STEP TWO: Option-click (PC: Alt-click) on that point, and then click back on your original point and drag to bend the final segment of your path inward (as shown in the image top right). Then press Command-Return (PC: Control-Enter) to turn you path into a selection.

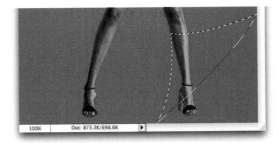

STEP THREE: Press "g" to get the Gradient tool, then up in the Options Bar, click on the Gradient thumbnail to bring up the Gradient Editor. Create a gradient that goes from a medium gray, to light gray, to medium gray, to white (as shown here).

STEP FOUR: Click on the New Layer icon in the Layers palette to create a new layer. Take the Gradient tool, click at the bottom of your triangle-shaped selection and drag upward toward the center point (as shown).

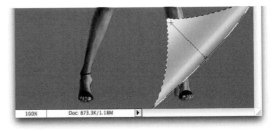

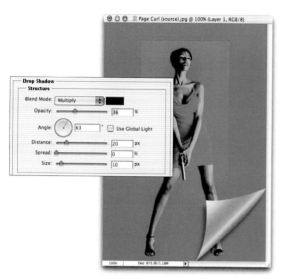

STEP FIVE: Deselect by pressing Command-D (PC: Control-D). Next, choose Drop Shadow from the Add a Layer Style pop-up menu at the bottom of the Layers palette. Increase the Distance to 20, the Size to 10, change the Angle to 63°, and lower the Opacity of the shadow to 36%. Click OK to add this drop shadow to your gradient, to create a sense of depth.

STEP SIX: Create a new layer below your page curl layer by Command-clicking (PC: Control-clicking) on the New Layer icon at the bottom of the Layers palette. Get the Polygonal Lasso tool and create a triangle shaped selection like the one shown here. In the Toolbox, click on the Foreground Color Swatch and choose a bright blue in the Color Picker. Then press Option-Delete (PC: Alt-Backspace) to fill your triangle shaped selection with blue (as shown here).

STEP SEVEN: Lastly, just add your text to complete the effect. It also helps, when placing the text that goes in the blue area, that you tuck it under the page curl a bit, to help with the idea that you're pulling back the corner and revealing another page (as shown here).

Quick Tip:
Don't like the Clouds pattern? Request a new one.

We often use the Clouds filter (Filter>Render>Clouds) for creating textured backgrounds or even creating lightning effects. One of the great things about the Clouds filter is that the pattern it generates is totally random, so if you don't like the way your clouds look, just redo the Clouds filter. Each time you do it, you'll get a different cloud effect.

There are a number of
changes and transforma-
tions you can apply to
multiple layers at once.
The first step is to go to
the Layers palette and
link together the layers
that you want to affect.
This is done by clicking
in the second column of
each layer you want to
link. A tiny link icon will
appear indicating that
the layer is now linked to
your currently active layer.
Once that's done, whatever
transformation (such as
scaling, rotating, etc.)
you do to your active
layer will also affect all
your linked layers.

Tag It!

One of *Photoshop User* magazine's readers sent me a newspaper ad, and asked "How do you do
this? Did they do it in Photoshop?" Yup, they did, and it's a pretty darn handy effect that you can
customize for a number of uses. The tag part is truly simple, but I was stuck on how to create the
cord. Luckily, one of our good friends, Colin Smith of PhotoshopCAFE.com, came to the rescue
with an easy way to create realistic cord, and how to bend it too!

STEP ONE: Open a new document in RGB mode. Create a new
blank layer by clicking on the
New Layer icon at the bottom of
the Layers palette. Get the Rectangular Marquee tool and draw
a large vertical selection in the
center of your image area. Click
on the Foreground Color Swatch
and choose a beige in the Color
Picker and fill your selection with
this beige by pressing Option-
Delete (PC: Alt-Backspace).

STEP TWO: Go under the Filter
menu and choose Filter Gallery.
Click on the right-facing triangle
next to the Texture folder, then
click on the Texturizer thumbnail (as shown here). From the
Texture pop-up menu choose
Canvas. Set the Scaling at 100%,
Relief at 4, and for Light choose
Top, then click OK to apply this
texture to your beige rectangle.

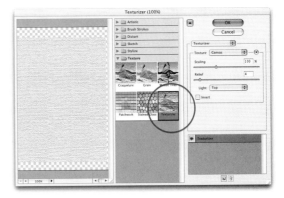

STEP THREE: Go under the Edit
menu and choose Fade Filter Gallery. Lower the Opacity to 40%
(to decrease the intensity of the
Texturizer filter, which was too
strong for this tag). Click OK to
fade the filter to 40%.

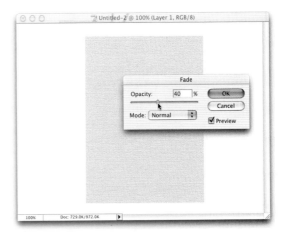

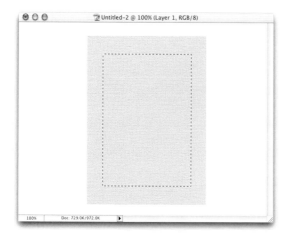

STEP FOUR: Take the Rectangular Marquee tool and drag a smaller rectangular selection within your beige tag area (as shown here). Press Command-J (PC: Control-J) to copy the selected area onto its own layer.

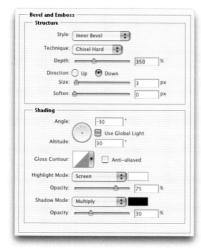

STEP FIVE: Choose Bevel and Emboss from the Add a Layer Style pop-up menu at the bottom of the Layers palette. For Technique choose Chisel Hard. Increase the Depth to 350%, and lower the Size to 3. In the Shading section of the dialog, turn off Use Global Light, set the Angle to -30°, the Altitude to 30°, and lower the Opacity setting for the Shadows to 30% (as shown). Don't click OK yet. Instead, click directly on the word Inner Glow in the list of Styles on the left side of the dialog.

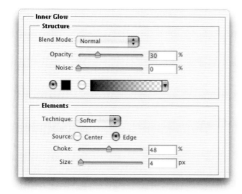

STEP SIX: When the Inner Glow options appear, change the Blend Mode from Screen to Normal, and lower the Opacity to 30%. Click on the Color Swatch and then set black as your glow color in the Color Picker. Increase the Choke to 48, set the size at 4, and click OK to apply a hard bevel to your smaller rectangle.

Quick Tip:
Detaching a Layer Effect from its layer

When you apply a Layer Effect, the effect is attached directly to your layer. So if you apply a Layer Effects Drop Shadow to a Type layer, that shadow is attached to your Type layer. If you'd like to separate that drop shadow onto its own layer, you can go under the Layer menu, under Layer Style, and choose Create Layer. When you do this, a new layer is created that contains just the effect (in this case it would contain the drop shadow). If you try this when you've applied a Bevel and Emboss Layer effect, it separates the highlights to one layer and the shadows to another. However, in the case of Bevel and Emboss, they're still grouped with the original layer as a clipping group. To remove the clipping group, press Shift-Command-G (PC: Shift-Control-G). You'll see that you now have three separate layers.

continued

Quick Tip:
Viewing only your active layer and hiding the rest

If you have a multilayered document, you can look at just the layer you're working on (or any one layer for that matter) by holding the Option key (PC: Alt key) and clicking on the Eye icon in the first column next to it in the Layers palette. This immediately hides all other layers from view, leaving only your chosen layer visible (and any Layer Styles you have applied to other layers). To show all the layers again, hold the Option key (PC: Alt key) and click again on the Eye icon for your layer, and the rest will instantly reappear.

STEP SEVEN: In the Layers palette, click back on your original beige rectangle layer. Choose Drop Shadow from the Add a Layer Style pop-up menu at the bottom of the Layers palette. When the dialog box appears, turn off Use Global Light, then set the Angle to 60°. Increase the Distance to 13, Size to 10, lower the Opacity to 40%, and click OK to apply a soft drop shadow behind your tag (as shown here).

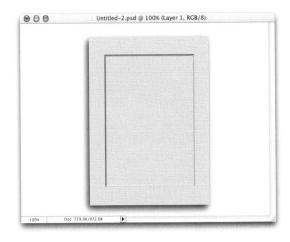

STEP EIGHT: Get the Type tool (from the Toolbox), press "d" to set your Foreground color to black, and create your type. The font used here is Minion (from Adobe). After your type is in place, create a new blank layer, get the Line tool (from the Shape tool flyout in the Toolbox), and draw two 1-pixel lines: one under the top block of text, and one under the center block (as shown here).

STEP NINE: Create a new blank layer, then get the Elliptical Marquee tool, hold the Shift key, and draw a small selection (like the one shown here) at the top of your tag. Press "d" to set your Foreground to black then fill this selection with black by pressing Option-Delete (PC: Alt-Backspace). Don't Deselect yet. Create another new layer, set your Foreground color to a medium gray, then go under the Edit menu and choose Stroke. When the Stroke dialog appears, for Width enter 4, set the Location to Center, and click OK to put a gray stroke around your circle (as shown).

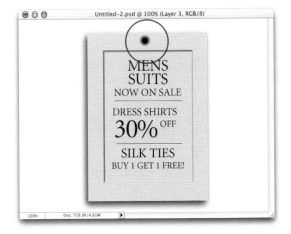

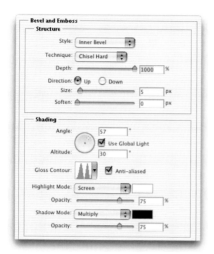

STEP TEN: Deselect by pressing Command-D (PC: Control-D). Choose Bevel and Emboss from the Add a Layer Style pop-up menu at the bottom of the Layers palette. For Technique choose Chisel Hard, and increase the Depth to 1000%. Set the Angle at 57°, the Altitude at 30°, and from the Gloss Contour picker, choose the "Ring-Double" contour that looks like two peaks (as shown here), and click OK to bevel the gray stroke and give it a metallic feel.

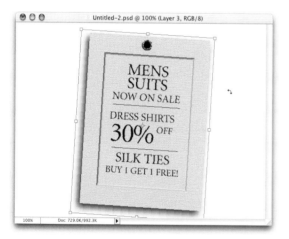

STEP ELEVEN: Go to the Layers palette, hide the Background layer by clicking on the Eye icon, then choose Merge Visible from the palette's pop-down menu to merge the entire tag into one layer. Then, press Command-T (PC: Control-T) to bring up Free Transform. Move your cursor outside the bounding box (as shown), and click-and-drag downward to rotate the tag a little. When it looks rotated like the one shown here, press Return (PC: Enter).

STEP TWELVE: Now for the cord at the top of the tag. Open a new document (RGB mode), create a new blank layer, and get the Rectangular Marquee tool. Drag out a horizontal rectangular se-lection (like the one shown here). Choose a medium gray as your Foreground color, then press Option-Delete (PC: Alt-Back-space) to fill your rectangle with gray (as shown here).

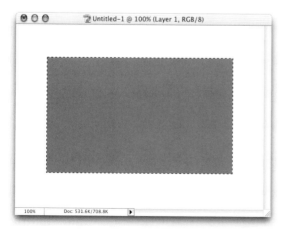

Quick Tip:
**Copying Layer
Styles to
other layers**

Once you've applied a Layer Style to a layer, you can apply that same effect (with the exact same settings) to any other layer. The slow sloth-like way is to go under the Layer menu, under Layer Style, and choose Copy Layer Style. Then go back to the Layers palette, click on the layer where you want the effects, then sloth your way back under the Layer menu, under Layer Style, and choose Paste Layer Style.

A much faster (and more fun) way is to hold the Control key (PC: Right-click) and click-and-hold on your layer in the Layers pal-ette. A pop-up menu will appear and you can choose Copy Layer Style. Hold the Control key (PC: Right-click) and click-and-hold on the layer in the Layers palette where you want to copy the effect. Choose Paste Layer Style from the pop-up menu that appears. Try it once, and you'll never go digging under the Layer menu again.

continued

Quick Tip:
How to move a layer to another document and have it appear in the exact same spot

There's a quick trick for duplicating a layer and having it appear in another document in the exact same position as in the original. In the Layers palette, click on the layer you want to duplicate, then in the Layers palette's drop-down menu, choose Duplicate Layer. When the dialog box appears, under Destination, choose your other document from the pop-up menu (or new if you want it to appear in a brand-new document), and click OK. Your layer will be duplicated to its new document in the exact same spot as in the original.

STEP THIRTEEN: Go under the Filter menu, under Sketch, and choose Halftone Pattern. When the dialog appears, set the Size to 2, Contrast to 33, and for Pattern Type choose Line. Click OK to apply a series of gray and white lines over your medium gray box. Press Command-D (PC: Control-D) to deselect.

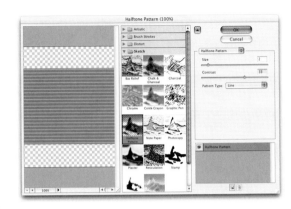

STEP FOURTEEN: Press Command-T (PC: Control-T) to bring up Free Transform. Move your cursor outside the bounding box and click-and-drag upward to rotate the entire gray lined box (as shown here). Press Return (PC: Enter) to complete your rotation.

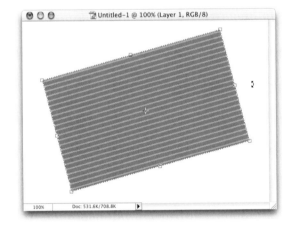

STEP FIFTEEN: Get the Rectangular Marquee tool and drag a thin horizontal rectangular selection though the center of your tilted box (as shown here). Press Command-J (PC: Control-J) to copy that selected area up onto its own layer. Drag the gray box layer to the Trash icon to delete it (you don't need it anymore). Press Command-T (PC: Control-T) to bring up Free Transform. Control-click (PC: Right-click) in the bounding box and choose Rotate 90° CW. Press Return (PC: Enter) to lock in your transformation.

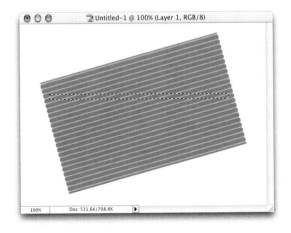

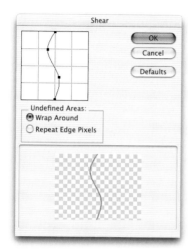

STEP SIXTEEN: Go under the Filter menu, under Distort, and choose Shear. A solid vertical line will appear in the center of the grid. Click on it once ¼ of the way down and drag to the left. Then click once again ¾ of the way down, and drag right to create a "squiggly line" (a highly technical term). Click OK to bend your thin bar of gray lines.

STEP SEVENTEEN: Choose Bevel and Emboss from the Add a Layer Style pop-up menu at the bottom of the Layers palette. Lower the Depth to 71 and click OK to add a rounded look to your cord. Press "v" to get the Move tool and drag this cord over into your tag document. Press Command-T (PC: Control-T) to bring up Free Transform (as shown here). Hold the Shift key and scale the cord down to size, and position it so the bottom end of the cord is in the hole at the top of the tag.

STEP EIGHTEEN: Once the cord is positioned where it looks like it's coming out of the hole in the tag (and extending off the top of the image area), press Command-J (PC: Control-J) and make a duplicate of this layer. Use the Move tool to position it as if it's the cord coming from the back of the tag, then go to the Layer palette and drag this layer beneath your tag layer to complete the effect (as shown here).

Dividing a Photo into Puzzle Pieces

I've seen this effect before, but what rekindled my interest in it was seeing it on Apple's new iLife product box. If you had to draw the puzzle pieces with the Pen tool, it could be quite a task, but luckily, four puzzle shapes are built right into Photoshop (as Custom Shapes). The technique can be used to make an editorial statement, a dramatic effect, a fun effect—it's pretty much up to you how you use it.

STEP ONE: Create a new document in RGB mode. Click on the Foreground Color Swatch and select a medium gray in the Color Picker, then get the Custom Shape tool from the Toolbox. Up in the Options Bar, click on the third icon from the left (to create pixel-based shapes), then click on the Shape thumbnail to bring up the Shape Picker. From the Picker's pop-down menu, choose Objects (then click Append) to import this set of Shapes.

STEP TWO: Once the set is loaded, scroll down in the Picker and you'll see four puzzle shapes. Click on the fourth puzzle shape (as shown here). Create a new blank layer by clicking on the New Layer icon at the bottom of the Layers palette. Hold the Shift key, and using the Custom Shape tool, drag out the first puzzle piece, and position it in the top-right corner (as shown here).

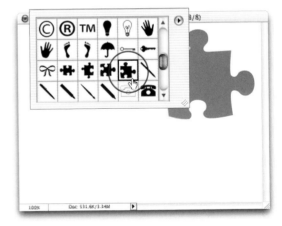

STEP THREE: Create a new blank layer, and then go back up to the Custom Shape Picker, and choose the second of our four puzzle shapes (as shown here). Hold the Shift key, and drag out a shape that is approximately the same size as your first shape.

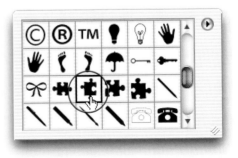

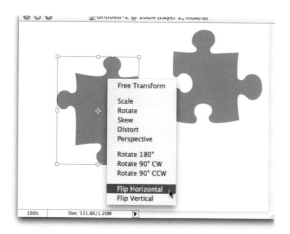

STEP FOUR: Press Command-T (PC: Control-T) to bring up Free Transform. Control-click (PC: Right-click) within the bounding box and choose Flip Horizontal from the pop-up menu. Press Return (PC: Enter) to lock in your transformation.

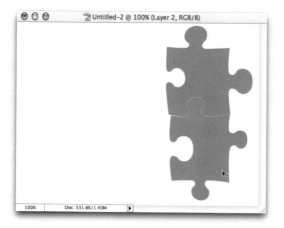

STEP FIVE: Press "v" to get the Move tool, then position this piece into the first piece, but make sure you leave a slight gap between the two (let them almost touch, but for this to work correctly, you need a tiny gap—it shouldn't look as if it's now one solid piece).

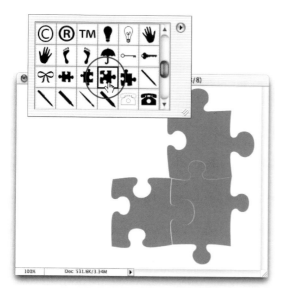

STEP SIX: Create a new blank layer, then get the Custom Shape tool again, and from the Custom Shape Picker choose the third of the four puzzle shapes (as shown). Hold the Shift key and drag out this puzzle shape, and then use the Move tool to position it up against the bottom puzzle piece. Again, make them very close, but leave a tiny gap between the pieces (as shown).

continued

Quick Tip:
How to make your small type for the Web look sharp

Without much fanfare, Adobe introduced a new level of Anti-aliasing back in Photoshop 7 that's very handy for creating small type for the Web. The level is called "Sharp" and it's accessed from the Anti-aliasing menu in the Options Bar, any time you have the Type tool selected.

STEP SEVEN: In the Layers palette, click on the layer with the bottom-right puzzle piece. Press Command-J (PC: Control-J) to duplicate that piece onto its own layer. Press Command-T (PC: Control-T) to bring up Free Transform. Click in the bounding box and drag the duplicate piece up to the top-left corner. Move your cursor outside the bounding box and click-and-drag to rotate it to the left. Press Return (PC: Enter) to lock in your transformation.

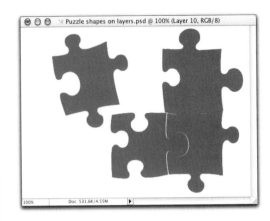

STEP EIGHT: Open the photo you want to apply the puzzle effect to. Press "v" to switch to the Move tool. Click-and-drag this photo into your puzzle document. In the Layers palette, drag this layer down in the layer stack until it appears below your puzzle pieces. Position the photo so the important parts that you want to keep are hidden by the pieces. Now you're going to apply a bevel effect to this photo.

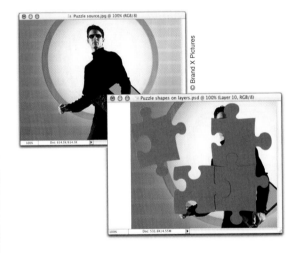

STEP NINE: Choose Bevel and Emboss from the Add a Layer Style pop-up menu. Lower the Size to 1, and increase the Soften amount to 1. In the list of Styles on the left side of the dialog, click on the words Inner Glow.

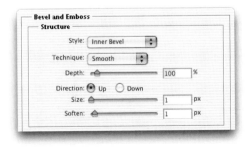

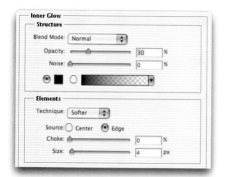

STEP TEN: Change the Blend Mode from Screen to Normal, lower the Opacity to 30%, set the Size to 4, and then click OK to apply both of these effects to the photo layer. You're applying them to this layer, so you can automatically apply this effect to the puzzle pieces later (as you'll see).

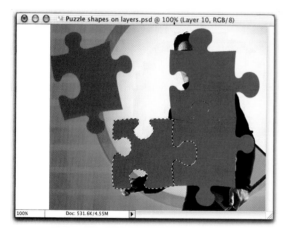

STEP ELEVEN: Go to the Layers palette, hold the Command key (PC: Control key) and click on the bottom-left puzzle piece layer. This puts a selection around the piece. Now, in the Layers palette, click on the photo layer to make it the active layer (don't deselect, just change layers). You can now delete this puzzle shape layer by dragging it to the Trash icon at the bottom of the Layers palette.

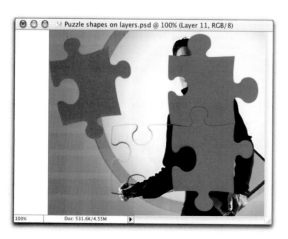

STEP TWELVE: Press Command-J (PC: Control-J) to copy the selection onto its own layer, in the shape of that puzzle piece. Because you applied a Bevel and Emboss and Inner Glow to this photo layer, when you copy that selection up on its own layer, that effect goes right along with it, giving the puzzle shape a bevel and inner glow (as shown here).

continued

Quick Tip:
Getting the Zoom tool while Curves or Levels is open

As you probably already know, opening the Curves or Levels dialog box switches you to the Eyedropper tool and you can't change to a different tool. However, if you want to zoom in tight on an area within your image, you can actually get the Zoom tool and zoom right in where you want, even though the Curves/Levels dialog is open. Just hold both the Spacebar and the Command key (PC: Control key). Your cursor will temporarily change into the magnifying glass, and then you can zoom right in on any area.

STEP THIRTEEN: Repeat this process for the other three pieces: Command-click (PC: Control-click) on each layer to put a selection around it, delete that layer, then switch to the photo layer and press Command-J (PC: Control-J) to copy the selected area up on to its own layer.

STEP FOURTEEN: Go to the Layers palette and delete the photo layer by dragging it into the Trash icon at the bottom of the Layers palette. This leaves just the beveled puzzle pieces (as shown here).

STEP FIFTEEN: In the Layers palette, hide the Background layer from view by clicking on the Eye icon beside that layer. Then choose Merge Visible from the palette's pop-down menu to merge all the puzzle pieces into one single layer. You can make the Background layer visible again by clicking where its Eye icon used to be.

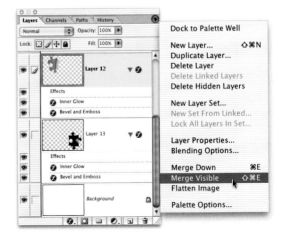

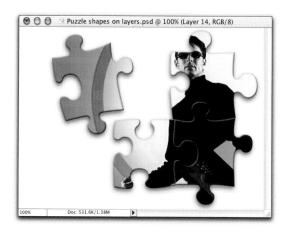

STEP SIXTEEN: Last, choose Drop Shadow from the Add a Layer Style pop-up menu at the bottom of the Layers palette. Lower the Opacity to 65%, increase the Size to 10, and click OK to apply the drop shadow and complete the effect.

STEP SEVENTEEN: Although the artwork I saw that made me want to learn this effect was from the product box for Apple's iLife software, here's the puzzle effect used in a completely different layout (a fictitious movie poster). The fonts used here are Minion (from Adobe) for the names at the top of the poster and the tag line under the name of the fictitious movie. The movie title uses the font Trajan (also from Adobe), and the type at the bottom of the poster is in Helvetica Bold Condensed.

MICHAEL BROOKS   ALBERT DOUGLAS

CYBERHOOD
a new breed of internet crime has arrived.

A ROBERT FORD FILM   DIRECTED BY FRANK LEE   IN COOPERATION WITH SCREENFILMS
STARRING ALBERT DOUGLAS FEATURING MICHAEL BROOKS AND A SPECIAL APPEARANCE BY BRUCE CHAN
PRODUCED BY MEL SMITH, MICHAEL LAWRENCE, AND KATE SUMMERSFIELD BASED ON THE NOVEL BY HARRISON TODD
MUSIC BY WILLIAM WILDER ORIGINAL SCORE BY PETER BANKS TELEPLAY BY CODY KNIGHT WRITTEN BY MAKE CALDER, FRANIS DRAY,
FROM NEW LIFE MEDIA PRODUCTIONS

Classified Ad Effect

You've probably seen this effect used in print ads and TV a dozen times. It's designed to look like someone has torn a classified ad out of the newspaper and highlighted the important points. The effect is easy to pull off—the only thing that takes any time is creating the fake classified ad (but I give you a sample one to download, in case you don't feel like doing it yourself).

STEP ONE: This technique starts with a fake classified ad. You can either create a fake one (as I did here) so that you can customize the text in the center ad (where the focus of the effect will be), or you can download my fake version (the same one shown here) from the book's site at www.scottkelbybooks.com/ csphotos.html.

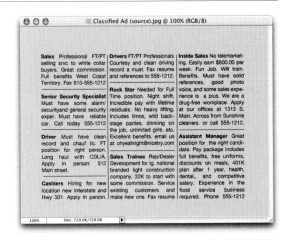

STEP TWO: Press the letter "L" to get the Lasso tool and draw a loose, jaggy (rip-like) selection around the classified ad that you want the viewer to focus on as shown here. (Note: I lowered the Opacity of the Background layer just to help you see the selection better). This selection should look a little jaggy, as if the section was torn from the newspaper by hand.

STEP THREE: Press Command-J (PC: Control-J) to copy the selected area up onto its own layer. Then go to the Layers palette and click on the Background layer. Press Command-A (PC: Control-A) to select the entire background, then press Delete (PC: Backspace) to delete the excess classifieds, leaving just your focus area on the layer above (as shown).

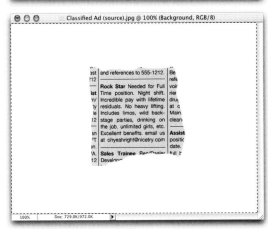

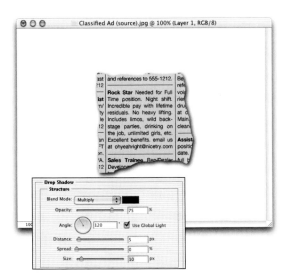

STEP FOUR: Deselect by pressing Command-D (PC: Control-D). Click back on the torn classified layer in the Layers palette to make it active. Choose Drop Shadow from the Add a Layer Style pop-up menu at the bottom of the Layers palette. When the dialog appears, make sure the Angle is set to 20 and set the Size to 10 pixels (try 40 for high-res, 300-ppi images). Click OK to apply a soft drop shadow to your torn newspaper (as shown here).

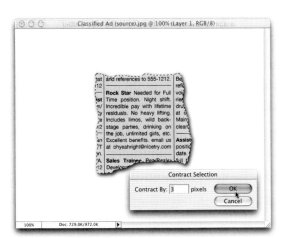

STEP FIVE: Hold the Command key (PC: Control key) and click on the torn newspaper layer to put a selection around it (as shown). Then go under the Select menu, under Modify, and choose Contract. When the dialog appears, enter 3 pixels then click OK to shrink your selection by 3 pixels.

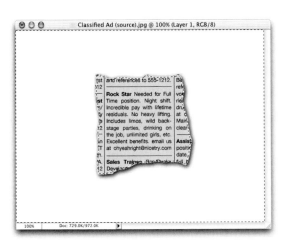

STEP SIX: Go under the Select menu and choose Inverse. This inverses the selection leaving only the 3 pixels on the outside edge of your newspaper selected. In the next step, you'll lighten those edges to help make them look more like they were really torn, so press Command-L (PC: Control-L) to bring up Levels.

Quick Tip:
Hide the grayed-out cropping area

When you use the Crop tool, the area outside the cropping border that will be cropped away appears dimmed (until you actually crop, of course). If you want to hide this dimmed area from view, just press the Slash key (/).

continued

STEP SEVEN: To lighten the edges, drag the bottom left Output Levels slider to the right (as shown). Deselect by pressing Command-D (PC: Control-D). Next, create a new blank layer by clicking on the New Layer icon at the bottom of the Layers palette.

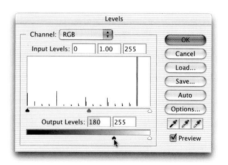

STEP EIGHT: Press "b" to switch to the Brush tool, then Control-click (PC: Right-click) in the document to bring up the Brush Picker. From the Picker's pop-down menu, load the brush set named Wet Media Brushes. Click on the 19-pixel tall vertical brush (the Light Oil Flat Tip as shown) and then use the Master Diameter slider to lower the size of the brush until it's the same height as a line of your type. Set your Foreground color to a highlighter yellow (I used R=216, G=209, B=0). Then paint strokes over the lines you want the reader to focus on.

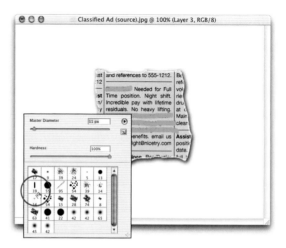

STEP NINE: To complete the effect, change the Layer Blend mode of this layer from Normal to Multiply in the Layers palette, and then you'll be able to see the words through the high-lighting (as shown here). In the ad here, I merged the highlight layer with the classified layer by pressing Command-E (PC: Control-E), and used the Move tool to drag it into the ad layout. Lastly, I rotated it just a bit using Free Transform. Make sure you keep a copy of the original with all its layers, because then you can easily update the text for any classified you'll need in the future.

Index

Symbols

100% view 93
16-bit 69, 99
3D 23, 65, 82, 85, 140, 212
3D Curved Video Wall 116
3D Drop Back Logo 75
3D Hardcover Book Effect 139
3D Photo Cubes 230
3D Transform filter 107, 139, 230, 231
8-bit 69

A

Actions 12, 121
    Action sets 12
Actions palette 12, 121
    Button Mode 121
Adams, Ansel 198
Adding Side Lighting After the Fact 34
Add Anchor Point tool 10
Add Noise 28, 63
    Monochromatic box 155
Adjustment Layer 51, 150, 198, 199, 205, 280
Adobe Illustrator
    import artwork from 42
American Typewriter 242
Angled Strokes filter 49
Anti-aliasing
    Sharp 300
Apple Computer 60
arrowheads 50
Art History brush 245
Attaching a Note to a Photo 135
Aurora Condensed from Bitstream 83
Auto Color 260

B

backgrounds
    eliminating 53
Background color
    fill with 277
Background layer 101
backscreen 135, 230, 231, 287
    Blurred Backscreen Effect 164
Bevel and Emboss. See Layer Styles
Bitmap mode 243
Black Chrome 77
Blending Options dialog 13
Blend Modes 18
    Color 52, 84, 257
    Color Burn 80, 168
    Color Dodge 26, 74, 126

Darken 55, 56, 175
Hard Light 173, 175
Multiply 84, 95, 97, 231, 251, 306
Overlay 50, 130, 176
    keyboard shortcut 129
Soft Light 66, 237
Blur tool 258
    removing blemishes and scratches 258
Brightness/Contrast 54, 56, 57, 150
Brushes. See also Brushes palette
    Blend Modes 23
    Brush Picker 19, 20, 24, 33, 61, 125, 248, 306
        loading sets 20
        Master Diameter slider 96, 224, 256, 306
    Brush tool 52, 53, 106, 125, 146, 154, 175, 218, 224, 280, 306
    changing size 26
    Opacity 52
    Rename Brush 21
Brushes palette 11, 20, 24, 25, 26
    Brush Preview 172
    Clear Brush Controls 26
    custom brush 253
    Delete Brush 24, 248
    loading sets 60, 306
    lock icon 141
    New Brush Preset 253, 254
    reorder brushes 61
    Reset Brushes 24, 61, 254
    Save Brushes 254
Brush Script MT 179
Brush tool. See Brushes
Bullet from House Industries 77
Burn tool 65, 255

C

Camera Raw plug-in 99
Cancel button 72
canvas color 33
    Canvas Extension Color Swatch 27
Canvas Size 27, 33, 40, 53, 135, 170, 199, 252
    Relative box 27
Channels
    Alpha 22, 36, 37, 46, 49, 78, 79, 163, 249, 280, 281, 289
    seeing full-color composite 165
Channels palette 49, 78, 163, 249, 264, 265, 289, 297
    New Spot Channel 264
Channel Mixer 198, 199
Character palette 16, 63, 64, 70, 71, 72, 73, 83, 91, 104, 105, 152, 172, 199, 201, 214, 241, 251, 278
    Reset Character 64
checkboxes 194

checkerboard pattern 37
chrome 280
Chrome gradient 152, 203
Classified Ad Effect 304
Clear Inline Type Effect 71
Clipping Group 61, 86, 125. See also Clipping Mask
Clipping Mask 61, 86, 105, 125, 126, 168
Clipping Path 125
Clouds filter 28, 77, 291
CMYK preview 81
Cochin 271, 273
collaging 92, 204
    Defringe 127
    Remove Black Matte 92
    Remove White Matte 92
Color. See Blend Modes
colorize an object 84
colorizing grayscale images 242
colorizing line art 244
Color Balance 150, 205
Color Burn. See Blend Modes
Color Dodge. See Blend Modes
Color Overlay. See Layer Styles
Color palette
    Grayscale Slider 263
Color Picker 6, 27, 43, 60, 78, 128, 135, 138, 242, 263, 279, 304
    Adobe 78
    Custom 43, 264
    H, S, B fields 304
Color Replacement tool 174
Color Sampler Eyedropper 54
Color Stops. See Gradients
Compacta 68, 104, 149, 158, 159
Conté Crayon 40
Contours 272. See also Layer Styles: Bevel and Emboss: Gloss Contour
Copperplate Gothic 111, 195
copy 146
copyright symbol 285
copy all visible layers 261
Copy and Paste 34
copy layer. See layers: duplicating
Crop 87
cropping boundary. See Crop tool
Crop and Straighten Photos 66
Crop tool 40, 124, 170, 210, 216, 274, 305
    cropping boundary 216, 305
    rotate 274
Cross, Dave 4
Curves 78, 150, 200, 205, 231, 280, 281, 290, 302
Custom Shape tool 50, 86, 136, 137, 283, 284, 285, 298, 299. See also copyright symbol; See also registered mark; See also puzzle shapes

COLOPHON

The book was produced by the author and the design team using all Macintosh computers, including a Power Mac G4 733-MHz, a Power Mac G4 Dual Processor 1.25-GHz, a Power Mac G4 Dual Processor 500-MHz, a Power Mac G4 400-MHz, and an iMac. We use LaCie, Sony, and Apple monitors.

Page layout was done using InDesign 2.0.2. Our graphics server is a Power Mac G3, with a 60-GB LaCie external drive, and we burn our CDs to a TDK veloCD 32X CD-RW.

The headers for each technique are set in 20 point CronosMM700 Bold with the Horizontal Scaling set to 95%. Body copy is set using

CronosMM408 Regular at 10 points on 13 leading, with the Horizontal Scaling set to 95%.

Screen captures were made with Snapz Pro X and were placed and sized within InDesign. The book was output at 150 line screen, and all in-house proofing was done using a Tektronix Phaser 7700 by Xerox.

ADDITIONAL PHOTOSHOP RESOURCES

ScottKelbyBooks.com
For information on Scott's other books, visit his book site. For background info on Scott, visit www.scottkelby.com.

http://www.scottkelbybooks.com

National Association of Photoshop Professionals (NAPP)
The industry trade association for Adobe® Photoshop® users and the world's leading resource for Photoshop training, education, and news.

http://www.photoshopuser.com

KW Computer Training Videos
Scott Kelby is featured in a series of more than 20 Photoshop training videos and DVDs, each on a particular Photoshop topic, available from KW Computer Training. Visit the Web site or call 813-433-5000 for orders or more information.

http://www.photoshopvideos.com

Adobe Photoshop Seminar Tour
See Scott live at the Adobe Photoshop Seminar Tour, the nation's most popular Photoshop seminars. For upcoming tour dates and class schedules, visit the tour Web site.

http://www.photoshopseminars.com

PhotoshopWorld
The convention for Adobe Photoshop users has now become the largest Photoshop-only event in the world. Scott Kelby is technical chair and education director for the event, as well as one of the instructors.

http://www.photoshopworld.com

PlanetPhotoshop.com
"The Ultimate Photoshop Site" features Photoshop news, tutorials, reviews, and articles posted daily. The site also contains the Web's most up-to-date resource on other Photoshop-related Web sites and information.

http://www.planetphotoshop.com

Photoshop Hall of Fame
Created to honor and recognize those individuals whose contributions to the art and business of Adobe Photoshop have had a major impact on the application or the Photoshop community itself.

http://www.photoshophalloffame.com

Kelby's Notes
Now you can get the answers to the top 100 most-asked Photoshop questions with Kelby's Notes, the plug-in from Scott Kelby. Simply go to the How Do I? menu while in Photoshop,

find your question, and the answer appears in an easy-to-read dialog box. Finally, help is just one click away.

http://www.kelbysnotes.com

Mac Design Magazine
Scott is Editor-in-Chief of *Mac Design Magazine*, "The Graphics Magazine for Macintosh Users." It's a tutorial-based print magazine with how-to columns on Photoshop, Illustrator, InDesign, Dreamweaver, GoLive, Flash, Final Cut Pro, and more. It's also packed with tips, tricks, and shortcuts for your favorite graphics applications.

http://www.macdesignonline.com

Adobe® Photoshop® with a Wacom® Pen

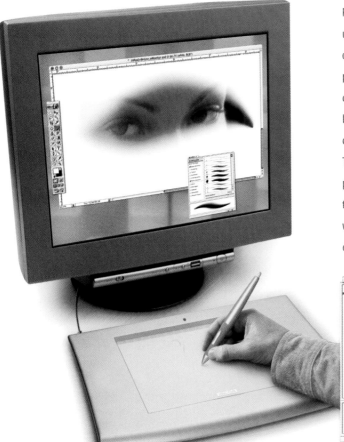

Take advantage of Photoshop's 21 pressure-sensitive tools

Pressure sensitivity opens up a new world of powerful options in Photoshop. Using pressure sensitivity, you can dynamically control things like brush size, opacity, color, texture, and more. Take a look in your Brushes palette to see firsthand all the tool characteristics that will respond to the natural control of your Wacom pen.

Pressure-sensitive control

Wacom pens are pressure-sensitive so you can control the amount of a software tool's effect by varying how firmly you press the pen tip to the tablet. Photoshop has 21 customizable tools that are specifically designed for use with a Wacom pen. You paid for them, why not use them properly?

Natural comfort

The Wacom Grip Pen is built for comfort. It has a cushioned, contoured grip-area and features Wacom's patented cordless, battery-free technology. Once you've experienced the natural comfort and superior performance of a Wacom pen, you'll wonder how you ever worked without one.

Time-saving productivity

With more control and comfort, you'll be more productive. Using a Wacom pen on your PC or Mac® is a very efficient way to work. Many Wacom customers tell us that switching to a pen has doubled their productivity. Try a Wacom pen for yourself and join more than 2,000,000 satisfied Wacom customers.

Visit www.wacom.com today to discover the Wacom pen that's right for you!

800-922-1490

www.wacom.com

Cintiq
Work Directly On Screen!
Cintiq starts at $1899

intuos2
Turn on Photoshop's power!
Intuos2 starts at $199

WACOM®

Penabled
WACOM

You've seen our images in this book, now search the entire collection online at BrandX.com

You'll find objects with clipping paths, people, backgrounds, textures, abstracts, locations, concepts, and more. Unique royalty-free images from Brand X Pictures are perfect for all your Photoshop® projects. Ready to manipulate or composite, they offer a world of possibilities. Best of all, Brand X Pictures are available online right now.

brand**X**pictures™

Unique Royalty-Free Images

Visit Peachpit on the Web at www.peachpit.com

- Read the latest articles and download timesaving tipsheets from best-selling authors such as Scott Kelby, Robin Williams, Lynda Weinman, Ted Landau, and more!

- Join the Peachpit Club and save 25% off all your online purchases at peachpit.com every time you shop—plus enjoy free UPS ground shipping within the United States.

- Search through our entire collection of new and upcoming titles by author, ISBN, title, or topic. There's no easier way to find just the book you need.

- Sign up for newsletters offering special Peachpit savings and new book announcements so you're always the first to know about our newest books and killer deals.

- Did you know that Peachpit also publishes books by Apple, New Riders, Adobe Press, Macromedia Press, palmOne Press, and TechTV press? Swing by the Peachpit family section of the site and learn about all our partners and series.

- Got a great idea for a book? Check out our About section to find out how to submit a proposal. You could write our next best-seller!

You'll find all this and more at www.peachpit.com. Stop by and take a look today!

VISIT OUR WEB SITE

WWW.NEWRIDERS.COM

On our Web site you'll find information about our other books, authors, tables of contents, indexes, and book errata. You will also find information about book registration and how to purchase our books.

EMAIL US

Contact us at this address: **nrfeedback@newriders.com**

- If you have comments or questions about this book
- To report errors that you have found in this book
- If you have a book proposal to submit or are interested in writing for New Riders
- If you would like to have an author kit sent to you
- If you are an expert in a computer topic or technology and are interested in being a technical editor who reviews manuscripts for technical accuracy

- To find a distributor in your area, please contact our international department at this address. **nrmedia@newriders.com**

- For instructors from educational institutions who want to preview New Riders books for classroom use. Email should include your name, title, school, department, address, phone number, office days/hours, text in use, and enrollment, along with your request for desk/examination copies and/or additional information.
- For members of the media who are interested in reviewing copies of New Riders books. Send your name, mailing address, and email address, along with the name of the publication or Web site you work for.

BULK PURCHASES/CORPORATE SALES

The publisher offers discounts on this book when ordered in quantity for bulk purchases and special sales. For sales within the U.S., please contact: Corporate and Government Sales (800) 382-3419 or **corpsales@pearsontechgroup.com**.
Outside of the U.S., please contact: International Sales (317) 428-3341 or **international@pearsontechgroup.com**.

WRITE TO US

New Riders
1249 Eighth Street
Berkeley, California 94710

CALL US

Toll-free (800) 571-5840. Ask for New Riders.
If outside U.S. (317) 428-3000. Ask for New Riders.

New Riders

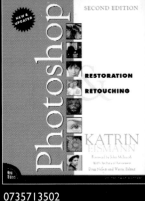
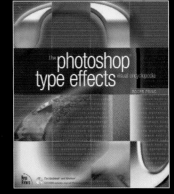

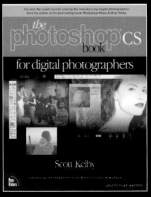